Perspectives on American Dance

UNIVERSITY PRESS OF FLORIDA

Florida A&M University, Tallahassee
Florida Atlantic University, Boca Raton
Florida Gulf Coast University, Ft. Myers
Florida International University, Miami
Florida State University, Tallahassee
New College of Florida, Sarasota
University of Central Florida, Orlando
University of Florida, Gainesville
University of North Florida, Jacksonville
University of South Florida, Tampa
University of West Florida, Pensacola

ALSO FROM THE EDITORS

Perspectives on American Dance: The Twentieth Century,
edited by Jennifer Atkins, Sally R. Sommer, and Tricia Henry Young

PERSPECTIVES ON AMERICAN DANCE

THE NEW MILLENNIUM

Edited by Jennifer Atkins, Sally R. Sommer,
and Tricia Henry Young

University Press of Florida
Gainesville · Tallahassee · Tampa · Boca Raton
Pensacola · Orlando · Miami · Jacksonville · Ft. Myers · Sarasota

Copyright 2018 by Jennifer Atkins, Sally R. Sommer, and Tricia Henry Young
All rights reserved
Published in the United States of America

First cloth printing, 2018
First paperback printing, 2020

25 24 23 22 21 20   6 5 4 3 2 1

Library of Congress Control Number: 2018932579
ISBN 978-0-8130-5499-5 (cloth)
ISBN 978-0-8130-6829-9 (pbk.)

The University Press of Florida is the scholarly publishing agency for the State University System of Florida, comprising Florida A&M University, Florida Atlantic University, Florida Gulf Coast University, Florida International University, Florida State University, New College of Florida, University of Central Florida, University of Florida, University of North Florida, University of South Florida, and University of West Florida.

University Press of Florida
2046 NE Waldo Road
Suite 2100
Gainesville, FL 32609
http://upress.ufl.edu

Contents

List of Illustrations   vii
Acknowledgments   ix
Introduction   1
  Jennifer Atkins, Sally R. Sommer, and Tricia Henry Young

PART I. VIRTUAL SPACE, REFRAMED DANCES

1. How One Awkward, Chubby, Bespectacled White Boy from New Jersey Got All of YouTube Dorky Dancing, and Why We Should Thank Him for It   15
   Latika L. Young

2. So You Think You Can Dance Straight? Same-Sex Ballroom and Reality Television   34
   J. Ellen Gainor

3. Syndicated Bodies: Expressions of American Identity in NFL Touchdown Dances   61
   Dawn Springer

4. Displays of Disruption: A Decade of Flash Mobs   82
   Kate Mattingly

PART II. INTIMATE SPACES, STAGED SUBVERSIONS

5. (Post) Pious and Porn Spectacles: Frontier Choreographies of the U.S. Jewess   111
   Hannah Schwadron

6. Pole Dancing for Jesus: Healthy Bodies, Healthy Souls   137
   Michelle T. Summers

7. Dancing the Brand: Striptease, Corporeality, and Corporatization   163
   Jessica Berson

8. Bgirls as Drag Kings 190
Ansley Joye Jones

PART III. PUBLIC SPACES, POLITICAL STATEMENTS

9. Receptions of *Descent* and Politics of *Agora*: 9/11 Changed the Way They Saw It; Everybody Jumped into the Pool 211
Sally R. Sommer

10. The Land of Dance Crimes: Social Dancing and the New York City Cabaret Laws 229
Ina Sotirova

11. Dancing in the Dark: Defining and Defending the Elusive Hipster Dance Aesthetic 251
Patsy Gay

List of Contributors 263
Index 267

Illustrations

Figures

1.1. Gary Brolsma in "Numa Numa Dance" 17
2.1. Women's Standard competitors 45
2.2. Men's Latin competitors 45
3.1. Cuba Gooding Jr. performing the Ickey Shuffle in *Jerry Maguire* 74
4.1. T-Mobile flash mob 91
4.2. *Step Up Revolution* flash mob 97
4.3. Official Beit Shemesh Women's flash mob 99
7.1. Dancer at New York City Club 169
7.2 Dancer at New York City Club 175
7.3 Dancer at New York City Club 180
8.1. Bgirl Ephrat "Bounce" Asherie in a "back-break" 193
8.2. Bgirl Ansley "Jukeboxx" Jones in a "Z" freeze 197
8.3. Bgirl Ansley "Jukeboxx" Jones in a one-armed "Y" freeze 202
9.1. Dancers on banisters in *Descent* 214
9.2. Dancers lying on stairs in *Descent* 220
9.3. Dancers in McCarren Park Pool in *Agora* 223
10.1. Francis Hall at a DLF dance action 231
10.2. Archie Burnett at a private dance party 235
10.3. No dancing sign at Von Bar, Bleecker St., NYC 240
11.1. Crown Heights, Brooklyn, house party 253
11.2. Hipster flail 256

Chart

2.1. Waltz Natural Turn 37

Acknowledgments

This project would not have been possible without the many people who provided inspiration and support. First, we would like to thank the authors who contributed the work that inspired these two volumes. For their expertise and generosity we are deeply grateful.

We would like specially to thank our colleague, Julie Malnig, for her encouragement and insights when this project was merely an idea. Julie is a kindred spirit who values dance and performance in its many incarnations, with particular affection for the social and idiosyncratic. We are grateful to the Congress on Research in Dance (CORD) and Society of Dance History Scholars (SDHS) for keeping dance at the forefront of scholarly research. Without the exchanges of ideas initiated by the presentations and presenters at their yearly conferences, the world of dance would be much less interesting and stimulating. In particular we are thankful for CORD's sponsorship of the "Dance and American Culture" Special Topics conference in 2011, held at Florida State University (FSU) and hosted by the Graduate Program in American Dance Studies. Some of the essays contained in this volume began as papers at that meeting.

Under the guidance of professors Michael Kirby, Brooks McNamara, and Richard Schechner of New York University's Performance Studies, dance scholarship was allowed to flourish. As they formulated what was "Performance Studies" (always a work-in-progress), they also opened our minds to rich possibilities of recognizing the performances and dances that surround us in all human exchanges. Their intellectual rigor aroused ours. Their theories about performance gave us tools to open new areas of study and redefined for us what kind of movement was dance. In turn, without our own wonderful graduate students, especially those in American Dance Studies, we would be much less knowledgeable. We thank them for their vitality and for teaching their teachers about the edges of the research frontiers.

In practical matters of moving this project forward, the list is also long. We thank Jessica Herzogenrath for her research expertise and Kathaleen Boche for her insights. We would like to express our deepest gratitude to Gianna Mercandetti, Anna Patsfall, Lucy Escher Kahn, and Madeline Kurtz whose assistance in maintaining order, communication, and momentum was invaluable. A special thank you from Jennifer Atkins, who values your positivity and camaraderie. Appreciation and profound gratitude to David Atkins, as well, who faithfully worked on images, computers, and morale.

Sally Sommer is grateful to Alessandra Larson for her willingness to take on extra responsibilities, for her intelligent advice about scheduling, and for her patience and sense of humor when times get tough. Hans Rasch and Nathaniel Hendrickson helped with the photographs, and Jamie Kight was able to stay calm while solving the computer's problematic programs. Thanks also to my husband, William Sommer, whose support makes my involvement in all dance projects possible.

Tricia Young extends appreciation to her husband, Martin Young, for his technical wizardry and steadfast moral support from the beginning of this project. I am also deeply grateful to Nancy Smith Fichter, whose vision for dance in higher education kept scholarly inquiry and artistic practice (literally and figuratively) under one roof at Florida State University, and who has made the field of dance a better place for us all. Thank you, especially, to my parents, Billie and J. D. Henry, who encouraged me always, and never asked if dance really had a history.

In the years that we have worked on this project, our institution, Florida State University, has generously provided us with financial support. We thank FSU for awarding us a Planning Grant, an Arts & Humanities Program Enhancement Grant, and a Small Grants Program Award.

Finally we would like to thank our readers for their suggestions about how to improve the quality and coherence of this collection; the University Press of Florida for its ongoing support of the field of dance; our project manager, Eleanor Deumens, for her assistance and expertise; and most especially director of the University Press of Florida, Meredith Babb, for her belief in this project.

Introduction

JENNIFER ATKINS, SALLY R. SOMMER, AND TRICIA HENRY YOUNG

In the new millennium, relationships between dancing and identity noticeably changed. The *sense* of dance and dancing became more social and interactive as new technologies opened an increasingly diverse range of performance settings and choreographic methodologies. The century began with the 9/11 terrorist attacks inside U.S. borders, followed by the sixteen-year war in the Middle East, the concurrent rise of extremism, and the Supreme Court's recognition of multiple gender identifications and rights. Civil protests about racial inequities and immigration policies continued, and the country was rocked by the great economic recession of 2008. However, the most pervasive transformations were wrought by the digital revolution that reconfigured communication, social patterns, and access to information worldwide.

The first generation to come of age in the twenty-first century, Generation Y, is defined by its technological savvy. As a group, their comfort with digital devices and nanosecond communications is the most distinctive marker between them and their parents' generation. In America, the widespread use of technology in making and distributing dance affected cultural expressions and provoked questions about the relationship between the individual and the group—identities that are played out in moving patterns and bodies.

Increased attention to social dancing, strongly influenced by YouTube, social media sites, and popular TV, is also a consequence of the harsh reality that many dance companies did not survive the economic downturn of the early 2000s, and fewer people and foundations are supporting the performing arts. A slowly developing trend has been to turn away from watching the work of a single choreographer or company and from regarding dancing as the exclusive purview of formally trained concert dancers. Following these changes a new generation of writers has shifted attention toward social dancing and everyday choreographies.

In selecting the essays for this anthology, the editors did not intend to provide a comprehensive view of dance in the early years of the new millennium. Instead, the focus is on a younger generation of writers/scholars engaged with dancing practices that indicate some of the new directions in dance scholarship. As participants and/or observers they write with familiarity about their own era, exploring new parameters of identity and evaluating a wide variety of movement practices being performed in spaces beyond traditional proscenium stages. The scope of what is considered and self-identified as "dancerly," and what is considered valid performance space is open-ended. Still, the range of the physical vocabularies and choreographies accumulate to form a composite sense of Americanness and identity in constant transition, filled with duality and contradiction. Some essay topics in this collection are atypical and idiosyncratic, scrutinizing, for instance, how religion and sex are being marketed through new physical practices. These investigations explore new parameters of identity, bringing into relief four interconnected themes (by no means an exhaustive list) that reveal how creative expressions negotiate some shared twenty-first-century concerns; they include innovative approaches to dance in terms of community, impermanence, paradox/doubleness, and space.

The Internet is now the center of an entire world of dance information and entertainment. Digital services generate circles of digital "friends," which expand in ever-widening circles that can become global, comprising billions of viewers who watch and practice the latest dance fads that quickly flare up and burn out. Generation Y is more interested in social cohesions arising from instant group communications; community takes precedence over the individual. This is enhanced by some important social-psychological influences. The participant has the pleasure of being an active part (or an active watcher) of an "insider-group" of communicants, who know because they are "in-the-know." These friend-circles have exponentially enlarged and diversified dance congregants, and spontaneous movement communities now rapidly arise and dissipate in digital spaces as well as actual physical places. Gathering together may seem more essential when life is experienced as unpredictable. Although friends and families may be scattered geographically, they are in closer communication than ever before through the Internet.

An excellent example of how the Internet has affected dance gatherings is the phenomenon of flash mobs, which emerged in the first decade of the 2000s and soon became an international sensation. One of the first flash mobs was orchestrated by Bill Wasik in 2003; following his e-mailed directions, five hundred people converged at the New York City Toys "R" Us store in Times Square to cower and chant before a massive "terrible god," a *Tyrannosaurus rex* robot. Kate Mattingly describes the duality at the heart of this political and socially humorous action, which distinguishes flash mobbing from other forms of political mobilizations. Drawing on elements of collective identity, accessible choreography, and celebratory atmospheres, "Flash mobs demonstrated how people could infiltrate and contaminate modes of capitalism, and [generate] a fundamental joy at seeing society overtaken." Everyday spaces were charged with the energy temporarily created by mass movement and the collective performance of ordinary people; as the event was instantly sent over the Internet the dance-space changed again, this time existing within the small frame of a phone, computer, or tablet screen. Ironically, flash mobbing was immediately co-opted by commercial capitalist interests that produced *faux* spontaneity by creating closely choreographed events that disguised the underlying advertisements. Exploiting the markets of easy accessibility and social-dance popularity, TV producers also ramped up a precipitous rise in TV dance shows (twenty-nine shows still existed in 2016). Formatted as dance competitions, the narratives are emotionalized and personalized by the contestants' real-life stories. Whether the dancing is on TV or YouTube, accessibility is crucial. Technically, the dances must look virtuosic yet quotidian, friendly even, as if anyone could do them with practice—a trope of hope that is the foundation of the entire genre. Watching involves one click, and with one more click a comment or parody can be circulated as friends and strangers join via Tweets, Instagrams, Facebook posts, or Snapchats. In this way a dance event—no matter if the spectators are scattered—can be transformed into an intimate, participatory social phenomenon.

Not only do the millennials have more digital technology and more platforms (texting, tweeting, snapchatting, etc.) that often operate in real time, they continue adding new data to the digital universe at staggering rates. As a consequence of immediate access, virtual dance communities can become a nexus of activism around a common cause, with interactive connections and tools that can manipulate the terrain. The viewer is able to pause, fast-forward, rewind, repeat, duplicate, repost, or personalize the material instantaneously, from a handheld smart phone. These concrete editing tools level the playing field, allowing the amateur to become choreographer and director. Video-sharing websites with user-upload content brought rapid distribution and hundreds of spinoffs. In her essay on pioneer Gary Brolsma's 2004 legendary video, "Numa Numa Dance," which featured this everyday guy doing his celebratory and sincere everyday dancing, Latika Young writes that it created a forum for Internet users to craft "their own embodied [video] explorations precisely in the realm where these investigations are most tangible: the body itself." The Internet, she states, removes "obstacles of dance production and distribution." All of these elements are built into the Internet and, at this point, remain free to access.

Interactive involvement in innovative spaces has likewise surfaced in choreographies made during the last fifteen years. In *Agora,* Noemie LaFrance invited the entire audience to jump into an empty 50,000-square-foot swimming pool for a celebratory finish; in *Descent* the audience became moving scenography as they descended a staircase, framed by dancers appearing above and below them. Stringent economics caused dance companies to become smaller, which has profoundly affected the intimacy of the narratives. As a result of diminished funding, solo artists and small companies are looking inward, making pieces that deal with issues of identification: "how do I fit in?" or "how do you fit with me?" in terms of gender, race, sexual fluidities, ethnic displacements, and performer-audience relationships. Whether it is participatory social dancing or choreographed works for an audience, these dances reconsider the relationships between the individual and the group.

In a generation for whom paradox is an everyday fact, the millennials are noted for "collective individualism," "gender fluidity," and "upbeat skepticism"—a series of multiple choices that seem to provide the possibility of balance in a period of great uncertainty. Hipster dance, for example, displays a multiplicity that simultaneously embraces social critique, humor, institutional resistance, communalism, and improvisational ingenuity. Patsy Gay discusses the benign "ideological paradox of self-denial" in the culture and dancing. "Hipsters, though they acknowledge the existence of the scene and follow all the appropriate trends, typically refuse to admit that they are, in fact, hipsters.... in this equation of mutually dependent, yet inherently conflicting, conditions, one can be a hipster and not a hipster all at once." It follows that hipster dancing embodies its own doubleness through its "intentional disregard for the standards of 'good' or 'attractive' dance," yet it still maintains superior regard for a kind of dancing that it finds "good," "professing instead an ironic and radical reverence for the un-cool."

New trends in scholarship reflect the changing landscape of twenty-first-century dance in several recent dance books. While they are significantly different in focus from this anthology, they share some common themes with this volume: the relationships between dance, space, and community; a growing focus on social dance; and expanded definitions of "dance" that extend to quotidian movement. One of the spaces most frequently chosen in these new studies is the city. One single-author book and two edited volumes discuss the relationships between dance and city spaces. SanSan Kwan, in *Kinesthetic City: Dance and Movement in Chinese Urban Spaces* (2013), investigates how both theatrical dance and movement in urban spaces shapes Chinese identity. *City Visions* (2000), edited by David Bell and Azzedine Haddour, presents dance as one of several art forms that construct space within the city. *Site Dance: Choreographers and the Lure of Alternative Spaces* (2009), a compilation edited by Melanie Kloetzel and Carolyn Pavlik, relies on interviews and writings of several artists to examine how different uses of space enable or affect engagement with communities. The authors investigate how dance in public sites (not always urban) may challenge exclusion to spaces according to race, class, and gender.

The screen provides another consideration of dance and space. In *Screendance: Inscribing the Ephemeral Image* (2012), Douglas Rosenberg discusses the lineage of dance on screen and argues that "screendance" is an inherently interdisciplinary, hybrid form where dance is mediated by what he calls "camera space." Rosenberg also edited the compilation *The Oxford Handbook of Screendance Studies* (2016), which includes thirty-six essays covering the history, theories, and practices of screendance. *The Oxford Handbook of Dance and the Popular Screen* (2014), edited by Melissa Blanco Borelli, presents twenty-four essays that concentrate on dance in feature-length movies, commercial videos, and television; dance and cyberspace; and how dance and space may challenge narratives of power. In *Dance, Space, and Subjectivity* (2001 original publication) Valerie Briginshaw uses various theoretical paradigms to describe how bodies interact with places, concentrating on postmodern dance. Markus Hallensleben, editor of *Performative Body Spaces: Corporeal Topographies in Literature, Theatre, Dance, and the Visual Arts* (2010), argues that artists' bodies are integral parts of artwork in the postmodern world. A series of essays, ranging from Holocaust literature to makeover reality TV, consider the body's image in relationship to cultural spaces.

The essays in *Perspectives on American Dance: The New Millennium* are organized according to three general themes related to the use of space. The chapters in part 1, "Virtual Spaces, Reframed Dances," investigates the ways in which spectators experience dancing in formats ranging from television to hand-held devices. Part 2, "Intimate Spaces, Staged Subversions," deals with live dance performances that torque normative conventions and ideologies to embrace diverse identities. Part 3, "Public Spaces, Political Statements," looks at dance as social activism that seeks to incite change. This organization accommodates the four interconnected themes previously mentioned: community, impermanence, doubleness/paradox, and space. These themes have recurred in American dance practices during the last fifteen years and are motifs interwoven throughout this volume.

The variety of screen formats, ranging from tiny handheld devices to giant, flat-screen home televisions, influences how we see the images, and our sense of time and space. Dances are now created or adapted for these smaller frames: Accessible Internet sites, streaming content, and copious amounts of data provide viewers with instant, on-demand, and interactive access to an unprecedented quantity of dance material. Performers and viewers meet in the digital world with unlimited screen time on completely transportable stages. The essays in "Virtual Spaces, Reframed Dances" discuss the effects of these transitions and how they changed *where* dance is seen and *how* it is created, received, and performed. The sheer size of the viewing audiences exponentially increases the significance of dancing, placing it in the paradoxical situation of having both a bigger immediate effect than ever that is transitory in its popularity.

"Dorky dancing," as defined by Latika Young, is the kind of dancing (usually reserved for the privacy of home or among friends) where people break out in hilarious, improvisational dancing of unadulterated, if uncoordinated, joy. The style perfectly fit tech-savvy teenagers, who delighted in mocking pop culture with lip-synching-dancing video creations shared online during bouts of adolescent boredom. Young's "How One Awkward, Chubby, Bespectacled White Boy from New Jersey Got All of YouTube Dorky Dancing, and Why We Should Thank Him for It" examines why Gary Brolsma—an unlikely creative leader who began a dance revolution that broke open the vlogging frontier with the global phenomenon of his 2004 "Numa Numa Dance"—is worthy of study. The deluge of homemade dance videos is watched by more people worldwide than any other form of dancing ever before. Dorky aesthetics thrive in the awkward, the amateur, the innocence of the self-produced. These videos, instantly made then dispersed throughout the virtual world "challeng[e] notions of who can dance, for whom, in what manner, and through what medium."

A growing assortment of other dance forms, including reality TV dance competitions like *Dancing with the Stars*, became wildly popular across media platforms. These shows began to reflect societal changes, including some same-sex dancing viewed by millions in 2008 (seven years before the Supreme Court legalized same-sex marriage). Ellen Gainor writes about the controversies provoked by this performance in "So You Think You Can Dance Straight? Same-Sex Ballroom and Reality Television." Because male/female movement vocabularies of competitive ballroom dancing (Dansport) are nearly identical, it is especially useful in assessing performances of sexuality and gender. Gainor deals with the challenges that serious same-sex ballroom artistry presented to the producers and hetero-normative codes of gendered performance on a mainstream TV dance show. The popular viewer reception of same-sex ballroom dancing validated how dance can embody and expand America's "visions of gender roles and sexual expression at issue in this moment."

Without the widespread reach of televised sports, the "touchdown dances" of professional football players would go unremarked. Witnessed by massive audiences, they are more than spontaneous entertainment; they are dances of identity and resistance, as analyzed by Dawn Springer in "Syndicated Bodies: Expressions of American Identity in NFL Touchdown Dances." Strictly regulated by NFL corporate leaders, touchdown dancing reinforces team solidarity and demonstrates how "football players' physical expressions embody and perform personal, political, and geographical identities, and resist structures of systemic racism and social dominance." Following initial TV broadcasts, these dances acquire ever larger audiences through the reach of YouTube and social media.

Internet communication and cell phones made flash mobs possible because large groups could be quickly assembled for semi-impromptu public events. In "Displays of Disruption: A Decade of Flash Mobs," Kate Mattingly describes how flash mobs were originally intended to be fun, but with serious intentions of interrupting public spaces and calling attention to commercialism, urban environments, and our role as citizens. Becoming instantly popular and prolific, they were quickly co-opted by corporations and Hollywood. Lacking activist goals, commercial flash mobs used images of everyday people dancing together to disseminate disguised advertisements. Whether commercial or not, flash mobbing's popularity demonstrates the pleasure that collective movement imparts and illustrates how embodied epistemologies can reconfigure relationships to our neighbors, ourselves, and our environment.

In a nation defined by the diversity of its citizenship, relationships between individual and group identity are mutable and complex. The second cluster in this anthology, "Intimate Spaces, Staged Subversions," considers dance practices that transgress conventional ideologies in order to accommodate more inclusive demographics. Unlike virtual spaces, intimate spaces are actual physical locations where people meet and interact in the flesh. The relative intimacy of these spaces—in terms of both physical proximity and live interactions—personalizes the performative acts. Agendas are brought into vivid relief as they take on sacred territory. Spaces demarcated for singular purposes and prescriptive codes of conduct (the gym, the synagogue) are juxtaposed with radically dissonant behaviors (pole dancing and Jesus, mechanical bull riding and a female rabbi). Shifting concepts of identity are enacted subversions, which become platforms for asserting, negotiating, and incorporating change.

In "(Post) Pious and Porn Spectacles: Frontier Choreographies of the U.S. Jewess" Hannah Schwadron looks at two American women—a rabbi and a porn star (both Los Angeles residents)—who manipulate traditional institutional boundaries to create spaces of agency for contemporary Jewish women. The rabbi makes Jewishness sexy, and the porn star makes sexiness Jewish. Rabbi Sharon Brous (who served as the official rabbi presiding over President Obama's Inaugural reelection ceremony) cultivates sexiness in her large congregation through an edgy unification of politics and religiosity. Adult film director and porn star, Joanna Angel, regularly spoofs her Jewish identity so that "her Jewish confessions seem to cancel any serious raunch with a self-ridicule that works to temper or justify any behavior that might be too outlandish." According to Schwadron, "as spectacular icons on the fringes of Jewish America," Brous and Angel both offer "positions of Jewish and female authority as funny, 'sexy' alternatives" to mainstream patriarchal directives.

Transgressing boundaries between sexiness and religiosity is the topic of Michelle Summers's essay, "Pole Dancing for Jesus." Ex-stripper Crystal Deans incited a media frenzy of fascination and outrage when she began offering Pole Dancing for Jesus classes at her Spring, Texas, fitness studio. Deans's classes, writes Summers, are just one of the many "ambivalent ways white Christian women are able to conjoin their sexuality and spirituality through an embodied rhetoric of the 'healthy.'" By framing her workout classes as physical and spiritual fitness lessons, Deans adds her voice to a larger conversation about health in America, arguing, essentially, that fit bodies equal fit souls. In this moral health agenda, dance is the primary mode through which Protestant women physically proclaim their Christianity. In "Dancing the Brand: Striptease, Corporeality, and Corporatization," Jessica Berson describes how the corporate system manipulates performers to standardize dancing "sexy." Berson examines how striptease is now part of the entrenched cultural phenomenon of branding. Corporate clubs, in particular, enter into the brand-scape by promulgating homogeneity in body types, dance styles, and in interactions between customers and dancers. For Berson, the depersonalized and commodified striptease contributes to important debates about the influence American corporations wield in our cultural and sexual lives, packaging desires and controlling expressions of identity.

In the world of breaking, bgirls follow masculinized, sexist conventions because they follow the bboys' rules—they master their moves, emulate their dress code, and adopt their vocabulary of "burns" (a gesture or movement so potent that it incinerates the opponent). Burns are notoriously misogynistic (often miming rape) and vividly scatological, used to one-up the rival in the art of physical insult. To better analyze her personal feelings and conflicts, and inspired by Kathryn Rosenfeld's article "Drag King Magic," Ansley Jones began looking at the bgirls' dilemma from a theoretical point of view in "Bgirls as Drag Kings." When bgirls move into "the masculinity of breaking, at the expense of femininity," they become "mimetic drag kings, taking part in their own suppression." Real power, Jones argues, exists with the "liminal" bgirl. Successfully merging femininity and masculinity, she gains androgynous power and creates alternative options for all male and female breakers.

The third group of articles turns to more public expressions of dance in relationship to shifting American identities. After a long period of quiescence and little mobilized political action, the turn of the millennium saw American young people begin to initiate and formulate public protests. A connection exists between the stirrings of political actions and the politicizing of dance. Both political protests and social dancing mobilize groups of people, resulting in increased interaction (intentionally or not) between them. This interplay between dancing and sociopolitical meaning is always occurring, but it is the core subject of the three articles that comprise the final section of this volume, "Public Spaces, Political Statements."

The trauma of the events of 9/11 had no precedent in American history. In the first essay of the last section, "Receptions of *Descent* and Politics of *Agora:*

9/11 Changed the Way They Saw It; Everybody Jumped into the Pool," Sally Sommer examines how post-9/11 sociopolitical contexts shifted perceptions of Noémie Lafrance's works *Descent* and *Agora*. In the post-9/11 environment, "a profoundly changed semiotics of bodies and stairs was operant." New York audiences saw the bodies of dancers lying in a stairway in *Descent* as an elegiac political statement rather than a meditation on women, as Lafrance intended. Then in 2005 Lafrance saw an abandoned 50,000-square-foot swimming pool in Brooklyn and instantly identified it as the choreographic locale for *Agora*. This time Lafrance knew her work would have a political impact on the site. But what she could not predict was how profound the ramifications would be. The politics of space is also central in "The Land of Dance Crimes: Social Dance and the New York City Cabaret Laws" by Ina Sotirova. Tensions between nightlife dancing, and the 1926 cabaret laws used to repress it, comprise a long and sordid history. Perverting the letter of the law, legal questions become reductive (but still deadly). NYC courts provided legal pathways for the real villains: real estate interests, residential zoning codes, and big-business capital investments, which served the more pervasive sexual, racial, and moral prejudices. Sotirova illustrates how NYC criminalized dancing, devastating a large and vibrant underground club culture, leaving serious club dancers with no place to go and the courts with unanswered legal questions about what constitutes "dancing."

The final article of the anthology, Patsy Gay's "Dancing in the Dark: Defining and Defending the Elusive Hipster Dance Aesthetic" discusses how political ideologies are displayed in the determinedly apolitical hipster social dance. Gay looks at dancing practices that take place on small impromptu dance floors in the back rooms of Brooklyn bars, where there is a tolerance of "anything-goes-any-style-is-OK." Hallmarks of the dance styles are cultural appropriation, movement bricolage, antivirtuosity, and anticool, which combine with the inherent flux of hipster identity to collectively establish a unique form of social transcendence on the dance floor.

The turn of the century, and the 9/11 terrorist attacks, were watershed moments delineating a period of time when Americans began to (re)assess the position of their nation in the world and their position as citizens in this nation. The hopeful optimism and technological infusions that characterized the turn of the twentieth century were tempered by ambivalence about entering into a new age. How would America grasp the future? What from the past would carry us forward? Then, months later, the traumatic events of 9/11 and the wars galvanized attempts to define what it means to be American.

Dancing is one of many actions Americans turn to when expression of ideas and feelings defies immediate verbalization. Movement practices follow new societal trends. This makes dance investigations extraordinarily useful frameworks for discerning important social issues in the first decades of the twenty-first century. Identity is always protean, and the way bodies express identity is always changing. However, as international boundaries dissolve through the Internet and mass migrations, American identities at the beginning of the new millennium are positioned as more intensely political and personal—creating more widely fluctuating perceptions of how the self fits with the other. Questions about self in relation to Americanness have expanded: from self as an individual to self as a member of community, to self as a citizen of a nation, to self as a member of a worldwide virtual community. This throws into relief the individual's choice of being exclusive or inclusive. These questions, and how they are expressed in motion by the individual and the group, are points of departure for the articles in this anthology.

I
Virtual Space, Reframed Dances

1

How One Awkward, Chubby, Bespectacled White Boy from New Jersey Got All of YouTube Dorky Dancing, and Why We Should Thank Him for It

LATIKA L. YOUNG

It is December 2004, and YouTube is still a few months away from being launched online; a grainy, heavily pixilated, pre-YouTube video opens with a chubby-cheeked, bespectacled, headphone-wearing young white male, framed by a tilted web camera in front of an aquarium and a window with a not-quite-long-enough blue curtain. For the first few seconds, this appears to be a subdued lip-sync to a song with unrecognizable lyrics. But no—at 16 seconds, Gary Brolsma, aka the "Numa Numa" kid, erupts into a frenzied explosion of arm-pumping, eyebrow-raising, unabashed dancing enthusiasm. Although at this time the world had not yet seen anything quite like this self-produced dance for the Internet, we would all soon be infected by the sheer giddiness of the Numa Numa–inspired, YouTube-driven, viral dorky dance revolution. For this, Gary deserves the sincerest of collective high fives.

* * *

Placed in his proper position in Internet history, the unassuming Gary Brolsma is a revolutionary who began the biggest popular production and distribution of dancing the world had ever seen. To appreciate the much-loved and subversive aesthetics of the self-produced and self-distributed dorky dancing that floods the Internet, it is necessary to know something about its beginnings. Today it is almost impossible to remember back to 2004 and relive how stunning (magical even) it was to watch the grainy and pixilated video on Newgrounds then YouTube—posted for all to enjoy, to critique, and even to emulate.

Memories are buried under our mindless acceptance of the ubiquitous cellphone-cum-tiny-computer, homemade Internet videos, and instant connectivity. User-uploaded content is what we *do*. From YouTube (still the reigning star) to Facebook, Flickr, Instagram, Twitter, Snapchat, Vine, etc., the proliferation of websites and apps obscure the reality that YouTube was only launched in 2005. The momentous impact YouTube and these other sites have had on the production and reception of dance is inestimable: They incited billions of self-produced dance performances—people dancing in their bedrooms and living rooms; on playgrounds, the streets, or mountaintops; in the sky and at the bottom of the sea. The viewership for this kind of self-produced dancing outstrips viewership of any other form of dancing, anywhere, at any time, throughout the world.

YouTube, in particular, has been instrumental in promoting "dorky dancing"—allowing what was once perceived as socially awkward or amateur movement to be embraced and celebrated. With the advent of video-sharing sites, first the youth (especially males) of America and then *everybody* found rapid-distribution and worldwide outlets for their physical expression. Dancing was the crucial gatecrasher. With YouTube, self-expression moved beyond words and still photography and entered the realm of moving images. People could control and distribute their own embodied explorations precisely in the realm where these investigations are most tangible: the body itself. And we have one awkward white boy from New Jersey—Gary Brolsma—to thank for getting this online dorky dance party started.

Although awkward dancing has been present since the first time a bumbling dancer elicited laughter, "awkward dance" is not necessarily the same thing as "dorky dance." Awkward dancing is certainly one substantial component of dorky dance. But the aesthetics of dorky dancing used here consider many other factors. Awkwardness is, of course, culturally specific. I am using "dorky dance" as would be perceived by Western audiences, primarily in the United States. It includes several common ingredients: uncoordinated, jerky, arrhythmic movement; hysterical (the term derives from the chaotic way a body moves when experiencing hysteria) movement that is off tempo from any musical rhythms, and off tempo from any sense of internal rhythm; the limbs move in unexpected directions; there is no kinetic logic when or how they stop and start; the dancer makes faces; and the dance cannot be aligned with any known style or technique.

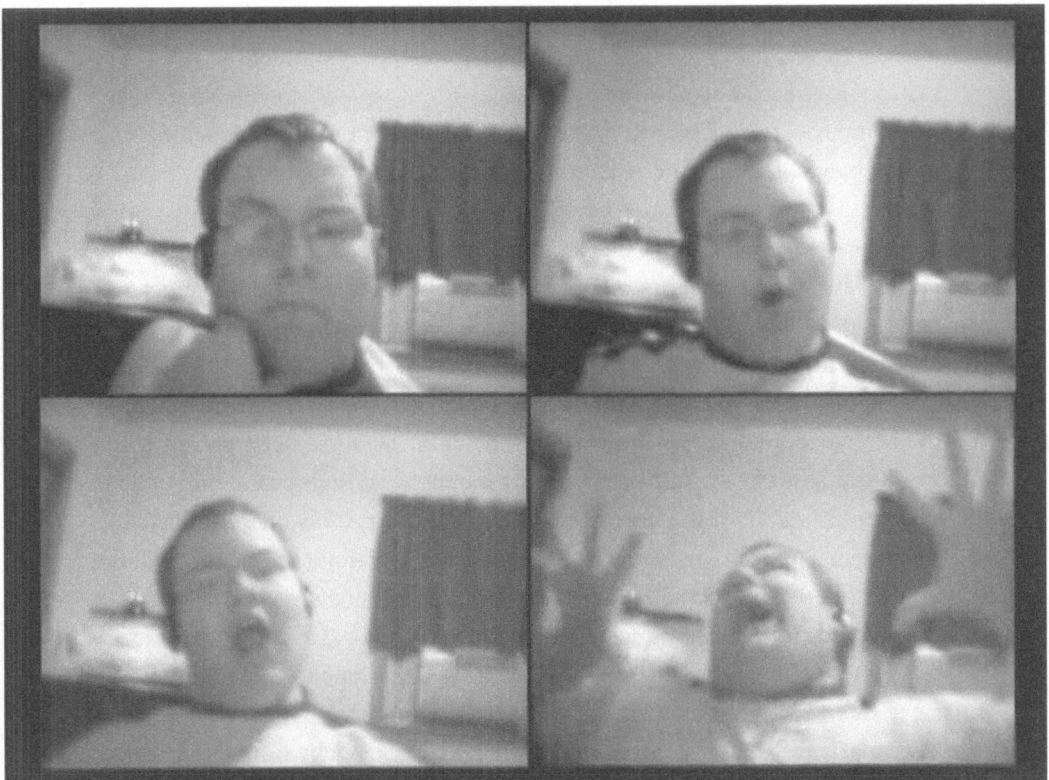

Figure 1.1. Still images of Gary Brolsma from "Numa Numa Dance" reflecting the original pixilated quality of the video upload. Image Source: http://livingromcom.typepad.com/my_weblog/2006/07/craft_is_not_en.html. By permission of Gary Brolsma.

Although dorky dance is rooted in awkward movement, other essential designators distinguish "dorkiness." A dance is read as dorky depending on the viewer's ideas about "proper" physical appearance/status, as much as it depends on the lack of any technical ability on the part of the dancer. However, at the time of Gary's debut, which set a standard, other "dorky" signifiers were being established. For example, the clothes of the dorky dancer are ill-fitting, badly matched, definitely *not* nerd-chic. The hair is odd or unkempt; badly fitted spectacles can be part of the mix. The physical stature of the dancer is uncomfortably out of the normative range: they are too short, too tall, too pudgy, too scrawny, existing on the physical fringes.

What makes dorky dancing so popular is its tenderness and vulnerability. Dorky dancing is humorous precisely because it is oblivious to any expectations. Gender plays a small role since male-produced movement (especially by white males) is still interpreted as inherently dorkier than that of females. American audiences are not as accustomed to watching men dance, and when they do, is usually in the sanctioned style of something like men dancing in boy bands. Dorky dances have an innocent, sincere quality that is both refreshing and witty, not merely naïve. They optimistically counteract the cynical and sarcastic impulses that fuel so much of our current humor. Dorky dancers express an overwhelming sense of believability. No spectator is expected to "suspend disbelief." In fact, as soon as the video feels in the least contrived or artificial, they are outed online as inauthentic "astro-turfs" or "sell-outs," and provoke a spate of negative dorky-dance video-responses. The genre is unapologetically unpretentious, militantly eschewing social expectations of dance propriety and any sense of artifice that comes with high production values. Who needs a state-of-the-art camera, film crew, and professional editing, when a stationary webcam or even a handheld bouncing cell phone camera will not only suffice—it will actually add to the aesthetic of amateuristic charm?

This veracity shines through when a video is produced for fun, not for financial gain. Genuine dorky dance videos cannot deliberately be made for profit, since this altered intention is not lost on the viewer, whose "purity" of viewing experience thus becomes tainted. Being commercially unfettered is what allowed user-generated YouTube dance in the first place. To fulfill the crucial criterion of dorky dance-dom irreproachably, and have the video accepted as amicably amateur, it must be self-produced and posted gratis on the web for a globe-spanning audience. The overriding intent of dorky dancing is to generate laughs, not profits. The sociability of the Internet removes traditional barriers between laborer and consumer and the financial obstacles of dance production and distribution. There is no need to rent a studio or a theater, to sell a required number of seats, or, in the case of film, to have hefty budgets and sales. On the contrary, dance in film reads as ultimately having financial aims, even in low budget productions.

People have always liked watching funny, awkward movers, and they have long figured prominently in the pantheon of beloved Hollywood characters. But these dancers could never be dorky because Hollywood is always driven by the bottom line. Since the earliest moving pictures, dancers have stumbled across the screen to generate laughs, from Charlie Chaplin and Buster Keaton to the more recent Pee-wee Herman and Napoleon Dynamite. In comparison to these consciously awkward silver-screen dancers, dorky YouTube dancers emit a sense of veracity, of being authentically amateur and genuinely vulnerable. They have not constructed their clumsiness to drive the plot of a big (or even small) budget film.

Significantly—just as it functions in the larger world of art-making—the indispensable ingredient of dorky dance is intention. Fun is fundamental. As much as dorky dance can comment on and critique society and our restrictive conceptions of dance aesthetics, its real purpose is to entertain. Therefore, it is no accident that dorky dance finds a perfect home on YouTube, the free forum where people can see funny dancing in a space that feels welcoming and unpretentious—utterly unlike the atmosphere of the concert performance hall.

YouTube was launched in February 2005 (just a few months after the "Numa Numa Dance" was first uploaded), was purchased by Google in October 2006, and grew quickly from its inception. Currently, according to YouTube's website, forty-eight hours of content are uploaded every minute, translating into eight years of content uploaded *every day* from the site's hundreds of millions of users.[1] According to the Pew Research Center, by 2015, 64 percent of American adults now own a smart phone, up from 35 percent in 2011.[2] The rate is even higher for young adults (18–29), 85 percent of whom were smart phone owners in 2015.[3] With so many smart phones in pockets, our expectations for privacy are altered. Any action we create in public—dance or otherwise—now has the potential to be captured and displayed online, transforming any such quotidian display into a virtual performance. The portability and speed of the smart phone allows all users to transition seamlessly from producer to viewer, from critic to distributor.

YouTube continues to develop as the most popular forum for meaningful, participant-driven communication and artistic creation, especially in the realm of dance. At the time of its inception, it was the perfect space to "broadcast yourself,"[4] as YouTube's early motto suggested. This platform allowed instantaneous communication and collaboration, at a temporal and geographical speed that connected across the nation and around the globe in seconds, which seemed miraculous at the time. Clips could be easily produced and quickly posted on the web from the privacy of home (or in public on one's smart phone or iPad) mere moments after a video was recorded. The sheer speed of this transmission and reception created the perfect forum for instant spoofs and parodies and invited a wider participation and dialogue in the dance-making process that still exists today.

This technology also revolutionized the role of the audience, who needed very little expressed interest in dance to be exposed to it.[5] Bombarded by dance images—particularly of the funny or awkward variety—the new viewer often adopted a more active role in this virtual world of dance. Those who were once spectators transformed into active dance collaborators; participation ranged from something as simple as reposting or e-mailing videos to adopting the role of the critic by writing commentaries about creations to becoming simultaneously an artistic-collaborator-critic-commentator by creating a dancing response-video. This dialogue occurred, and continues to occur, in an atmosphere that makes participation in dance fun, rather than grandiose or laborious.

Many of the most popular initial self-posted videos on YouTube—the ones that so quickly became viral—were those of dorky dancers. The infamous "Numa Numa Dance" is a deliciously dorky dance that exploded on the Internet as the first user-uploaded video that became popular primarily because of its dorky dancing. It should rightfully be placed into the annals of Internet history as the first dorky dance "viral video."[6] The video's creator, Gary Brolsma, has even been lauded by YouTube anthropologist Michael Wesch as "the first guy on the dance floor of this global mixer" (that is, the YouTube community of collaboration).[7] Although "Numa Numa" originated on a flash video-sharing site called Newgrounds (which predated the existence of YouTube and was especially popular with video game players and early technology adopters), the video quickly established its home on what would soon become the most popular video-sharing site, YouTube. Then-nineteen-year-old Brolsma (from Saddle Brook, New Jersey) created the clip and intended to share it with a small group of friends, but "Numa Numa" became an overnight sensation. One estimate proclaims that it has been viewed over 700 million times on various sites[8] and, by June 2014, the first copy uploaded to YouTube had been viewed nearly 54 million times.[9] But Brolsma never expected his creation to explode in this way: "I've always been a fan of making little video clips to entertain friends, by making mini-documentaries on stupid things, or just plain old goofing around. Honestly, the original Numa Numa Dance was exactly that. I'm just a regular guy that sits in front of his computer bored out of his mind messing around on the Internet looking at funny videos and other websites to pass the time. The video was originally intended to make a few friends laugh by just goofing off. It only took one take and about 15 minutes to put all together. A lot of people ask me if I planned the video out or took multiple tries with it. The real answer is . . . no."[10]

Brolsma's minimal movements, performed while seated in a chair, consist of precise lip-syncing, well-timed facial expressions, frenetically pumping arms, sparkly fingers, tongue flicks, and, the grand climax, musically synchronized eyebrow raises—two in quick succession, with the right eye in isolation. Brolsma himself labels the video as "dance," and this is the context in which it has been received—not as a mere video of lip-syncing, but as inceptive, choreographic movement. Brolsma never rises from the chair. All that is visible is his upper shoulders and head behind the computer. Because of this, Brolsma's dancing occurs primarily with his arms waving enthusiastically, victoriously above his head. The "dorkiness" of this video shines through in its obvious amateur dance presentation, a routine so simple that anyone could repeat it. And, as with any good dance template, many people *have* picked up the movement, both mimicking the original and adding fresh new variations to the mix.

"Numa Numa Dance" also highlights other "dorky" physical designators—Brolsma is a tad plump, wears glasses that seem a tad too small with too-large headphones. The video negotiates layers of cultural representation in humorous ways, by coupling his well-accepted dorky movements with an incomprehensible but addictive Romanian pop song by O-Zone called "Dragostea Din Tei" (or "Love from the Lindens"). Had Brolsma been lip-syncing to an already popular song with English lyrics, it would have read quite differently, and likely would have been less successful. Though the song was a huge hit throughout Europe in the summer of 2004, even topping the charts at number one for many weeks, it was virtually unknown in the United States before being adopted by Brolsma for his webcam romp.[11]

Moving deeper into dorky dance territory, it is clear that Brolsma did not create the original "Numa Numa Dance" for financial gain. Although dorky dance on the Internet is now being adopted and sponsored by large companies seeking financial profit (as we will read later with the "New Numa"), this was not true when the "Numa Numa Dance" entered into the cyberstream. Claiming the spot of being the first dorky dance video to go viral, there was no precedent by which to evaluate it. "Numa Numa Dance" set the standard for the aesthetic that is still operant today. "Numa Numa Dance" is an archetype of viral videos in general, and in the minds of the larger Internet community, it is *the* viral video.[12]

In fact, Brolsma himself tinkered with the video by altering it to focus even more on the earnestness that made the dance so appealing in the first place. The very first version he created had images—flashes of random people, presumably friends or perhaps other Newgrounds users, many with heads photoshopped onto fictitious alien or cop bodies, a steak, feta cheese, and text like "Give Me Lots of Kiss"—spliced with his dancing. The earliest viewers, however, felt these arbitrary images detracted from what was most appealing about the video: Brolsma dancing. In order to underscore the movement (however minimal), he very quickly posted a second, movement-only version of the video; this is the version that went viral, ultimately concretized the "Numa Numa Dance" as Internet Phenomenon, and launched Brolsma into Internet celebrity status. Self-created, produced, and distributed intentionally for the web, Brolsma's "Numa Numa Dance" erased the remnants of artifice that lingered in some well-known precursors, such as Spike Jonze's "Praise You" video[13] or Napoleon's magical but crafted-for-the-big-screen dance (discussed further later). Brolsma simply presented himself—not a theatricalized or edited version of himself.

Brolsma's notoriety quickly exploded, and he was interviewed for or featured in numerous articles and television news programs of the time, from ABC's *Good Morning America* to VH1's *Best Week Ever*.[14] Joe Levy of *Rolling Stone* magazine wrote, "You're wondering for a second when you're watching it, is this for real? Is it a phenomenon? Oh yeah. Are people richly amused? Oh yes, very much so."[15] Alan Feuer and Jason George of the *New York Times* even wrote an article about the Numa Phenomenon on February 26, 2005, which explored the pitfalls of Internet celebrity as experienced by Brolsma after achieving his instant notoriety, though they perhaps did not quite appreciate the true beauty of Brolsma's appeal, describing his virtual performance as "earnest but painful."[16]

The reaction to the original "Numa Numa Dance" by fans, however, was overwhelmingly positive. As of June 2014, the first copy of the video posted to YouTube had received 344,583 likes to only 25,576 dislikes.[17] Although the comments section for this video is now disabled on YouTube, many early reviewers on the original Newgrounds site admired Brolsma's courage for posting such a video. One reviewer, swordman321, acknowledged: "Wow. I never give good reviews on movie imports, but this was too hilarious ... and the fact that you had the courage is admirable. Very funny. You actually pulled off a video clip that will be remembered."[18] Another response by Tripps exclaimed "kudos man, that takes balls, but lord knows I'm glad you did it. I'm still laughing. I watched it like five times 20 minutes ago and I just can't stop."[19] Viewers seem to be impressed that a performance can be so simple and accessible while simultaneously acknowledging how daunting it can be to expose oneself in such a dancerly manner, especially to what turned out to be millions of viewers.

The immense popularity and distribution of this video would not have been possible without the participation of a virtual community. Initially this occurred through viral-video sharing—e-mailing friends a link or reposting the video on other social media forums. Within days of the original posting, however, users quickly became true collaborators by posting parody or copycat videos, starting with simple videos of others performing the moves, to animated characters performing Numa, then to videos borrowing the song and not the movement, resulting in a myriad of Numa manifestations. The logistics of the Numa explosion can be more clearly understood by exploring its relation to memes. In his 1976 book, *The Selfish Gene,* zoologist and evolutionary scientist Richard Dawkins introduced the "meme" concept to signify a "unit of cultural information transferable from one mind to another."[20] A meme is thought to operate similarly to genes (thus the derivation of the word) by propagating itself as a unit through cultural evolution and diffusion, although the term has been adopted by various disciplines including linguistics and anthropology. Memes range from commercial jingles and catchphrases to the technology of building arches or transmitting religious tenets. The concept of "meme" can itself be considered a meme, as it has permeated popular culture in ways that most scientific theories do not.[21]

Internet Memes are spread through the Internet. Once these memes have gained enough popularity to be recognized beyond the Internet community, they become "Internet phenomena."[22] According to this terminology, the "Numa Numa Dance" began as a posting to a video-sharing site, which then transformed into an Internet Meme when most members of that site became familiar with the video; then, as it traveled to YouTube and other websites, onto television, and even began being copied in the nonvirtual world, it metamorphosed into a veritable Internet phenomenon. Because memes transfer by imitation, they are subject to mutation, crossover, and adaptation,[23] which was precisely the way the Numa phenomenon spread. A recent search on YouTube for "Numa Numa Dance" results in around 1.2 million hits, meaning these submissions all reference Numa in more or less overt ways.[24] More Numa Numa response videos are continually posted online, even now, more than ten years after the original.[25] These copycat videos generally maintain the integrity of the Numa concept by incorporating enough characteristics of the original so that the lineage is obvious. Yet it remains clear that alterations and adaptations arrive at a rapid pace, forging a hyperspeed cultural evolution possible only on the Internet.

One favorite example of this memetic drift actually involves another meme, the similarly awkward but addictive dance of Napoleon Dynamite, from the eponymous film released around the same time (2004).[26] Clad in oversized glasses (complete with noseguard) and high-waisted jeans while sporting a voluminous tuft of disheveled curls, Napoleon (Jon Heder) boogies down on a high school auditorium stage with an impressive range of dance moves and hip undulations, all the while akimbo in stance, staring at the floor with an open mouth. Napoleon, while certainly a talented mover, cannot escape the awkward trappings of the overall display. The result of the mash-up is the "Napoleon Numa Numa Dance," (or, perhaps more succinctly, the "N(um)apoleon") which shows Napoleon dancing to the Numa soundtrack. Its creator, NeoScriptor, wrote "[f]or the first time in history, Napoleon Dynamite reveals his true love of the Ozone song 'Dragostea Din Tei.'"[27] This popular cult film demonstrates the commitment that exists to actively forge connections between various awkward and dorky dancers.

Users could orchestrate filmic and television content into reimagined forms or make straight-up parodies. The "Numa Numa Prance" surfaced on Newgrounds shortly after the Numa Numa rage ignited. In a webcam-shot video, a young man in white shirt and headphones waves his arms and lip-syncs lackadaisically. But this forced display[28] has none of the enthusiasm that made the original so endearing. Nevertheless this video secured its role as an Internet Phenomenon precisely for being the "official first Numa parody."[29] Another spinoff, an animated "American Idle," features cartoon Gary performing on the popular TV show *American Idol* to resounding applause from the "live" studio audience, while an animated Paula Abdul dances alongside with the same pumping arm movements.[30] Numa Coop is another animated character[31] that looks nothing like Brolsma. Brolsma's movement is transferred onto an entirely different masculine stereotype,[32] a muscular, spiky haired, goateed, weightlifting man wearing a shirt with cut-off sleeves; the environment has changed. A poster of a bikini-clad babe lounging on a hot-rod car replaces Brolsma's fish tank. The cartoon dancer faithfully performs many Numa moves, including moving toward the "camera," simulating a close-up shot with the infamous eyebrow raises (perhaps even more satisfying when seen performed in animation). But toward the end, the Numa Coop man takes a decisively divergent path from the original inspiration and headbangs for several measures. However, this cartoon character's performance is infused with palpable awkwardness arising from the juxtaposition of a hypermasculine character dancing with dorky abandon and glee.

It is difficult to pinpoint *exactly* why dorky dance video creations like the "Numa Numa Dance" are so immensely popular. On one hand, these YouTube dances indulge our voyeuristic inclinations, allowing us a chance to watch a dancing style often considered socially inappropriate. We are literally offered a glimpse into private dance habits that are mostly confined to the private terrain of home kitchens and dorm rooms. YouTube is the disembodying mask that enables movers to feel safer in their dance explorations. A constant incongruity exists between the vulnerability of displaying oneself publicly versus the safety that accompanies such displays in the privacy of one's home or having that creation remain in the virtual world.[33]

YouTube is a kind of virtual dancehall or online cypher.[34] It emboldens people (especially men) to put themselves out there—quirks and all—while entering into this "circle of a global mixer," as Michael Wesch explains in his 2008 presentation to the Library of Congress, "An Anthropological Introduction to YouTube." This is especially true for people making copycat videos utilizing the original meme as a template to test some of their dorky moves. They might not be quite brave enough to make a completely original dorky dance submission but find the process of riffing off the established dance a little less daunting. We see this in the explosion of the "Gangnam Style" copycat videos, modeled after the original wildly popular music video from South Korea, by the musician Psy, released in July 2012. Currently the record holder as YouTube's most-watched video, it has been viewed well over 2.6 billion times.[35] Copycat versions include everything from dancing Gangnam babies[36] to a rather elaborate Gangnam danced by zombies in New Zealand,[37] to "Gangnam-Style Mom and Son"—a mash-up of hip hop, line dancing, and Gangnam moves, which became so popular on the Internet that the mother-son team were invited to perform live on the *Ellen* show.[38]

Some online viewers might indeed give a thumbs down on these videos, but more often than not the posse of admirers will have the video-poster's proverbial back, posting positive feedback through written commentary or creating their own video riff. This type of collaboration occurs without having to be in the same room, street corner, or dance hall, much less the same country. Despite its immense scale and geographic reach (from the individual to the world and back), the fact that people can actually create—and not be embarrassed by—dorky dancing acts (paradoxically) as a site for real dialogue and exchange. It celebrates the not-quite-talented dancing and the not-quite-perfect body, the site where explorations of identity formation take place. Numa Numa and dorky dancing created the first important virtual act of community ritual. As journalist Douglas Wolk observed about those who have participated in the Numa Numa collective experience: "[T]hey start to look less like an infectious joke than a new cultural order. These kids aren't mocking the Numa Numa Guy; they're venerating him . . . and they're beautiful to see, because they're replicating and spreading his happiness. They're following a ritual that's meaningful if not yet venerable: learning the dance, lip-synching the song, documenting their performance just so, making it available for the world to see.[39]

Viewers are profoundly attracted to the sheer simplicity, genuineness, and admirable courage of the dancers because dorky displays resonate on a personal level. At some point all of us experienced the awkwardness of adolescence, when our bodies underwent changes beyond our control. Generally we try to forget these awkward stages, not revel in them. But dorky dancing also evokes images of the awkward toddler, whose body, despite grasping for control, evidences an endearing perseverance to remain upright. The best dorky dancers express both of these awkward sensibilities in a single body.

Because its main impetus is fun, participation in dorky dance is also motivated by pleasure, though the direct and meaningful consequences that emerge from dorky dancing can spark real personal transformation. People may not be bold enough to project themselves in goofy grandeur to millions, but they can find great value in these video contributions—value that ranges from sheer entertainment to experiences as in XxJojexx's case: "I just wanted you [Brolsma] to know that I played your video every morning while I was caregiver for my husband in his fight with lung cancer. I would play it when I got up and dance and sing and it gave me an upbeat frame of mind so that I could smile and go on with what I needed to do. When that dear man died I still played your video mostly when I was at my worst, when the darkness was tight around me and bouncing around to your Numa Numa dance would help me find my way back to the light. I still come and play it when being alone gets to be a little too much. I just wanted you to know that while this is a very funny and entertaining video it has served a higher purpose and helped save me in the darkest times of my life. For this I thank you very, very much."[40]

As much as we must credit Gary Brolsma for being the first guy on the Internet dance floor, he was also quick to commit the biggest party faux pas, the metaphorical "spilled drink" at the global dorky dance mixer: He agreed to do a polished yet utterly unthrilling sequel video, "New Numa." Although the relationship between commercialism and dorky dance is complex,[41] any marketing of dorky dance distorts and taints its charm, destroying its sincerity and authenticity, and creating in its place a contrived, obvious, and annoying awkwardness.

Big business sunk its talons into the dorky dance world with the creation of "New Numa," "released" on September 8, 2006, on its own website, newnuma.com. Even the word "release" is antithetical to the homegrown, improvisational nature of dorky dance and viral videos. "Release" conjures images of Hollywood movies or new X-box games. The original "Numa Numa Dance" was not released—it was just posted for the amusement of a couple of Brolsma's friends and accidentally garnered immense popularity. "New Numa" was planned, promoted, and packaged. "New Numa" was a brand: when visiting newnuma.com, one could click on a "gear" icon link and purchase New Numa shirts, coffee mugs, bumper stickers, a throw pillow, and a Numa T-shirt-bedecked teddy bear, all imprinted with a cartoonish version of Gary—a smiling face with arms thrown high in dorky dance victory style. As if this wasn't enough, visitors could also purchase Brolsma's style of headphones made famous in the original Numa video.

The "New Numa" begins in Brolsma's bedroom, the same setup as the original video. Brolsma's phone rings; he answers, "Halo," (the signature song lyric from the original song/video) and a female voice exclaims "Oh my goodness. Is this Gary Brolsma, the Numa Numa guy?" His affirmative response prompts the female caller to ask: "Will you please, please do a new Numa video, please?" Brolsma responds, "Hmmm, I wonder" and the video quickly transitions into a fantastical dream sequence of what a new Numa video might look like. Brolsma maintains the pumping arms from side to side and sparkly fingers of the original, but the video shows him in full screen, at times accompanied by a trio of other "dorky looking" young men. The background changes to various locales, transporting Gary away from his room. Obviously shot in a film studio, advanced technology enables the producers to add lightning effects and transpose graffiti-covered brick walls onto the scene.[42]

Although it strives to appear amateurish, the polished veneer of "New Numa" unmistakably signifies professional production, which likely included a creative triad of director, editor, and even choreographer. The video was produced by Gary Voelker and Andrew Lee of Seattle-based Experience Studios and despite the bevy of creative talent, the "New Numa," floundered and never garnered the attention or respect of Brolsma's original. This constructed dorkiness could never register as authentic. The new song "New Numa" (sung in Russian) was created specifically for the "New Numa" by Variety Beats and could be purchased on the official website along with other downloadables or ringtones. iTunes reviews of the song ranged from a few positives to the more common lukewarm responses: "This song is okay, but not [what] started the whole revolution,"[43] and "Twas moderately entertaining. . . . nothing is ever as good as the original."[44] Then there was an abundance of scathing criticism. Wooden Tree commented: "The original Numa, Dragostea Din Tei, was a great song. This, however, is trash for multiple reasons. . . . The only similarity is the use of the word "Numa."[45] Another commenter, Imdafox, best sums up the sentiments of many: "This boy used to be one of us, an Internet person. Now he's trying to make a quick buck, what a bastard."[46]

Since its release, "New Numa" has been viewed over 16.7 million times on YouTube alone.[47] Like the reviews for the song, viewers sense the sequel's deficits and articulate their disapproval online. Sockglue wrote: "The first Numa video was good, not because you [Brolsma] put a lot off effort into it, but because it was almost . . . innocent. You should have just let it go. You had your time of fame, this video (that wasn't bad, just disappointing) won't bring you back up to fame."[48] Another reviewer clarified further that the essential lacking component was rooted in the choreography of the video. Jinitron noted: "I like the song but you're missing what was cool in the first one. Your close-ups, your facial expression. That was great. You [had] facial rhythm and the arm movements were good, too."[49] Another reviewer, djkuhl, agreed: "Jinitron is right. The facial expressions [were] priceless" but goes on to emphasize its obvious commercial production values. Djkuhl continued, "I'd like to know how many people were involved beyond Gary. The video feels like something . . . wrapped in someone else's finishing touches."[50] Others are more vocal in their criticism of commercializing grassroots creations, foreseeing the overwhelming co-optation to come: "This is the first of many overdone viral marketing campaigns we will see involving Internet memes. It was only a matter of time until the authenticity and innocence of the true viral Internet phenomenon was violated. And here, in the flesh, is one of the beautiful accidents cashing in on his unsolicited fame. Good for Gary—shame on the backer of this project. What's next? (Star Wars Kid on Ice?) I'll pass."[51]

However, one response-video favorite is "New Numa: The Animation" by Dustball.[52] It loosely follows the plotline of the original "New Numa" video, but in animated form. It differs in the beginning; the woman's voice and script are replaced. Now a man (sounding like a showbiz talent scout or a fairground carnival spieler) calls Gary and pitches an idea: "Look kid, we loved your last video, it was phenomenal. But we wanna' make a New Numa video that is even better than the last one. . . . It's gonna' be huge I tell you, huge! This new video is not gonna' be on some crappy webcam. We got a full crew this time and it's gonna' be totally slick and MTV style. That's what the kids want these days. We're flying you out to Hollywood tomorrow and we'll get started right away. We're gonna' put your name in lights, kid. You're gonna' be a staaaar!"[53] Gary responds: "That sounds terrible. I wonder . . ." then the animated video proceeds into a re-creation of the actual "New Numa" video—again as if Gary were imagining what the final product might look like. After this dream sequence, animated Gary utters to himself: "Holy crap, that was awful." The phone rings again and the show businessman exclaims, "That was brilliant. Here's what we're gonna' do with your next video. You're gonna' dance the Numa Numa while you eat your own poop."[54] Animated Gary's imagined retort seems to summarize what many in the YouTube-viewing community wish the real Gary had said when approached to undertake "New Numa." He shouts with a hitherto unheard aggression: "You know what, that video was total crap. Just leave me alone while I still have some shred of dignity . . . It worked the first time but that was a fluke. And it worked because it was genuine and I wasn't trying to be a hit. It's impossible to re-create that. Don't you get it? You're a slime ball for trying to make money off of me! Screw you!"[55]

"I Will Not Pay for Numa" by Mr. Safety is a direct response to the hawking of the "New Numa" song on their website—where it sells for 99 cents per download.[56] Mr. Safety has created numerous parody YouTube videos and has his own subscription channel. His version of the "New Numa" has song lyrics that investigate the Numa phenomenon from its inception to its current form. The refrain for this video is "I will not, will not pay. The song's okay, but I still will not pay."[57] On a fundamental level, however, Mr. Safety's video reads as an outright rejection of the entire phenomenon of "New Numa" and the corruption of the Internet's homemade productions, with the inevitable result of the increasing commercialization of virtual space.

What this suggests, then, is that the Internet (and YouTube in particular) *really did* create a space where blended identities can exist in a less problematized realm. The reduction of commercialistic incentive, at least at its inception, created a freer space for the trying on and commixing of personalities. The minimally restricted space of the Internet (at least in the United States), in which anyone could participate with little governmental or big-business mediation or censorship, gained an unprecedented boost with the advent of video-sharing websites, especially YouTube.

The popularity of the dorky dance phenomenon demonstrates a change in attitude about dancing. Of course it makes us laugh. But we reside in an era when this dancing style (like nerdiness) is embraced and celebrated. We enjoy watching this kind of dance because it reflects *us*, and we are watching it by the millions. Dorky YouTube dancers are breaking down discouraging barriers and established conceptualizations of what dance should be. Instead they are creating a place for amateurs of varying body shapes and sizes and abilities to embrace a variety of fashion, music, and other cultural styles. Internet dorky dance participants are challenging notions of who can dance, for whom, in what manner, and through what medium. As they engage in an instantaneous process of production, reception, and reaction, they become millions who are fighting for (gently, with humility and wit) their right to dance, awkwardly or not. If they are ridiculed, an army of potential virtual-copycats rises up to praise them. As user-generated dance on YouTube and the wider web becomes increasingly sophisticated, polished, and commercialized, the original "Numa Numa Dance," in all its pixilated glory, remains enduringly endearing. This is the *Ur*-usermade dancing video. And for this, Gary Brolsma, the father of dorky dance, deserves the biggest (virtual) standing ovation of all.

Notes

1. "YouTube: Frequently Asked Questions," YouTube, accessed August 1, 2012, http://ww.youtube.com/t/faq.

2. Susan P. Crawford, "The New Digital Divide," *New York Times*, December 3, 2011, accessed June 7, 2014, http://www.nytimes.com/2011/12/04/opinion/sunday/internet-access-and-the-new-divide.html.

3. Aaron Smith, "U.S. Smart Phone Use in 2015," *Pew Research Center*, accessed October 7, 2016, http://www.pewinternet.org/2015/04/01/us-smartphone-use-in-2015/.

4. "YouTube Brings Back its Popular Motto 'Broadcast Yourself,'" The Utube Blog, accessed August 10, 2012, http://theutubeblog.com/2008/02/07/youtube-brings-back-its-motto-broadcast-yourself/.

5. The involvement of the virtual audience as critics was clearly seen in the response to Miley Cyrus's "twerking" display at MTV's 2013 Video Music Awards. Many more viewers were witness to her dancing—and its accompanying critiques—online, through Facebook and Twitter, than those who watched it live on television. The response was so widespread, even the *New York Times* posted an article in response, "Explaining Twerking to Your Parents," while other critiques examined the issue of cultural appropriation, e.g., Demetria Lucas's "Twerking Miley Cyrus Starts Trend in Overanalyzing 'Black' Dance."

6. A viral video is "video content which gains widespread popularity through the process of Internet sharing, typically through e-mail or IM messages, blogs and other media sharing websites" (http://en.wikipedia.org/wiki/Viral_video).

7. Michael Wesch, "An Anthropological Introduction to YouTube," (lecture presented at the Library of Congress, June 23, 2008), accessed August 12, 2012, http://www.youtube.com/watch?v=TPAO-lZ4_hU.

8. Michael Strangelove, *Watching YouTube: Extraordinary Videos by Ordinary People* (Toronto: University of Toronto Press, 2010), 130.

9. "Numa Numa," YouTube, accessed June 7, 2014, http://www.youtube.com/watch?v=600g9gwKh10.

10. "The Numa Story: Interview with Gary Brolsma," New Numa, accessed February 6, 2007, http://www.newnuma.com/story.html.

11. "Dragostea Din Tei," Acharts.us, accessed August 15, 2012, http://acharts.us/song/1600.

12. Jay Dedman and Joshua Paul, *Videoblogging* (Indianapolis: Wiley, 2006), 13.

13. Spike Jonze, the director, crafted a fictitious personality, Richard Koufey, and performed amateur-looking dance with the fictitious Torrance Community Dance Group in public spaces in LA. The resulting video, shot on handheld cameras, was made into the official video for Fat Boy Slim's song, "Praise You."

14. "The Numa Story: Interview with Gary Brolsma."

15. "You Go, Gary! 'Numa' Takes Web by Storm," MSNBC, February 17, 2005, accessed August 16, 2012, http://today.msnbc.msn.com/id/6987134/ns/today-entertainment/t/you-go-gary-numa-takes-web-storm/#.UDwnpKDwSuk.

16. Alan Feuer and Jason George, "Internet Fame Is Cruel Mistress for a Dancer of the Numa Numa," *New York Times*, February 26, 2005, accessed February 12, 2007, http://www.nytimes.com/2005/02/26/nyregion/26video.html?ex=1174708800&en=401d2538d98cd1e2&ei=5070.

17. Eventually numerous copies of the video appeared on YouTube; these comments refer to the first posting of the video, accessed on June 7, 2014, https://www.youtube.com/watch?v=600g9gwKh10&feature=kp.

18. Swordman321, "Numa Review," Newgrounds, accessed February 8, 2007, http://www.newgrounds.com/portal/readreview.php?sort=date_mr&id=206373&page=1031.

19. Tripps, "Numa Review," accessed February 8, 2007, http://www.newgrounds.com/portal/readreview.php?sort=date_mr&id=206373&page=1031.

20. Richard Dawkins, *The Selfish Gene* (Oxford: Oxford University Press, 2006).

21. It is important to note that the meme concept has met with criticism from semioticians who view meme as a distortion of their use of "sign" or other critics who view it as reductionist or inadequate; J. T. Burman, in his article "The Misunderstanding of Memes" (2012), prefers the use of the term "infectious idea."

22. "Internet Meme," wikipedia, accessed on February 12, 2007, http://en.wikipedia.org/wiki/Internet_meme.

23. "What Is a Meme?" *Daily Meme*, accessed August 12, 2012, http://thedailymeme.com/what-is-ameme/.

24. With more recent postings, the word "Numa" might be included in the description of a YouTube video just to entice users into watching something else completely unrelated.

25. "Numa Numa Dance Search." YouTube, accessed August 12, 2012, http://www.youtube.com/results?search_query=numa+numa+dance&oq=numa+numa+dance&gs_l=youtube.3. .3515 9j0l9.854.2302.0.2795.6.4.0.0.0.0.150.432.2j2.4.0 . . . 0.0 . . . 1ac.-7laRx74a58.

26. The Napoleon Dynamite dance clip has nearly 1.8 million views and 10,383 likes on YouTube alone, as of August 2013.

27. "Napoleon Numa Numa Dance," Newgrounds, accessed February 7, 2007, http://www.newgrounds.com/portal/search.php?ms=numa+napoleon&kind=j&x=0&y=0.

28. Around 6,000 views, as of August 2013.

29. "Numa Numa Prance," Newgrounds, accessed February 7, 2007, http://www.newgrounds.com/portal/view/207440.

30. "American Idle," Newgrounds, accessed February 7, 2007, http://www.newgrounds.com/portal/view/227808; 1,028,976 views as of August 2013.

31. Interestingly, "Numa Coop" was created by female animator, Katie Henderson, though the animated dorky dancer was still a male.

32. "Numa Coop," Newgrounds, accessed February 7, 2007, http://www.newgrounds.com/portal/view/237597, 173,584 views as of August 2013.

33. Even if a creator wishes to later remove a posting, once it has been copied or reposted, it is impossible to contain.

34. Cypher is a term used in hip hop for the circle in which spontaneous art-making (dance, poetry, graffiti) is created by collective improvisation.

35. "Gangnam Style," YouTube, accessed June 7, 2014, https://www.youtube.com/watch?v=9bZkp7q19f0.

36. "Baby Gangnam Style," YouTube, accessed June 7, 2014, https://www.youtube.com/watch?v=mP1DPTY4Y70.

37. "Gangnam Style Zombie Style," YouTube, accessed June 7, 2014, https://www.youtube.com/watch?v=47XPuiKOjdk.

38. "Gangnam Style Mom and Son," YouTube, accessed June 7, 2014, https://www.youtube.com/watch?v=rr5Z0SHBNv0.

39. Douglas Wolk, "The Syncher, Not the Song: The Irresistible Rise of the Numa Numa Dance," The Believer, June/July, 2006, accessed August 20, 2012, http://www.believermag.com/issues/200606/?read=article_wolk.

40. xxJojexx, "Numa Review," accessed February 8, 2007, http://www.newgrounds.com/portal/readreview.php?sort=date_mr&id=206373&page=1031.

41. There *are* examples of dorky dances that accidentally became marketable, like OK Go's "A Million Ways" music video, YouTube, accessed on August 13, 2012, http://www.youtube.com/watch?v=M1_CLW-NNwc.

42. "New Numa—The Return of Gary Brolsma," YouTube, accessed on August 13, 2012, http://www.youtube.com/watch?v=3gg5LOd_Zus.

43. Posted by Freakin'Nuts, iTunes.

44. Posted by patman216, iTunes.

45. Posted by Wooden Tree, iTunes.

46. Posted by Imdafox, iTunes.

47. "New Numa—The Return of Gary Brolsma."

48. Sockglue, "New Numa Review," accessed February 18, 2007. http://www.youtube.com/comment_servlet?all_comments&v=3gg5LOd_Zus&fromurl=/watch%3Fv%3D3gg5LOd_Zus.

49. Jinitron, "New Numa Review."

50. Djkuhl, "New Numa Review."

51. In reference to another early Internet celebrity, known as the Star Wars Kid, whose parents sued his classmates for posting video of him using a light saber onto the Internet without his permission; Medianox, "New Numa Review."

52. "New Numa: The Animation," Newgrounds, accessed March 3, 2007, http://www.newgrounds.com/portal/view/348166.

53. Ibid.

54. Ibid.

55. Ibid.

56. "I Will Not Pay for Numa," YouTube, accessed March 3, 2007, http://www.youtube.com/watch?v=SLMZdwOc4Ds.

57. Ibid.

2

So You Think You Can Dance Straight?

Same-Sex Ballroom and Reality Television

J. ELLEN GAINOR

A search of Google images for "ballroom dancing" displays page after page of photographs and line drawings of a man and a woman holding each other in close embrace or stylized pose, dressed in elegant formal wear or colorful, tight-fitting spandex costumes. Significantly, what is not readily found in these pages are representations of two people of the same sex dancing together, despite the burgeoning global phenomenon of same-sex ballroom dance. In the context of Western partnered social dance traditions, the notion that men would dance with men, and women with women, rather than in heterosexual pairs, defies historical conventions. While American film and television have long featured images of men dancing with men, or, less frequently, women with women, in a closed couple embrace, such same-sex dancing is almost always fraught with homosexual anxiety, deflected into broad physical comedy routines and raucous audience laughter (often with added laugh track).

By contrast, representations of a man and a woman ballroom dancing together have become synecdoches for romance or (sometimes illicit) passion. Ballroom and other partner dance forms have long been part of the American social milieu,[1] and these dance tropes are now so ubiquitous and potent that they have become default choices by advertisers: older couples who take Centrum Silver vitamins will enjoy swing dancing together well into their golden years, while women who shave with Venus razors need never fear bare-legged caresses from seductive male Argentine tango partners. This heteronormative and homosocial imagery is enormously powerful and omnipresent. Therefore, the 2008 and 2009 broadcasts in the United States of same-sex ballroom dance, especially as performed by serious dancers in the context of the wildly popular medium of reality television, represented a significant cultural disruption and challenge.[2]

The first two decades of the twenty-first century have, of course, already seen both polarized conflict and remarkable cultural transformation around LGBTQ concerns. We might usefully consider the emergence of same-sex partner dance into broader American consciousness toward the end of that first decade as reflecting these debates and transitions. Indeed, as scholar Caroline Picart notes, the ballroom form "constitutes a crucial site upon which negotiations on how to package bodies as racialized, sexualized, nationalized, and classed are staged," reflecting "larger social, political, and cultural tensions." For Picart, ballroom offers a "template for values concerning masculinity and femininity, heterosexuality and homosexuality, nationalism and xenophobia, among others."[3]

Since the early twentieth century, ballroom dance has occupied three overlapping locations within global culture: as a social form practiced within variously defined communities; as an exhibition form performed for audiences; and as a competitive form—now commonly known as DanceSport—that has, for a number of years, been progressing toward formal recognition by the International Olympic Committee, largely through the efforts of the World DanceSport Federation (WDSF, previously called the International DanceSport Federation [IDSF]), which oversees sanctioned DanceSport competitions worldwide.[4]

For purposes of this essay, I will focus primarily on international DanceSport, the dominant version of ballroom with an established, formalized movement vocabulary shared by dancers globally. Although dancers in the United States (and some sections of Canada) may enjoy and perform American ballroom, which has some notable distinctions from international DanceSport, competitors understand that working only in the American form may limit them since this style is not practiced in most other countries.[5] Additionally, in the latter half of the twentieth century, as the number of ballroom dancers from other countries coming to teach in and compete for the United States grew, the prevalence and popularity of the international style has expanded. Precisely because there is a common movement structure within international DanceSport (and thus fewer "variables"), this form of competitive ballroom becomes a compelling site in which to explore the performance of gender and sexuality.

A brief history of this competitive form may help frame the discussion. After the First World War, England's Imperial Society of Teachers of Dancing began to codify its "Technique of Ballroom Dancing," which, through the processes of political and cultural imperialism, subsequently became the international standard for dance instruction and competition.[6] In competitive international ballroom, there are ten dances that fall into two categories, Standard and Latin. The Standard dances are: waltz, fox-trot, tango, Viennese waltz, and quickstep. The Latin dances are: rumba, cha cha cha, samba, paso doble, and jive. Couples may compete in either category, or in both.

The manuals published by the Imperial Society provide detailed information on the proper execution of the figures comprising each dance as well as combinations of steps that can be grouped in sequences. For purposes of training, licensing, and competition, the figures are categorized by level of difficulty: bronze, silver, and gold, with gold being the most advanced. As the opening pages from *The Revised Technique of Latin American Dancing* show, for example, the manual offers guidance on correct body positions and a list of abbreviations that will help dancers decode the instructions for executing the sanctioned movement patterns. The details include exact foot angle, alignment, and placement; the movement of the shoulder(s) in relation to the lower body; the amount of turn within figures; interpretive options within the lead; and definitions of specified holds and body positions (see this chapter's appendix).

Each named figure within a dance is broken down into its component elements for each partner, always designated as "man" and "lady." The explanation of the "Natural Turn"—one of the most common figures used in waltz choreography—illustrates how the Imperial Society's other volume, *The Ballroom Technique*, provides both a step-by-step guide for each partner (literally what one does with each foot movement), and instructions on other physical elements (such as contra body movement) and placement of the body relative to the "line of dance" (the imaginary oval inscribed on the dance floor, around which the couples move counterclockwise). The suggested sequences of steps at the bottom of the chart aid choreography at the different skill levels (Associate, Licentiate, and Fellow) but also assist dancers to be aware of others' potential movements, which in turn helps them avoid collisions or entanglements on the dance floor (see Chart 2.1).

Anyone studying these manuals can readily observe two important details: there are many steps danced identically by each partner, regardless of sex; and,

Chart 2.1. Waltz Natural Turn

STEP	FEET POSITIONS	ALIGNMENT	AMOUNT OF TURN	RISE & FALL
MAN				
1	R.F. fwd	Facing D.W.	Com. to turn R.	Com. to rise e/o 1
2	L.F. to side	Backing D.C.	1/4 between 1–2	Continue to rise on 2&3
3	R.F. closes to L.F.	Backing L.O.D.	1/8 between 2–3	Lower e/o 3
4	L.F. back	Backing L.O.D.	Com. to turn R.	Com. to rise e/o 4. NFR
5	R.F. to side	Pointing D.C.	3/8 between 4–5. Body turns less.	Continue to rise on 5&6
6	L.F. closes to R.F.	Facing D.C.	Body completes turn.	Lower e/o 6

FOOTWORK: 1. H.T.; 2. T.; 3. T.H.; 4. T.H.; 5. T.; 6. T.H.
C.B.M. on 1 and 4.
SWAY: S.R.R.S.L.L.

LADY				
1	L.F. back	Backing D.W.	Com. to turn R.	Com. to rise e/o 1. NFR
2	R.F. to side	Pointing down L.O.D.	3/8 between 1–2. Body turns less.	Continue to rise on 2&3
3	L.F. closes to R.F.	Facing L.O.D.	Body completes turn	Lower e/o 3
4	R. F. fwd	Facing L.O.D.	Com. to turn R.	Com. to rise e/o 4
5	L.F. to side	Backing centre	1/4 between 4–5	Continue to rise on 5&6
6	R.F. closes to L.F.	Backing D.C.	1/8 between 5–6	Lower e/o 6

FOOTWORK: 1. T.H.; 2. T.; 3. T.H.; 4. H.T.; 5. T. 6. T.H.
C.B.M. on 1 and 4
SWAY: S.L.L.S.R.R.
Precede: (A) L.F. Closed Change—Natural Turn (corner)—Chassé from P.P.—Outside Change—Reverse Corté—Basic Weave
(L) & (F) Weave from P.P.—Closed Telemark—Outside Spin—Turning Lock
Follow: (A), (L), & (F) R.F. Closed Change—Natural Turn (corner)

by extension, there is nothing inherent in the steps that would preclude their being danced by someone of either sex. In other words, the historical social convention of ballroom dance being executed by male-female couples can be separated from the kinetic basis of the dances; there is no reason why ballroom "must" be heteronormative. Although ballroom dancers in the United States and elsewhere perceived these social strictures,[7] it was not until the late twentieth century that some dancers proactively chose to explore alternative same-sex modes within the form, first socially, and then competitively.

In 1982, American Olympic athlete Dr. Tom Waddell founded the Gay Games in San Francisco. This competition was envisioned as "a vehicle for education and change regarding the perception of homosexuality."[8] Modeled on the Olympics,[9] but welcoming athletes of any sexual orientation, and focusing on inclusion and community, the Gay Games have become "the largest sports and culture festival in the world open to all."[10] In 1998, the International Federation of Gay Games included DanceSport, featuring same-sex dance partnerships from multiple countries, as one of its official competitive events for the Gay Games V in Amsterdam.[11] By the summer of 2006, with Chicago hosting the Gay Games VII and with Montréal hosting the first international Outgames (a similar event that resulted from a dispute with the Federation), DanceSport had become one of the most popular competitive events, drawing sizeable international pools of entrants and attracting among the largest audiences at both games. In the United States, same-sex ballroom had originated within LGBTQ communities, attracting social dancers and competitors who wanted to dance in same-sex partnerships. Although it was popular earlier in Europe and Australia—locations with older and stronger ballroom dance cultures than in the States—by the time of the Chicago Gay Games there were enough well-established U.S. competitors and same-sex ballroom communities to support dedicated instruction and competitive events at such locations as the Sacramento DanceSport Project, a studio, performance, and competition venue that opened in 2001.[12]

Notably, the Gay Games and Outgames chose to foreground DanceSport. Not only do such events showcase same-sex ballroom, they also provide enhanced visibility as well as a "home" for these dancers whose athleticism and artistry has been denied them in mainstream athletic competitions.[13] Subsequently, the games helped foster a global community of dancers who may now encounter each other regularly, at these Federated events, as well as at stand-alone international ballroom competitions. Indeed, many dancers at the 2006 games not only appeared at both venues but (from my perspective as an observer) also seemed to know each other—greeting each other warmly and dancing with various partners from countries other than their own in the less formal "general dancing" periods in between competitive events.

Significantly, the WDSF explicitly refuses to sanction same-sex competitions.[14] Some countries specifically prohibit dancers from participating in WDSF-sanctioned events and same-sex events, most probably because of assumptions surrounding same-sex ballroom and sexuality. In other words, dancers who choose to participate in same-sex competition may forfeit the right to represent their country in WDSF events, including, potentially, the Olympics. As was obvious from the homophobia that emerged in the months leading up to the 2014 Winter Olympics in Sochi, the issue of athletes' sexual orientation remains volatile. Thus dancers' decisions about where to compete, and with whom, have real and lasting consequences.

In July 2004, on the occasion of a competition hosted by the Massachusetts Institute of Technology, the *New York Times* published an article on the growing controversy surrounding same-sex ballroom dance within the United States and internationally.[15] The *Times* article identifies several concerns central to the rejection of same-sex partnerships within mainstream international competition. Some believe the tension stems from the high stakes for DanceSport to gain a firmer place and greater visibility within the Olympics, a goal that could be compromised if DanceSport were perceived to be gay.[16] A closely related issue is the potential for positive economic impact if DanceSport were to become an official Olympic event. As the article notes, "the Olympics might well bring endorsements, exposure and respect." But having same-sex couples competing could "hurt the image" of the form, thus reducing or eliminating the potential of the Olympics to be a financial boon to dance studios, dance teachers, and dancers alike. Moreover, according to Jim Frasier, the IDSF spokesman quoted in the article, the international organization is "looking at televising the sport and obtaining sponsorship, and there may be implications there" if it were to endorse same-sex dancers.

When questioned further by *Times* reporter Eric Marx about the IDSF position on same-sex ballroom, Frasier explained: "Just as the [Ukrainian] Hopak [folk] dancers do not have to start adding other ethnic groups' elements to their dances because to do so would fundamentally contradict what the dance is about, DanceSport does not have to start adding dances about some other relationship." For example, Frasier continued, the [DanceSport] paso doble "is performed by a man and woman because it is about the relationship between a man and a woman, using the metaphor of the matador and the cape."[17]

This stunningly heterosexist (and xenophobic) quotation would require an entire essay to unpack, but we might consider briefly two of the central assumptions reflected by this statement. First is the idea that the inclusion of same-sex couples would necessitate "adding dances" to competitions,[18] and second is the idea that a specific kind of interpersonal relationship inheres in any ballroom form—in this case, the paso doble. These notions have at their core a kind of biological essentialism that same-sex ballroom directly challenges.

Ironically, of course, same-sex ballroom poses a threat precisely because it *does not* necessitate the *addition* of any dance to the established structures of Standard and Latin competition. Indeed the same-sex competitions that have sprung up worldwide over the last two decades largely follow the WDSF rules for competition—with the signal difference that the established competitive ballroom dances are performed by same-sex couples.[19] The North American Same-Sex Partner Dance Association (NASSPDA), for example, provides clear information for competition dancers about the parallels to and distinctions from the WDSF regulations.[20] The recently formed International Federation of Same-Sex Dance Associations (IFSSDA), of which NASSPDA is a member, seeks "to serve as a worldwide umbrella organization for same-sex dancing,"[21] and may well become the central resource for international same-sex competitors and competitions, potentially solidifying globally these regulation parallels.

Within the codified structure of traditional international ballroom, the "man" leads and the "lady" follows. Yet we should note in this regard that most contemporary professional dance instructors and coaches, regardless of their sex, must learn to execute both the "man's" and the "lady's" figures, in order to teach and choreograph them; this professional necessity, then, already reveals some cracks in the "separate spheres" ideology of the WDSF.[22] Same-sex dancers, moreover, consciously substitute the designations "leader" and "follower" for "man" and "lady" so as to distinguish between gendered traditions in ballroom and the actual mechanics of partner dance.[23] And while some same-sex dancers choose to execute only the movements assigned to the leader or to the follower, other dancers choose to alternate these roles. To switch the lead in the midst of a dance is actually quite complicated. For competition, the lead change must be carefully choreographed into the routine, and, in Standard, it necessitates strategically timed and aesthetically pleasing exchanges of arm, hand, and head positions, as well as shifts in body weight within the dance frame hold. In Latin, where the dancers' bodies are often farther apart, the choreographed change may be more seamless, as the lead flows through the arm and handhold from one dancer to the other to initiate turns, directional changes, or poses. During competition, judges take away points if the switch is not well and smoothly executed. Same-sex dancers' decision to switch lead is, of course, both political and aesthetic. This choice speaks to their desire for a greater artistic range within the prescribed movement vocabulary of the dances and to embody a partnership reflecting equality and balance (in fact, some of these dancers participate in a form of same-sex ballroom known as "Equality Dance").[24]

The inherent threat to mainstream ballroom competition, then, is the visible, kinetic proof that same-sex dancers are able to execute the established ballroom forms—with identical technique and adherence to the highly codified movement structures—as their mixed-sex counterparts. But the other assumption underlying Frasier's dismissal is, arguably, even more complex, that is, same-sex competitors pose a profound challenge to the hegemony of interpretation—to the meaning of a (heteronormative) metaphor. The idea that ballroom dance could represent anything other than narratives of male-female relationships, and, even more specifically, narratives defined by the nexus of male dominance ("lead") and female submission ("follow"), is unimaginable within the paradigms of these mainstream international organizations.

With such theoretical and historical considerations in mind, we can more fully explore how issues surrounding same-sex ballroom manifested in mainstream American popular culture earlier in the twenty-first century. Within the context of reality television, U.S. audiences have had, for over a decade, access to two popular programs that regularly feature ballroom dance: *Dancing with the Stars* (devoted primarily to ballroom) and *So You Think You Can Dance* (which includes ballroom among other dance forms). Both series originated in England, which has long enjoyed a strong ballroom culture, but now there are distinct national versions of these programs aired in many countries around the world, featuring that region's competitors.[25] These reality programs have heightened awareness of and interest in ballroom dance wherever they are broadcast, even in locales that did not previously have a strong cultural tradition in the form. In the United States, the fact that local dance studios air advertisements during episodes of these shows indicates that such programs are perceived to enhance viewers' desire to participate in dance.

The ABC network's *Dancing with the Stars* pairs ballroom professionals with celebrity amateur dancers, who are the title's implied "stars."[26] Weekly broadcasts feature snippets of the partners' training sessions, culminating in the performance of the week's routine, and postperformance critiques and scoring by a panel of professional judges. Through the combination of judges' scores and viewers' votes, couples are eliminated one by one until the season's winner remains. Over the course of any season, the partners will usually perform a number of different ballroom dances, the quickstep being notoriously the most challenging for the amateur "stars." In choreographing ballroom routines, the dance professionals often draw liberally from the more flexible exhibition ballroom vocabulary, and both American and international ballroom styles are represented. The performances must entertain television viewers and demonstrate (as well as possible) dance technique and artistic expression. Using the two styles provides more variety for audiences and more strategic options for the professionals, who must be acutely sensitive to the strengths and weaknesses of their partners. It is always understood that the judges will be assessing the amateur dancers' ability to execute steps from the codified ballroom syllabi that are woven into the routines. Indeed, if the judges perceive an inadequate inclusion of steps and figures from the syllabi in the choreography, the partners may receive a lower score. Significantly, however, there is never any discussion of the fact that, in almost every instance, the dance professionals—male or female—have to "lead" each routine to assist their "stars" in the execution of what is often quite complicated choreography. In this way the program also silently displays the ruptured façade of gender roles embedded in the "pro-am" dynamics of this televised ballroom competition.[27] Particularly when the dance professional is female, we can observe how she must carefully modulate her dominance in training with a less assertive persona in performances and in postperformance interview segments with her male "star."

In spring 2008, audiences of *Dancing with the Stars* unexpectedly witnessed what for many was their first glimpse of quasi-serious same-sex ballroom dance. In this sixth season, the program featured married ballroom champions Anna Trebunskaya and Jonathan Roberts as two of the dance professionals. Trebunskaya, paired with film star Steve Guttenberg, became ill and was temporarily unable to work with Guttenberg on that week's routine, a tango. Roberts, who with his "star" partner had already been eliminated from the competition, came to the rescue and coached Guttenberg while his wife recuperated. Because Guttenberg was dancing the man's part, Roberts had to dance "as lady." *Dancing with the Stars'* producers obviously decided to exploit Trebunskaya's unforeseen illness, and the "training footage" they assembled for that week's episode fascinatingly wobbled between choreographic parody, homosocial anxiety (complete with laugh track, added to accompany the studio practice sessions), and serious same-sex dancing.[28] Trebunskaya recovered sufficiently by the time of the broadcast to perform the routine, but it appears that the segment with Roberts and Guttenberg worked so effectively that the show's producers decided to pursue their unanticipated partnership further, by having them formally execute the entire routine the following week in a special "one-night-only" performance dubbed "The Mango."

Guttenberg was costumed for both performances in tailored black trousers, shirt, and vest. Trebunskaya wore a spectacularly sequined, bare-backed red gown for the routine's first showing, while, for the second iteration, Roberts sported a white shirt and black tuxedo with tails. This choice could, of course, simply be read as traditional male Standard competition attire (which it was), and/or, in this context, more ambiguously, as a feminized costume, with the swinging, swirling tails echoing the swish, swirl, and flow of Trebunskaya's gown. Guttenberg, embracing a macho persona, maintained similar facial expressions and physicality for both renditions. And while the choreography in both performances was essentially identical, careful viewing reveals an important difference between the two versions. In Standard competitive ballroom, partners usually maintain close physical contact through the lower torso region. If this close contact is not maintained—a phenomenon informally referred to as "too much daylight"—the dancers are penalized. When Trebunskaya led Guttenberg through the routine, she ensured that this contact was appropriately maintained. In "The Mango," however, Roberts kept their bodies farther apart, avoiding the appearance of any pelvic (and intimate or sexually suggestive) contact. To underscore this message, the pair concluded their "Mango" exhibition with a chest bump, (re)affirming their normative masculinity.

This televised tango, as performed by these three competitors, illustrates vividly how dancers (or choreographers) take what is essentially neutral movement—the foundational ballroom positions and figure sequences that comprise a routine—and layer onto it gendered gesture and expression.[29] We can observe identical figures danced by Roberts and Trebunskaya, and watch what—if we had only seen Trebunskaya dancing with Guttenberg—we might assume unquestioningly are "female" steps and gestures. But a comparison of both segments shows how Roberts vacillates between moments in which he *straightforwardly* executes many of those same tango steps "as lady" on the one hand, and, on the other, displays specific movements and expressions that suggest parody or panic. It is precisely these latter movements and expressions, I would argue, that reveal heteronormative perceptions of gendered motion in ballroom (here, specifically, feminized motions).

Significantly, Roberts's footwork and body position in the foundational figures of the tango routine remain neutral when he dances "as lady," following the ballroom syllabus (such as promenade steps and the hand and arm positions in the dance frame). Roberts uses certain other instances in the routine to signal parody of the "lady's" choreography and thereby reveal gender anxiety through exaggerations of facial expression and body posture. He does this especially when executing steps drawn from the exhibition style at the opening and closing of the routine, as well as in his gestures; these are moments the syllabus leaves more open to individual interpretation (such as the tango's increasingly iconic head shakes and snaps). The fact that it was Roberts, and not Guttenberg, who demonstrated the anxiety is equally significant; we could speculate that this was because he was dancing the "lady's" part; because of his professional position within the dominant structure of competitive ballroom; because of the concerns of the program/network, or its perceptions of what would entertain its viewers most; or still other factors.

Regardless, this tango analysis suggests that the tropes of masculinity and femininity, which the WDSF would argue inhere in the dances themselves, such as the "lady's" extended bending in the upper back in both Standard and Latin, may instead emerge as cultural coding, artistic interpretation, and/or the performance of a gendered role. And while the *Dancing with the Stars* example happens to be from the tango, these issues apply to all the competitive ballroom dances. The photographs of same-sex ballroom dancers included here, one from Standard and the other from Latin, illustrate how such body postures reflect interpretations of form and style in the dances, rather than the sexual or gender identity of the dancers themselves. The form of competitive ballroom that has evolved over the course of the twentieth and twenty-first centuries demonstrates, moreover, an increasingly stylized execution of such expression and movement.

In May 2009, about a year after audiences were treated to "The Mango," millions of viewers across the United States were introduced to the first intentional pair of same-sex ballroom dancers on network television. For the audition phase of the Fox program *So You Think You Can Dance* season five, the show's producers decided to feature aspiring competitors Misha Belfer and Mitchel Kibel, two amateur ballroom dancers from Colorado. Their samba routine thus represented the first premeditated depiction of same-sex competitive ballroom on United States reality television. Three months later in 2009 another pair of same-sex ballroom dancers auditioned for season six: Willem de Vries and Jacob Jason. Exploring these two audition sequences illustrates how *So You Think You Can Dance* constructed same-sex ballroom and its participants, as well as some of the broader implications of this dance form, both politically and culturally, for this early twenty-first-century moment.

Modeled on the highly popular *Idol* singing competitions, *So You Think You Can Dance* aims to discover "America's favorite dancer," as selected by viewers who call or text the show each week to vote for their chosen competitors.

Figure 2.1. Women's Standard competitors. Photos by Raphael Coffey (2009). www.raphaelcoffey.com.

Figure 2.2. Men's Latin competitors. Photos by Raphael Coffey (2009). www.raphaelcoffey.com.

A panel of expert judges initially selects a group of contestants from among thousands who audition "in their own style," which may include what the program designates as jazz, contemporary, ballet, hip hop, Broadway, tap, and folk, among others. Ballroom dancers may audition singly (performing with a partner who is not auditioning) or jointly; if both dancers move on past the audition phase, however, they are treated as individual competitors and are rarely put together as partners. Over the course of several months, this initial group is winnowed down to a small number of finalists who perform routines in a range of dance forms and styles set by leading choreographers. Most contestants have some advantage when they are assigned a routine in their area of expertise; however, dancers must come to excel in the full range of dance forms if they are to remain in the competition. Throughout the season, televised segments alternate between off-stage rehearsals or "candid" footage of the dancers and their fully realized performances.

The entire structure of such audition-based reality television programming consciously fosters audience engagement. As media theorist Henry Jenkins notes: "Many more people watch the series than try out; many more try out than make the air; many more make the air than become finalists. But, at every step along the way, the viewers are invited to imagine that 'it could be me or someone I know.'"[30] Two interconnected elements of Jenkins's analysis merit closer scrutiny here. First, consider the calculated choices producers make to feature certain contestants on air. Second, ask how those choices enhance viewers' connections or identification with the contestants, thereby ensuring viewers' continued desire to watch the programs. Why did the producers of *So You Think You Can Dance* decide to feature same-sex partners Belfer and Kibel from among the thousands of dancers who auditioned? Why did they package this pair's appearance on the program as they did? And what did they think this segment would offer the viewers they hoped to capture for season five? While it is impossible to access the producers' full intentions, it seems demonstrably clear that Belfer and Kibel's segment did not play out with viewers as the producers had anticipated.

The Belfer/Kibel audition sequence starts with a voiceover by *So You Think You Can Dance* host Cat Deeley. The camera reveals Belfer waiting in the theater's lobby area, and, after a strategic pause for dramatic effect, Deeley introduces his dance partner Kibel, emerging from the men's room, dressed in a Latin blue spandex costume identical to Belfer's.[31] As the camera zooms in for a close-up of the men's room symbol on the lobby wall, the disco hit "It's Raining Men" (added as a sound track) accompanies the pair's walk toward the auditorium for their audition. The segment then cuts to an interview with the dancers, who explain that Belfer is gay, while Kibel is straight. Kibel acknowledges that "it was a little awkward at first" to dance with his partner, but he also explains that the partners both know the judges are "looking for masculine dancers, and I actually think that's something that's going to be a strong point for us... two men dancing together is a very masculine thing."

It is important to recall here that while many same-sex ballroom dancers identify as part of the LGBTQ community, others do not; regardless of one's sexual orientation, the same-sex ballroom community welcomes anyone who wishes to participate in the dance form, conforming to the principles of inclusion articulated for the Gay Games and Outgames. Nevertheless, the WDSF and the mainstream media appear to equate same-sex partner dance with gay and lesbian identity and sexuality. This allows such representatives of the dominant culture to compartmentalize and marginalize same-sex partner dance, and to ignore its potential to examine and expand the ballroom form narratively and choreographically.

Most unfortunately, the Belfer and Kibel audition did not go as well as the dancers had hoped; despite some strong moments that displayed solid Latin technique, they lost their balance and fell during the routine. While it must be admitted that it would have been preferable to have had more accomplished dancers as the first representatives for same-sex ballroom on the show, it is not clear that a higher quality of performance alone would have significantly changed the responses of the judges. The panel of experts at the audition that day included the show's executive producer Nigel Lythgoe, professional ballroom champion Mary Murphy, and professional choreographer Sonya Tayeh. What follows is a transcript of their televised postaudition critique (with ellipses used only to indicate pauses):

NIGEL: I don't really know what to say... It was a bit like watching Will Ferrell in *Blades of Glory*... I think you probably alienate a lot of our audience... We've always had the guys dance together on the show, but they've never really done it in each other's arms before... I'm certainly one of those people that only like to see guys be guys and girls be girls on stage. I don't think I liked it.

MARY: This is the first time honestly for me to see it. I'm confused because I see that sometimes you're both being the female role and sometimes the male . . . so it confuses me.

[Belfer and Kibel explain to Mary that they switch lead and follow roles to emphasize the strengths of their dancing, which Mary then acknowledges]

MARY: It would have been easier for me . . . if one had been playing the female role and one was playing the male role.

NIGEL: I don't think you want to see two guys there and think male, female.

SONYA: OK, but what do you do with the feminine qualities of it? *[She demonstrates an arm gesture toward Mary that presumably for her is coded as "feminine," then apologizes for inadvertently touching Mary, to which Nigel comments, "Same-sex judging"]* I relate to it *[i.e., such gesture]* more as a female . . . I was just confused in terms of the classical form.

NIGEL: You know what—I'd like to see you both dancing with a girl.

MARY: I would, too.

SONYA: Me, too.

NIGEL: You never know; you might enjoy that.[32]

A full essay would be needed to unpack the assumptions and attitudes underlying this exchange. Nevertheless, some salient details stand out from the segment, especially recalling Jenkins's analysis of reality television and the questions about the producers' intentions that this episode raised. Lythgoe's statement that these dancers "probably alienate a lot of our audience" indicates Jenkins's theory of audience identification within reality programming. What do the producers think they know about their viewers? And, again, why choose to broadcast this segment if it would be alienating?[33] Lythgoe wants "guys to be guys . . . on stage"—meaning, of course, appear to be heterosexual men. Over the show's thirteen seasons to date, Lythgoe has consistently sent the message that boys should be encouraged to dance, but that any dancer's personal sexual identity is not relevant for the show: male dancers are uniformly to appear strong and masculine and establish "chemistry" with their female partners, while female dancers are to be sexy and feminine.[34] Dance scholar Juliet McMains observes that such programs as *Dancing with the Stars* and *So You Think You Can Dance* routinely model compulsory heteronormativity and rigidly enforced gender roles through their ballroom choreography.[35] Such normative ideology indeed emerges in these programs on many levels: in the choreography, in the televised dialogue between the judges and with the dancers, and in the overall framing of dancers in the televised episodes.

For several seasons, *So You Think You Can Dance* also trumpeted interest in exposing contestants and viewers alike to "world dance." This pedagogical mission might appear to resonate with the creative decision to broadcast the Belfer and Kibel audition, as both world dance and same-sex ballroom dance might be considered gestures toward "diversity." However, on closer examination, the underlying political structure of that mission appears to be highly selective. "World dance," in the context of this program, usually means already-popularized cultural dance forms such as Bollywood and Argentine tango, or it means interpretations of regional folk dances that underscore heteronormative paradigms or that suggestively showcase the female dancers' bodies. So here, too, choices the producers make are consistent with McMains's analysis regarding gender and choreography.

Why, then, feature Belfer and Kibel, and risk what Lythgoe deemed negative viewer response—or, even more dangerous, remembering the WDSF concerns—negative advertiser response? Lythgoe is both executive producer of the show and its lead judge, so he plays a significant role in deciding what is aired each week. It seems plausible that the producers actually wanted to play it both ways: Feature competitors who would appeal to the segment of the audience friendly to same-sex dancers while simultaneously not appearing to endorse the form. If this hypothesis is correct, then their strategy backfired badly. Lythgoe's follow-up commentary the next day on Twitter, that he was not a fan of "'Brokeback' Ballroom," only amplified what became a firestorm of criticism following the May 21, 2009, episode. Public commentary roundly condemned the homophobic comments made by the judges and the insulting treatment of Belfer and Kibel. This suggests that the producers either misjudged the makeup of their audience (or at least its tolerance levels) or underestimated the power of a given audience segment to respond to what it saw as blatant discrimination. The Gay and Lesbian Alliance against Defamation issued a Call to Action, and Lythgoe was quickly forced to make a formal, public apology for his remarks.

Although Lythgoe was the focus of much of the backlash, there are related implications for the female judges' remarks. Even though Murphy and Tayeh did not express the same level of homophobia as Lythgoe, their observations exemplify the heterosexist bias inherent in the ballroom world and the culture at large. One of this essay's opening points bears repeating here: For Western culture, ballroom offers among the most powerful corporeal signifiers of both traditional gender roles and heterosexual romance and passion. Same-sex ballroom thus poses a much larger threat to this symbolic cultural system than the comparatively smaller size of its participant community would suggest.

Since its inception Mary Murphy has been the show's primary expert on ballroom dance. A professional ballroom dancer since the 1980s, as well as a former competitive champion, Murphy clearly knows the ballroom world. Yet, perhaps disingenuously, she claims an inability to grasp, technically or symbolically, the strategic interventions Equality Dance has wrought on the traditional structure of ballroom.

Sonya Tayeh, then a recent addition to the *So You Think You Can Dance* roster of choreographers, specializes in what she calls "combat jazz," and is known for her eclectic, highly energetic, and innovative routines that push dancers to their physical limits. Both her personal affect and her jazz-dance vocabulary eschew traditional gender roles. It is therefore surprising for her to describe the ballroom movements in biologically essentialist ways. She, too, is confused by the male dancers' transgression of what she calls "the classical form" of traditional ballroom, with what she believes are its inherently "feminine" and "masculine" "qualities." Ironically, it is precisely these notions of culturally codified, gendered gesture that same-sex ballroom dancers seek to expose, interrogate, and resist. This resistance emerges through the same-sex audition sequences, which grate against the heteronormative strictures of the reality programming that seeks to contain it.

In fall 2009, to capitalize on the growing popularity of *So You Think You Can Dance*, the Fox network decided to air another season of the program immediately after its usual spring/summer slot. A few months after the Belfer and Kibel imbroglio, America was introduced to another same-sex ballroom partnership, that of Willem de Vries and Jacob Jason. Interestingly, the dancers, who had known each other for many years, claim that they decided to form their partnership after having participated as individual contestants in season two of the program. They began competing together soon thereafter, representing the United States at the Gay Games in summer 2006 as well as at the Outgames that same year, where they won the gold medal in the men's Latin division. In the intervening years, de Vries and Jason also became the reigning United States same-sex men's Latin ballroom champions.

It is reasonable to speculate that the producers of *So You Think You Can Dance* seized the opportunity to redeem themselves when de Vries and Jason decided to audition again as same-sex ballroom partners. Their rumba routine demonstrated unequivocally the artistry of two technically accomplished, captivating ballroom dancers. But this episode also revealed how the program exploited the chance to regain the favor of the viewership that the producers so woefully misjudged just a few months earlier.

As with the previous audition sequence, host Cat Deeley begins in voiceover, introducing the next competitors, "same-sex dancers" de Vries and Jason.[36] This segment features none of the coy preliminaries or musical jibes of the Belfer and Kibel audition. The camera simply tracks the dancers, dressed casually in jeans and (nonmatching) black shirts, entering the theater. The segment then cuts to an interview sequence, where DeVries provides a brief history of their partnership, including their decision to work together after auditioning for season two, as well as details of their competitive triumphs thereafter.

As we watch the dancers in the lobby area running through their audition routine, de Vries further explains: "There are a lot of same-sex couples out there that are now afraid to come out and audition for shows like *So You Think You Can Dance*. We just want America to know that there's a whole forest of same-sex dancers"—and Jason cuts in with "there's a *world* of same-sex dancers," a correction that de Vries emphatically echoes; de Vries' and Jason's comments are, of course, situated as a direct response to the events of season five. De Vries and Jason are allowed by the producers not only to be visible but to be taken seriously. By reviewing their competition history, the dancers cite their artistic and technical accomplishments and, further, attest to the worldwide existence of this dance community, suggesting that such excellence may be found globally.

The segment then moves to the theater for their audition. Within seconds, their choreographically and emotionally compelling rumba routine accomplishes a number of unstated objectives: it demonstrates excellence of technique commensurate with the dancers' international competitive ranking; it puts to rest questions that the Belfer and Kibel audition may have raised about the performative capabilities of same-sex dancers; and it confirms that same-sex ballroom dancers use identical technique to, and can reach the same level of accomplishment as, mixed-sex partnerships. Even more strategically, it showcases how same-sex ballroom transcends stereotypically gendered movement. Drawing on Latin ballroom and exhibition movement vocabularies, Jason and de Vries both employ not only the traditional "man's" lead, posture, footwork, hip action, and rumba holds, but also a series of back arches, partial splits, penchés, and développés that, in a mixed-sex routine, would have been assigned to the "lady." The seamless fluidity with which they exchange lead and interweave "man's" and "lady's" figures demonstrates efficiently and unarguably how same-sex ballroom can reveal new choreographic and narrative vistas.

Throughout the audition, the cameras cut between footage of the routine and snippets of the judges' intense visual focus on the dancing. The panel consists of Lythgoe, Murphy, and Emmy Award–winning choreographer Mia Michaels. Lythgoe briefly acknowledges in an aside to Murphy, "I've really got to say that there's great lines to it" (the dancers' full arm/hand and leg/foot extensions, as well as the overall geometry and flow of the rumba choreography). When Lythgoe signals that the judges have seen enough, the dancers move downstage to rapturous applause from the other dancers in the auditorium, and we are again allowed to hear what the dancers want the panel and the viewers to understand about their performance, when Jason observes: "You know it's amazing—brings tears to my eyes—amazing for young gay people to be able to express themselves, and that's the dance [the rumba] that I think that represents that the most." The judges simply respond, "Wow."

Lythgoe then calls on Murphy for her feedback. Murphy, turning to Michaels, whose eyes have filled with tears, comments in a choked voice, "Well I can understand why you're welling up, and I have to say I'm just really proud of you two. And that showed all the emotion, and passion, in a strong way. It had great line, great technique. Well done. I'm really proud of the two of you."

Lythgoe asks Michaels for her input, and she observes: "All I know is that I celebrate the courage that you guys have to just expose yourselves, and your hearts, and your passion, and who you are." De Vries and Jason both thank Michaels, which then allows Lythgoe to pick up his cue: "Thank you for showing me that same-sex ballroom dancing can be very strong and very good. You know, I got myself into trouble last time saying I'm going to ask you to dance with girls. I would very much like you to do the choreography [the section of the audition where some dancers are taught a male-female pairs' routine to see how they dance with a partner][37] and see if there is any difference in how you handle that, to be honest with you." To which de Vries responds, "I'd actually like to point out that we do both enjoy dancing with girls as well." Lythgoe acknowledges this comment and tells the dancers that the judges will see them again later, and the segment ends.

What the producers hoped viewers would take away from this second exposure to same-sex ballroom is revealed in their comments. The judges' repeated emphasis on strength suggests that the routine succeeded in two ways: it read favorably as "masculine" (strength, in their lexicon, when applied to male dancers, is usually a synonym for normative masculinity) and it also read favorably as technically skilled. But the female judges' remarks about "passion" and "courage" point, even if obliquely, to the dancers' decision to appear on the program in the wake of the Belfer and Kibel debacle. The audition thus provided *So You Think You Can Dance* with an opportunity to appear supportive of gay identity through the combination of equation of same-sex ballroom techniques and specific sexual orientations. In other words, the segment became as much, if not more, about the competitors as (assumedly) representative figures for the LGBTQ community as it did about them as dancers. But in moving de Vries and Jason on to the choreography round, Lythgoe signaled that, should they continue in the competition, they, like all the other dancers, would have to conform to the structures of heteronormativity, including the choreography of male/female partners that emphasizes the dancers' "chemistry" as well as traditional gender roles, that the program routinely showcased.[38] Thus the innovations that same-sex dancers can bring to ballroom as a form remain outside the scope of this particular American popular culture vehicle; it is still to be seen what, if any, inroads same-sex dance may make within the established ballroom world.[39]

While the American version of *So You Think You Can Dance* has not subsequently featured any other same-sex ballroom partnerships, it is clear that the judges' commentary is now carefully monitored, and we are seeing more "clarifications" of response—especially around hot-button areas such as race and sexuality—than before. So Belfer and Kibel, and de Vries and Jason have opened cracks in the heteronormative veneer of *So You Think You Can Dance*, even if same-sex ballroom is not formally represented on the program.

Media theorist Misha Kavka has observed that an interesting tension inherent to reality television is its need "to peddle the mores of the status quo back to an audience that is as broad, and hence commercially viable, as possible." At the same time, this programming "seeks to skew the hetero-ordinary in order to keep that same audience watching." Moreover, for Kavka, "the performances of [heteronormative] intimacy on reality TV," through their "effects of excess" and "over-exposure"—and I would add especially in the dance competition programs that so blatantly traffic in the objectification and sexualization of dancers' bodies—"queer the public/private divide . . . and draw the audience's attention to this queering" precisely because they "make for 'good TV.'"[40] In retrospect, it should not surprise us that we saw these same-sex partnerships featured at the same time as gay marriage, employee benefits for same-sex couples, and many other related social, economic, and political issues were dominating the media. The televised same-sex ballroom sequences, and the controversy that surrounded them, contributed to the buzz around these programs and exemplified the contested and unresolved place of queerness in contemporary popular culture. Within the arena of same-sex ballroom today, we are seeing new partnering options sanctioned for competition that reflect more fully the complexity and the politics of LGBTQ identities and relationships. The form is also expanding to allow for greater choreographic and narrative expression. These options include, most recently, the expansion of categories to allow for female/male couples where the female leads for the majority of the dance, and partnerships determined by the dancers' gender identity, as opposed to sex. Such dynamic responses to contemporary culture suggest that same-sex ballroom will continue to offer aesthetically rich and narratively diverse representations of our twenty-first-century world.

* * *

This research would not have been possible without the welcoming support of the same-sex ballroom community. My special thanks to Auriel, Winter Held, Richard Lamberty, Benjamin Soencksen, and the late Camille Wojtasiak for sharing their time and expertise. Many of my academic colleagues also provided valuable feedback during the development of this essay. My thanks to the organizers of, and participants in, the 2011 CORD conference at Florida State University, as well as to colleagues at the University of Toronto, Brown University, and Cornell University who responded to earlier drafts. I am particularly grateful to Christopher Martin, Julie Malnig, Allan Hepburn, Erin Hurley, Patricia Ybarra, Eng-Beng Lim, Nick Salvato and the editors of this volume for their comments and suggestions.

Notes

1. For a sampling of these various dance forms and their sociocultural significance in North America, see Julie Malnig, ed., *Ballroom, Boogie, Shimmy Sham, Shake: A Social and Popular Dance Reader* (Urbana: University of Illinois Press, 2009).

2. The reality television programs I discuss here are increasingly global, but each has nationally produced versions, targeting a national audience and culture. For the purpose of this essay, I will focus only on the U.S. versions of such programs and their relationship to American culture.

3. Caroline Joan S. Picart, *From Ballroom to DanceSport: Aesthetics, Athletics, and Body Culture* (Albany: State University of New York Press, 2006), 1, 6.

4. For a discussion of the various amateur and professional dance organizations in the United States and abroad, including the IDSF, see Jonathan S. Marion, *Ballroom: Culture and Costume in Competitive Dance* (Oxford: Berg, 2008).

5. American ballroom has two forms, Smooth and Rhythm, which correspond to international ballroom Standard and Latin. American Smooth includes the American forms of waltz, tango, fox-trot, and Viennese waltz, while American Rhythm includes cha cha, rumba, swing, bolero, and mambo. In general, American ballroom is distinguished by more open dance holds and figures than international ballroom. Couples who train and compete in the American ballroom style do not usually compete outside North America, and do not usually also compete in the International style.

6. *The Ballroom Technique* (London: Imperial Society of Teachers of Dancing, 1948, rev. ed. 1993). *The Revised Technique of Latin American Dancing* (London: Imperial Society of Teachers of Dancing, 1971–74, rev. ed. 1983).

7. See, for example, Sally Peters, "From Eroticism to Transcendence: Ballroom Dance and the Female Body," in *The Female Body: Figures, Styles, Speculations*, ed. Laurence Goldstein (Ann Arbor: University of Michigan Press, 1991), 145–58.

8. www.gaygames.org.

9. See www.gaygames.org for Federation history and information on the organization's legal battle over the use of the term "Olympics."

10. www.gaygames.org.

11. For a full list of events and winners by year, see www.gaygames.org.

12. Becca Costello, "Dance Dance Revolution," *Sacramento News and Review*, February 26, 2004.

13. There is ongoing controversy about whether DanceSport will ever be truly embraced as an athletic, as opposed to an artistic, form. While further consideration of this debate lies outside the scope of this essay, the constellation of issues including sexuality, artistry, and athleticism embedded in such discussions is certainly relevant. For a detailed analysis of these issues as they pertain to ballroom, see Picart, *From Ballroom to DanceSport*, chpt. 4.

14. See World DanceSport Federation Competition Rules #13: www.worlddancesport.org.

15. Eric Marx, "In the Ballroom, a Redefinition of 'Couple,'" *New York Times*, July 14, 2004, accessed October 9, 2008, http://www.nytimes.com/2004/07/14/arts/in-the-ballroom-a-redefinition-of-couple.html.

16. For a discussion of the tensions between dancers' sexual orientations and their performance of heterosexual identity in ballroom dance, see Juliet McMains, *Glamour*

Addiction: Inside the Ballroom Dance Industry (Middletown, CT: Wesleyan University Press, 2006).

17. Eric Marx, "In the Ballroom, a Redefinition of 'Couple.'"

18. While it is certainly true that what comprises a competitive event would have to be reenvisioned, were same-sex couples to compete together with mixed-sex couples, that is a different issue from what I believe Frasier implies here.

19. Same-sex competitions do often separate events by male-male partnerships and female-female partnerships, largely to accommodate anatomical factors, such as center of gravity, that can impact dance movement.

20. See the competition rules detailed by the North American Same-Sex Partner Dance Association: www.nasspda.org.

21. See www.ifssda.org.

22. It is also worth noting that even for dancers who do not teach or choreograph, there is great benefit to learning their partners' figures, as that allows for a fuller understanding of how the dancers, and the individual dance components, can work together most effectively.

23. See www.nasspda.org.

24. See, for example, the website for St. Louis Equality Dance: www.stlequalitydance.org.

25. The United States has attracted individuals who have participated in other countries' versions of *So You Think You Can Dance*. Choreographer Stacey Tookey, who began her work on the Canadian show, is now frequently featured on the American program, and in season ten, dancer Paul Karmiryan, who had previously won the Armenian version of the program, became a finalist on the American show.

26. With each new season, however, the "stars" of this program have increasingly been understood to be the remarkable dance professionals—many of whom have appeared repeatedly and developed fan followings—who are able to transform amateur personalities into creditable ballroom dancers in just weeks. See Brooks Barnes, "A Realignment of Star Power," *New York Times*, September 25, 2011, accessed September 26, 2011, http://www.nytimes.com/2011/09/26/arts/television/dancing-with-the-stars-is-turned-on-its-head.html.

27. For a detailed discussion of the professional/amateur dance nexus, see McMains, *Glamour Addiction*.

28. Clips of Guttenberg's performances of the tango with both Trebunskaya and Roberts may be seen on YouTube. See, for example, Codebear 4's upload of November 10, 2010, http://www.youtube.com/watch?v=fLN6CobxnEw and Greg Yamane's upload of April 2, 2008, http://www.youtube.com/watch?v=aJZqk2eObFk.

29. For broader considerations of gendered movement in dance, see Judith Lynne Hanna, *Dance, Sex and Gender: Signs of Identity, Dominance, Defiance, and Desire* (Chicago: University of Chicago Press, 1988).

30. Henry Jenkins, *Convergence Culture: Where Old and New Media Collide* (New York: NYU Press, 2006), 71.

31. Although not always the case in same-sex competition, identical costuming may be a signal that the dancers adhere to the practices of Equality Dance.

32. http://www.idolstartv.com/component/seyret/video/1664/Misha-Belfer-and=Mitchel-Kibel-SYTYCD-Audition.html. March 8, 2011. Unfortunately, this clip no longer appears to be publicly available.

33. Particularly in the audition phase of any season, we see a number of dancers who are clearly unqualified to enter the competition. However, the foundational form of dance with which these individuals audition is not the object of critique, as was the case with the Kibel/Belfer sequence.

34. While the show appears to have become more willing to acknowledge the gay identity of some dancers, it has yet to focus any attention on lesbian dancers. Season thirteen (Summer 2016), with its focus on dancers ages 8–13, also necessitated some modification of the sexual dimensions of costuming and choreography.

35. See McMains, *Glamour Addiction*.

36. All quotations are transcribed from a recording of the broadcast. The audition sequence is no longer accessible on the program's website or on YouTube.

37. Dancers who are not immediately rejected or approved to go on to the next round participate in this choreography section. Because most dancers audition with a solo routine in their own preferred style, this round allows the judges to assess the dancers' ability to work in other dance forms, and with a partner, both of which are critical for further success on the program.

38. Both dancers did, indeed, continue in the competition, but were eliminated before the program identified its "top 20," the group that becomes the focus of the duration of the season.

39. The Manhattan Amateur Classic competition has recently added a same-sex division to its roster of events, perhaps signaling a transition toward the inclusion of same-sex dance in mainstream competition.

40. Misha Kavka, *Reality Television, Affect, and Intimacy* (London: Palgrave Macmillan, 2008), 134–35.

Appendix

General Notes for Latin American Dance Technique

How to Study the Charts

The technique has been published in chart form and it is necessary to understand the headings used in these charts. These are explained below.

Body Positions

These always refer to the Lady's position in relation to the Man. An analysis of Holds and Body Positions is given later.

Feet Positions

These refer to the position of one foot in relation to the other foot: Forward, Back, Side, Diagonally Forward (or Back), Side and Slightly Forward, etc. P.P. (Promenade Position), Counter P.P.; R. Side-by-Side Position, etc., are also given in the Feet Positions column for clarity. Other terms used are O.P. (Outside Partner); preparing to step O.P.; C.B.M.P. (Contra Body Movement Position), etc. The term Left (or Right) shoulder leading is also used as it will slightly alter the position of the foot. A Shoulder lead denotes the turning of the same side of the body to the foot that is moving forward or back and is normally used prior to an outside step.

Contra Body Movement Position (C.B.M.P.) denotes a step that has been taken across the body when the body is already in position.

Alignment

This refers to the position of the foot in relation to the room. Terms used are "Facing," "Backing" and "Pointing," the latter being used on side steps where the alignment of the body differs from that of the foot. "Pointing" is often used when in Promenade Position. Both alignment of the foot and the direction in which the step is taken are given together where these differ, notably when in Promenade Position in the Paso Doble.

Alignment appears in the charts of Samba and Paso Doble as these two dances progress around the floor in a counter-clockwise direction.

Amount of Turn

This has generally been measured between the feet on each step and is given as a guide. More or less turn can often be made when actually dancing the figures. In some figures where the feet are turned out the turn has been measured from the body for simplicity. Where a slight turn out of the toe is indicated in the Feet Positions column and does not result in a turn of the body, no turn is given, for example, Samba Whisks.

Footwork

This refers to the part or parts of the feet used when taking a step.

Leads

Whenever the Lady's steps are not the normal opposite to those of the Man it is necessary for the Man to lead her into position. These leads are described as a guide but have not been explained in great detail to allow for individual expression and interpretation.

Precedes and Follows

The lists of precedes and follows are all that are necessary for the theoretical part of the professional examinations and are clearly classified for the Associate, Member, and Fellow Examinations. In medal tests and the dancing section of professional examinations, any standard figure may be introduced as a precede or follow but only the complete figure may be used unless a part of a figure is specified in this book.

Abbreviations Used

L.	Left
R.	Right
L.F.	Left Foot
R.F.	Right Foot
P.P.	Promenade Position
C.P.P.	Counter Promenade Position
O.P.	Outside Partner
C.B.M.P.	Contra Body Movement Position
S.	Slow
Q.	Quick
F.	Flat
B.	Ball
H.	Heal
T.	Toe
B.F.	Ball, Flat
H.F.	Heel, Flat
W.F.	Whole Foot
I.E.	Inside Edge
L.O.D.	Line of Dance
D.W.	Diagonally to Wall
D.C.	Diagonally to Centre
A.	Associate
M.	Member
F.	Fellow

Analysis of Holds and Body Positions

1. CLOSED FACING POSITION—Facing partner, slightly apart, normal hold; or Man holding Lady's R. hand in his L. hand, double hold or without hold.
2. CLOSE FACING POSITION—Normal hold, facing partner, with light body contact.

3. OPEN FACING POSITION—Facing and away from partner, Man holding Lady's right hand in his left hand. (Or her right hand in his right hand, double hold, or without hold).
4. FAN POSITION—Lady at right-angles to Man on his left side, her right hand in his left hand.
5. PROMANDE POSITION—A V-shaped position with Lady on Man's right side.
6. COUNTER PROMENADE POSITION—A V-shaped position with Lady on Man's left side.
7. FALLAWAY POSITION—As Promenade position but with Man and Lady moving back.
8. RIGHT SIDE-BY-SIDE POSITION—Lady on Man's right side, both facing the same way.
9. LEFT SIDE-BY-SIDE POSITION—Lady on Man's left side both facing the same way.
10. RIGHT SHADOW POSITION—Lady on Man's right side slightly in advance, both facing the same way with weight on the same foot, normally with Man's right hand on Lady's right shoulder blade and her left hand in his left hand.
11. RIGHT CONTRA POSITION—A position where Man and Lady are moving towards partner's right side, both using the same foot.
12. LEFT CONTRA POSITION—A position where the Man and Lady are moving towards partner's left side, both using the same foot.

3

Syndicated Bodies

Expressions of American Identity in NFL Touchdown Dances

DAWN SPRINGER

On a corner in Milwaukee, a bar erupts as a Green Bay Packer crosses into the end zone and scores a touchdown. The player spikes the ball and leaps into the crowd, performing the iconic Lambeau Leap. The fans at Lambeau Field reach out and hold onto the athlete as his body falls back into their outstretched arms. The Milwaukee bar-goers jump for joy and embrace. Across Wisconsin, bodies move in simultaneous celebration with the signature Packer touchdown dance on their televisions.

* * *

Since the inception of the Lambeau Leap by Leroy Butler in 1983,[1] many Green Bay Packer athletes have charged the crowd and leapt backward over the barrier that separates fans from the field. The jump into the stands is a patriotic expression for Packer fans—a physical expression that speaks of place, of Wisconsin. The Lambeau Leap is one of many end zone celebrations performed by athletes across professional American football. On the surface, these dances are performances of collective joy and victory for players and their fans. The evolution of their choreography through the game's history, however, has brought strict league regulations against "excessive celebration." When athletes dance their way into the end zone, how they choose to move their body is under exacting scrutiny. These moments of individual expression in the NFL therefore hold the potential to become acts of defiance.

Policing of movement is not new in the United States. Throughout American history, formalized rules have enforced social codes of so-called acceptable behavior when mobilized dancing bodies challenged the status quo. The

Cabaret Laws of early twentieth-century New York City, for example, emerged when Americans flocked to Harlem to dance together, interracially, in the 1920s. This is just one instance of America's historical penchant for bodily regulation. In fact, the Supreme Court removed "social dancing" from First Amendment Protection in 1989.[2] In 2008, eighteen people were arrested at the Jefferson Memorial in Washington, D.C., for performing a silent dance in honor of Thomas Jefferson's 265th birthday.[3] Thus, the NFL's "excessive celebration" rules are part of a larger history of sanctions on dancing in the United States. Dance often acts as a vehicle for inciting controversy, depending on the type of movement, who is dancing, and where the dancing occurs. In America, the public moving is inherently political. Touchdown dances are no exception.

Since Leroy Butler's first leap into the stands in the early eighties, end zone celebrations and touchdown dances have become more elaborate and more culturally relevant. The way a person dances signifies a great deal, either through their movement, the perception of their moving body, or both. When football players dance, it is a highly visible display of the intersection between dance and public perception. From the figure eight of the hips in a salsa, to the bent knees and polyrhythmic movements of African American dancing culture, to the erect spine of Irish jigs, what America sees when a football player dances is much more than the celebration of a touchdown. This essay examines touchdown dances and personal choreographies in American football culture to reveal how football players' physical expressions embody and perform personal, political, and geographical identities, and resist structures of systemic racism and social dominance.

Thousands of screaming fans cheer for the touchdown and for the dance that ensues. Countless video compilations are made on home computers that highlight the moves. America's obsession with the dancing football player has evolved into marketing campaigns that use end zone dancing to promote products such as credit cards[4] and life insurance.[5] The connection between dance and football is a compelling element of American pop culture. For example, as of January 2014, eleven NFL players have appeared on the wildly popular television reality show *Dancing with the Stars*.[6]

Just two years after the first Lambeau Leap, the iconic "Super Bowl Shuffle" rap song and music video were performed by members of the 1985 NFL Chicago Bears Champion team. The video premiered during the height of Music Television's (MTV) popularity, and millions of Americans watched as the team represented Chicago with simple hand gestures and sidesteps while rapping the lyrics: "You know we're just strutting for fun, strutting our stuff for everyone!" The video became a media phenomenon, and was even nominated for a Grammy Award.[7] The record produced a substantial sum, which was donated to city charities. When the Bears went on to win the Super Bowl that year, the Shuffle became a citywide virtual touchdown dance.[8]

Nationwide television coverage elevated players to epic celebrity status. Wide receiver Will "Speedy Willy" Gault explains: "We were so big that year. There had been the Black and Blues Brothers poster for the linemen, and a lot of commercials, so it wasn't against the norm to do this. It was just like a commercial, almost. Except that this would be for charity. Everyone in the video would be paid some nominal fee, but the main purpose was we would give money to the neediest families in Chicago."[9] Several of the players have short features in which they introduce themselves and have solo dancing/rapping moments. Gault's lyrics, for example: "I practice all day and dance all night, I gotta get ready for the Sunday fight. Now I'm as smooth as a chocolate swirl, I dance a little funky so watch me girl!" showcases him with fluid, rhythmic steps while he bends at the waist and circles his hips. He describes his choreography, "Actually, I didn't plan it, I just went with the beat. It was totally ad-libbed. It may have seemed like I did because it was so smooth, but there goes that smooth-as-chocolate-swirl thing."[10]

"The Super Bowl Shuffle" was beloved by many. The song is an American ode to one of our nation's favorite pastimes. On closer inspection, it reveals the tensions created by commercialized, fabricated demarcations of race in the United States. In retrospect, performed stereotypes in the song's lyrics are obvious. African American Walter Payton's lyrics, for example, proclaim, "Well they call me sweetness, I like to dance. Running the ball is like making romance." These lyrics, as well as Gault's, overtly reference a connection between physicality, sexual prowess, and race. Caucasian players Jim McMahon and Steve Fuller are labeled "punky" players who "can't dance." African American athletes like Mike "LA Mike" Richardson's lyrics declare that he "plays it cool," and linebacker "Mama's Boy" Otis Wilson's lyrics tell us, "the ladies all love me for my body and my mind."[11] These lyrics form the framework through which we watch each of the players move. In this way, their two-step dance enforces racial stereotypes that the song's language suggests: black men are better dancers than white men, despite a seemingly even range of movement capabilities across team members' various ethnicities. Dance scholar Brenda Dixon Gottschild explains in her book *The Black Dancing Body: A Geography from Coon to Cool*: "The 'inborn sense of rhythm' stereotype is so entrenched in the Euro-American imagination that it still holds sway in the most learned of settings ... and it is a fallacy. Not all Blacks have rhythm. Like other 'either or' arguments, the nature or nurture debate is a generalization, a stereotype in and of itself with so many exceptions that the rule demands revisions."[12]

Historically, the perception that black men were more "physically capable" than white men was integral to the inception of American slavery that forced many Africans and African Americans into positions of manual labor. It further perpetuated a stereotype that black skin negated intellectual capacity and helped maintain white privilege in the workforce. This reduction to the body is still evident in arenas like the NFL, where more than half of the athletes are black. Racism reinforced the perception that African American athletic ability is a characteristic of ethnicity.[13] On the other hand, white privilege in the United States enabled white men to pursue a range of professions, so athletic prowess does not seem to mark Caucasian racial identity. The ways in which American culture has held on to or discarded these racial ideologies become readily apparent in examining the performances in "The Super Bowl Shuffle." The video molded the mid-1980s hip hop aesthetic into a consumable package for Americans while it underscored familiar racial boundaries disguised as athletic choreography.

While its performance and lyrics still play to imagined binary oppositions between black and white athletes, the Shuffle and other performances on the football field—including dance—simultaneously transcend overly simplistic categories of ethnic culture. The Shuffle, with its soulful downbeat, hip-hop lyrics, and specifically Chicago Blues instrumentation, unifies team and fans alike with the sweet-home Chicago sound, transforming it into a regionally specific celebration, and situating it within the most American of institutions—professional football. As "The Super Bowl Shuffle" characterizes the winning spirit of 1985 Chicago with its victorious song, it also acts as a barometer for understanding race as a hybrid, fluid landscape in the mid-1980s United States. In fact, MTV broadcast "The Super Bowl Shuffle" and other iconic interracial collaborations (Run DMC and Aerosmith's "Walk This Way," for example) to millions of Americans who watched their music videos as religiously as they tuned into ESPN. Just as the dancing, rapping football players in "The Super Bowl Shuffle" epitomize the mid-eighties MTV generation, we can also consider how football culture in general—stadium arenas, game configuration and rules, professional organizations, televised games, and instantly accessible video clips and commentary via the Internet—connects diverse populations across economic, ethnic, and spiritual divisions. Touchdown dances not only celebrate a team's score but illuminate the intersections of the demographic mosaic of America.

If you type "touchdown dance" into the search engine on YouTube, an entire world of dance sensation opens up at your fingertips. There are thousands of video compilations of athletes performing end zone celebrations and fans' imitations of their favorite players' signature moves, from the late 1980s "Ickey Shuffle" to the 2011 "Tebowing" craze. These five-second performances have become widespread markers of American culture, increasingly recognizable to millions of fans through after-game replays and thousands of online views. The dances have also become geographic emblems for the specific cities that players represent.

Victor Cruz, wide receiver for the New York Giants, was born in 1986 in Paterson, New Jersey—a mere twelve miles from the Giants Metlife Stadium in East Rutherford, where his professional football career began. His father, Mike Walker, was African American and a firefighter. His mother, Blanca Cruz, was born in Puerto Rico. When he graduated from the University of Massachusetts in 2010, Cruz went undrafted during that NFL season.[14] He was signed by the New York Giants later that year, and in 2011 he set a New York record for the most yards ever received in a single season.[15] While his statistics are strong, he is also famous for another type of performance: a phenomenal touchdown dance.

Victor Cruz enacted his first end zone salsa on the Philadelphia Eagles Lincoln Financial Field in 2011.[16] Not only did his dance fuel the epic rivalry between New York/New Jersey and Philadelphia, but Cruz performed it during the American National Hispanic Heritage Month. Cruz explains that his coach encouraged him to honor his Puerto Rican roots; he states, "And without much second thought, I broke out the very same salsa dance my grandmother had taught me on East Twentieth Street twenty years before. Step, step, step. Move your arms. Shake your hips. The salsa!"[17]

The short basic salsa of forward and backward rock steps that Cruz performs has an easy figure eight action in his hips and isolated circular movements of his bent arms. These movements hold particular significance for American football. According to Latino Fox News, major league baseball has seen a 218 percent increase in the number of players who identify as Latino over the past twenty years, but Latino and Puerto Rican players are less visible in the NFL.[18]

Cruz's salsa marks an inherent Puerto Rican identity in an American game commonly stereotyped as a sport for black and white players.

As a member of the multibillion dollar NFL franchise, Cruz is conveniently positioned to cultivate a marketable multicultural narrative for the NFL—an organization that has faced increased scrutiny about its racial politics. Critics caution that the dance runs the risk of reinforcing a stereotype of the so-called suave, sexy Latin man. David J. Leonard, an interdisciplinary scholar of race and popular culture, addresses Cruz's conundrum. Leonard writes: "The reduction of his background and identity to dancing, to a commodifiable practice that reaffirms stereotypes and erases the history and diversity of the community for the sake of an easily digestible cultural practice, is emblematic of contemporary multiculturalism."[19] According to Leonard, this invisibilized not only Cruz's blackness, but also a more complicated conversation surrounding location, community, and identity.[20]

Mass media images of Latin culture often create this dilemma. Actress and television producer Eva Longoria describes the negative feedback she received after the TV show *Devious Maids* (a remake of the Mexican series *Ellas Son la Alegria del Hogar*) aired. She stated that, "When we get backlash [from the Latino community] saying 'Oh they're playing the stereotypical maids,' my immediate response is 'so you're telling me their stories aren't worth telling? That they have no complexity in their lives?' That's what angers me, especially in the Latino community." She goes on to explain that, when playing affluent Gabrielle Solis on *Desperate Housewives*, she received similar criticism from the Latino community for misrepresentation. She argues, "Sometimes you can't win and I think that people really need to look at the paradigm of television and realize this is a very powerful medium for Latinos to have a voice. Let's support it so that they will make more."[21] Each time Cruz dances his salsa, it makes Latin heritage in American culture visible on millions of Americans' televisions but, as Leonard suggests, that visibility runs the risk of playing into reductive conversations about ethnicity.

Eduardo Vilaro, Artistic Director of Ballet Hispanico, recently responded to criticism that the inclusion of Asian American and African American dancers in the company defeats the mission of Ballet Hispanico. He explains: "For me, being Latino is a complex and personal experience that cannot be neatly branded. It is not a color, a mood, a look, an interjection or a language, even though those are all a part of my complex identity. Rather, it is a narrative that changes from person to person, and that is informed by the claims that each person (and their family) have to the rich histories brought to our country by Hispanics."[22] Both Vilaro and Longoria's examples highlight the complexity involved in performances of ethnicity. Within this realm, Cruz's dance provides an interesting glimpse into American obsessions with the proverbial and reductive "what are you?" race question. This is not an insignificant inquiry, apparently. There are entire Internet message board threads dedicated to the discussion of Victor Cruz's race. From *Yahoo Answers*: "What race is Victor Cruz?": "Is VC Mexican or Mexi-American? He has the name of one but he looks black but does look a little Mexican . . . He also does his 'Salsa' dance which is a Mexican term. Anybody know?"[23]

Whether it's on-screen as a sitcom, in a theatrical dance concert, or in an end zone salsa, performances with cultural markers in public spaces become inherently political. They can cause conflict and highlight misconceptions, but may also encourage conversation. Cruz's dance pushes against attempts to fix ethnicity as a static notion. Performances highlighting Latin culture, like his salsa, are impossible to appreciate within simplistic conversations about ethnicity. Cruz's dancing moves beyond binary and reductive racial conversations and locates itself instead within the broad New York City area (including the Jersey suburbs), making his salsa a geographic symbol. Here, if we consider Cruz's dance as embodying a more nuanced layering of both ethnicity and regional identity, we can move from the current version of categorical "either or" racial thinking and into a new kind of dialogue. Dance is critical to this conversational shift.

Cruz's salsa dancing is evidence of a rich history that goes beyond a simple genetic inheritance and illuminates a multifaceted narrative of location. Cruz says he learned to dance from his maternal grandmother, Lucy Molina.[24] In his grandmother's lifetime, Tito Puente helped create the sounds of Latin Jazz in Manhattan.[25] The same city that is filled with bars of cheering Giants fans on any given Sunday gave birth to many of the sounds we as Americans identify as "salsa" music. For young Nuyoricans like Cruz, the cultural revolution sparked by Cuban and Puerto Rican musicians who immigrated to the United States (especially living and playing music together in New York City) is part of their personal heritage. "I have to tell you that Victor is a real Boricua that reminds me of the millions of youngsters who were not born on the enchanted island," said Julio Pabon, founder of latinsports.com after an interview with

Cruz. "Many of them," Pabon continued, "are from only one parent of Puerto Rican descent, but when you ask them, 'What are you?' They answer Puerto Rican."[26]

Cruz is part of an American generation that openly identifies with a fluid and multifaceted sense of personal history. It is common, especially in the New York area, to hear people move swiftly and seamlessly between Spanish and English in conversation. In a similar vein, Cruz's end zone celebration speaks to the interwoven cultures that comprise the identity of many young New Yorkers. From the salsa clubs in Newark to 53rd and Broadway, where the Palladium ballroom once stood, many New Yorkers and citizens of New Jersey have a special connection to salsa music and dance as members of the area that created it.[27] When Cruz performed his New Jersey–grown salsa during the Giants' victorious 2012 Super Bowl, an estimated 111.3 million viewers tuned in to watch.[28] And even though several members of the NFL franchise, including Cruz, might work to capitalize on the media opportunity, people across the Tri-State identified with that touchdown salsa as more than a media stunt; it was a moment that spoke of home. With one of the highest percentages of people of Puerto Rican descent in the nation, Giants fans of all stripes in New York and New Jersey celebrated a truly hometown victory alongside Cruz's salsa in Superbowl XLVI.[29] Yahoo Answers user Lonesome Rhodes summarizes, "His dad is half-Black, half-Puerto Rican and his mother is Puerto Rican. He was born in *New Jersey*, so he's an American of mixed foreign heritage."[30]

The same stadium where Victor Cruz dances his salsa was where another athlete (if only for a short time) also became a cultural phenomenon, this time for on-field spiritual gestures. Quarterback Tim Tebow was traded to the other New Jersey Metlife Stadium home team—the New York Jets—in 2012. Just a year earlier, the *Global Language Monitor* officially recognized the word "Tebowing" as part of the English language.[31] The phenomenon of Tebowing ignited when fans began posting to the Internet photographs of themselves in the same kneeling prayer position that Tim Tebow assumed on the sidelines during every game. Tebow's signature posture consists of dropping one knee to the ground in genuflection; placing an elbow on his other knee, he supports his head with a clenched fist while his other arm often rests on his helmet, positioned on the ground next to him. His on-field prayer has been the source of extensive controversy in the United States surrounding public displays of faith.

Timothy Richard Tebow, the son of a Baptist preacher, was born in the Philippines while his American parents were there conducting missionary work.

The narrative surrounding Tebow's birth illuminates the complexity of his in-game spirituality: doctors expected him to die in utero and thus recommended that his mother have an abortion.[32] His mother resisted the advice and gave birth to a professional athlete who is also a champion and symbol of the pro-life movement. During the 2010 Superbowl, the millions of fans who tuned in to watch Victor Cruz salsa his way across the end zone also watched Pamela Tebow discuss the miracle of her son's life during commercial breaks in an anti-abortion "Focus on the Family" advertisement.

As a professional athlete, Tebow was known for leading his team to miraculous comebacks in the last moments of a game.[33] While still playing for the Denver Broncos in 2011, Tebow was able to lead them to victory against the Miami Dolphins from fifteen points behind with less than three minutes left.[34] After his victory, Tebow performed his customary prayer movements when he pointed to the sky and dropped to one knee. In postgame interviews, Tebow customarily began by offering thanks to his "Lord and Savior, Jesus Christ" and ending with the words "God bless."[35] His genuflections during games made his religious passion obvious, even to spectators who missed his interviews.

As political debates over contraception and religious institutions flared in anticipation of the 2012 presidential election, Tebow's gestures on the field became a symbol for the political pendulum's swing in the direction of social conservatism. Many Christian conservatives cite examples of mandates to remove religious icons, such as the U.S. Army ordering the removal of a crucifix from an Afghanistan Army base chapel, as proof of a homogenized, overly sensitive, and politically correct–obsessed society that disallows their freedom of religious practices. So when Tebow prayed in an arena as hyperpublic as professional American football, it was a concentrated performance of Christianity in an era when many conservative groups argued that their rights were under attack. His body in prayer spoke to hundreds of thousands of Christian Americans and served as a kind of spiritual protest for the Christian right.[36] Some sports pundits criticized and questioned Tebow's NFL readiness and athletic prowess while his defenders said he was unfairly targeted by the liberal media as a direct result of his expressions of spirituality. David Leonard suggests that this argument within professional American football (a historically conservative community) is an attempt to use Tebow's religious gestures to presumably negate notions of white privilege.[37]

Despite the charged rhetoric surrounding Tebow and conservative advocates' political and religious stances, fans from all walks of life seemed to literally get down with the NFL athlete as people continued to Tebow and take pictures of themselves all across the globe. A Google image search yields pictures of children; brides and grooms; celebrities on red carpets; Marines; tourists at the Eiffel Tower, Times Square, and London; as well as dogs, snowmen, and even soft pretzels Tebowing. Tebowing became both a novelty and a symbol of spiritual pride, especially for young Americans. As Dan Barry explained in the *New York Times*, "it can be hard to tell whether people Tebowing are celebrating or mocking Tebow for his virtuous ways."[38] The sense of irony, as well as instantaneous mass-communicated replications of Tebow's gesture via social media, speak of a generation who more than likely do not remember a time before Facebook, Twitter, and text messages existed, and are not accustomed to such public and secularized displays of personal faith. Therefore, the ability of individuals to instantly replicate Tebow's genuflection via social media combined with the extraordinary nature of an athlete overtly praying in front of millions created a social phenomenon.

There is a significant difference in the location of Tebow's gestures and the end zone dances of wide receivers like Victor Cruz. Tebow genuflects on the sidelines, among his teammates, usually without his helmet.[39] The sidelines of a football field are a sort of "off stage" area for athletes despite the hundreds of cameras on them at all times. So when Tebow bowed to pray in that space and his fans saw him without his helmet, it offered the perception of something genuine and personal. His proximity to his teammates supported the rhetoric of Tebow's moral example via an assumed team player attitude, rather than an individual moment of glory in the end zone.

The end zone is a more overtly public space than the sidelines on which Tebow prays. When an NFL player scores a touchdown, the proximity to fans serves as a simultaneous celebration of the touchdown, the city, and teams they represent. It also creates a vicarious, proximal connection to fans watching at home. Taken together, these elements build excitement that erupts in triumphant, and particularly contagious, dances. The fleeting dance performances in the end zone, or on the sidelines, can elevate a player like Tim Tebow from athlete to celebrity.

Increased publicity is often accompanied by greater scrutiny for the athletes. Some touchdown dances began to be viewed as gloating on the part of the wide receiver, in contrast to the image of Tim Tebow praying on the sidelines. Cincinnati Bengal Ickey Woods, who crafted the iconic Ickey Shuffle[40] in the late 1980s, explains: "The entertainment or the things that they're doing now is more me-oriented. They're geared more for the player than the fans. My thing was geared toward the fans. I never did it on the road. I always did it at home. It was something for our fans."[41] As Woods suggests, the so-called excessive dances pull the attention solely to the wide receiver and away from the collective expertise of the team, which is required in order to accomplish every touchdown. In the years since Woods retired both his jersey and his shuffle, a number of players have employed much more elaborate choreographies to celebrate their victories. Players like Chad "Ochocinco" Johnson and Terrell "T.O." Owens (who consistently tried to outdo each other) became media superstars with their preplanned celebratory dances and dramatic stunts, such as hiding cell phones in goal posts and pantomiming calls to their mothers. Johnson once mocked the Tiger Woods golf scandal by pretending to putt the football with an orange end zone cone. Owens placed a towel over his arm like a waiter and served the football to the opposite team after he scored. Another T.O. choreography included a hidden sharpie in his sock so he could autograph the football and give it to a fan (rumored to be his financial advisor) after a touchdown. Johnson, who some credit with prompting the regulations by nicknaming them The Chad Rules,[42] rose to iconic touchdown dance stardom when he removed his helmet, got down on one knee, and proposed to a cheerleader from the opposing team. Johnson and Owens became increasingly famous for their celebratory performances. Like an NFL b-boy battle, fans soon began to create YouTube compilations of the two athletes in virtual competition[43] and the pair earned the nickname "Batman and Robin."[44] The elevated hype surrounding Owens and Johnson's touchdown dances even inspired a skit with Justin Timberlake on *Late Night with Jimmy Fallon*.[45]

In response, the NFL began to enforce "excessive celebration" penalties. In keeping with the rules, Victor Cruz, for example, is careful to keep his dances brief with both feet on the ground to avoid NFL penalties.[46] Teams are penalized fifteen yards and players can face individual fines if the athlete "leaves their feet" during end zone celebrations, if they use props, use the football as a prop, or if their victory dances are too long in duration.[47] These restrictions are the league's response to an increase in elaborate touchdown dances since the Ickey Shuffle and the Lambeau Leap. Critics in support of the new rules felt that the dances had become unsportsmanlike.

However, the lenses through which we define appropriate bodily behavior in conjunction with spectatorship, participation, and sportsmanship are complicated and varied in cultural perception. Misconceptions about dances and their meanings are certainly not new to the American experience. Seventeenth-century plantation owners, for example, feared that secret codes were being communicated through movement and music, and regulated how enslaved Africans were allowed to dance.[48] In contemporary professional football, the censorship of end zone dancing seems to be a policing of African American cultural values while the dances themselves comment on the NFL's power structures.

According to the annual report from the Institute for Diversity and Ethics in Sports, in 2012 66.3 percent of athletes in the NFL identified as African American, 30.1 percent as Caucasian, 0.7 percent as Latino, and 1.1 percent as Asian. However, 79 percent of all professional quarterbacks—a position regarded as a leadership role in football—are white. A mere 21 percent of quarterbacks identify as African American, a percentage that has more than doubled since 1998. While this change is significant, other leadership roles, like head coach, remain in the realm of white privilege. Only 9 percent of NFL head coaches are African American. At the highest positions of NFL management, demographic changes are only now beginning to appear. The year 2012 marked a historic change when the San Francisco 49ers hired Korean-American Gideon Yu as president/CEO. This was the first year in the history of the game that a person of color served in such a capacity.[49] Despite the vast majority of African American athletes involved in the NFL, leadership positions in the franchise are dominated by white men.[50] In a recent interview about black quarterbacks with Showtime's *60 Minutes Sports*, former NFL quarterback Warren Moon explained: "Not only did you have to play well for yourself, but you were playing for your race. It was a burden that you played with, but you played with it proudly because you knew you were doing something that was going to help another generation of guys."[51] A quarterback like Moon carries a weighted responsibility that is unknown to his white counterparts. His performance is scrutinized in a culture that historically speculates about whether he can or should be a leader, solely because of the color of his skin. Despite his remarkable athletic talents, his statement acknowledges that he had to prove himself again and again so that younger black athletes might also be appointed to the position he played. Moon was one of the few African American quarterbacks in the league's history when he signed to the Houston Oilers in 1989. At the time, he was the highest paid player in the NFL, and held the record for the highest-passing yardage in professional football until 2006.[52] He explains the racial politics of his career: "In the pros you can hear the N-word and all those other things far, far more than once. I mean, I got death threats in different places we went. This is [in] like 1990."[53] This describes a painful, not-so-distant NFL past and exemplifies tensions surrounding perceptions of race and leadership in twenty-first-century America. The countless, undocumented verbal attacks toward some of the most accomplished athletes in the world—by teammates and alleged football "fans"—provide a glimpse into the terrain on which athletes still play, and dance, over twenty years after Moon's own personal experiences.

Eighty-seven percent of wide receivers—the position that most frequently dances in the end zone—are black.[54] Terrell Owens had trouble advancing in his career when his emotional displays began to be viewed as a liability by the NFL. Sports journalist Dexter Rogers explains, "The white male dominated media often have problems covering African-American athletes that are demonstrative like Owens. His behavior is depicted as arrogant, selfish and divisive when, in actuality, it's not. . . . lack of diversity in the media has led to Owens being characterized in a negative fashion which has induced teams to be wary of signing someone who can obviously still play."[55] In recent years, scholarly attention has focused on how African American culture and aesthetics have influenced professional sports in the post–Civil Rights era. In the final chapter of his seminal work, *Am I Black Enough for You?* Todd Boyd discusses what he calls a "Black Athletic Aesthetic" in professional basketball. Boyd outlines the ways the game shifted from what he calls a textbook or "white" style of play to more improvised and spontaneous methods on the court.[56] He writes, "Like jazz before it, basketball now had a substantial body of cultural producers who, through their communal exchange, spurred by competition, created a distinct style and aesthetic specific to African American culture."[57] The communal exchange Boyd describes is exemplified in football as well, especially in the competition and "cultural production" between the touchdown dances of Terrell Owens and Chad Johnson. Their dances became a type of end zone call-and-response, intensifying week after week. In this way, athletes like Johnson and Owens cultivated unique moments where the hypermasculine athleticism of the NFL met an extraordinary wealth of individual bodily expression and humor that quickly and exponentially multiplied on the Internet. This type of bodily expression and humor is, in fact, grounded in an African (and, by extension, African American) aesthetic.

"High-Affect Juxtaposition," for example, is often seen in end zone dances where "a forceful, driving mood may overlap and coexist with a light and

Figure 3.1. Rod Tidwell, played by Cuba Gooding Jr., performing the Ickey Shuffle. Screen capture from *Jerry Maguire*, directed by Cameron Crowe (TriStar Pictures, 1996).

humorous tone."[58] Jamal Anderson embodies this "aesthetic of contrariety" when he dances his "dirty bird"—a percolator and chicken dance hybrid of flapping both his knees and bending his arms like a chicken. The playfulness of his movement is presented in stark contrast to football's intense competition. Moreover, Anderson navigates this tension with a kind of nonchalance that is reminiscent of West African dance traditions of "spiritual coolness" or "dwo."[59]

Other elements of the Africanist aesthetic are evident in touchdown dances like the Ickey Shuffle, which utilize polyrhythmic articulation, bent knees, a sense of weightedness in the lower half of the body, and movements of the pelvis.[60] Today this embodied cultural legacy is clear as NFL players dance The Dougie, The Jerk, and The Bernie Lean on the field.

The Bernie Lean exemplifies how movements in the NFL not only embody Africanist attributes that have come to be a bedrock of American body language and dance, but also how touchdown dances reflect and perpetuate cultural production. The dance was made popular in the NFL in 2011 when Baltimore Ravens player Ray Rice performed it in the end zone. The Bernie Lean originated as zombie-inspired movement in a music video that spoofed the

1980s movie *Weekend at Bernie's*. The lyrics describe the movement,[61] which consists of throwing the pelvis forward, dropping the head back, and shaking the arms with dead weight behind your body. The lyrics:

> We lit the weekend, we move it like Berney
> We move it like Berney
> Hey! yeah, so awesome, gotta dance too
> You gon' start movin' even at first glance too
> Believe us, it's not as easy as steps one two,
> Hold yah head back like a nosebleed comin' through.[62]

Ray Rice's on-field Bernie Lean created a moment of recognition for fans as he acknowledged his own participation in American pop culture. End zone dances like this are highly public moments that bring worldwide visibility to the dancing body when broadcast to millions of people during NFL games. And, like other end zone dances, The Bernie Lean became an Internet sensation; the number of viewers and media variations multiplied exponentially with videos inspired by the dance, notably in music video productions like the one released by the major league baseball team, the Oakland A's,[63] as well as the viral Daddy Daughter Iggy Azalea dance off.[64] The Bernie Lean also crept into local sports games. A men's high school soccer team at Perry Hall in Baltimore County, Maryland, adopted Rice's signature dance when they performed it during games throughout their 2011 season. When parents from a losing team became upset, claiming that the dance was too sexually explicit, the Perry Hall principal suspended the team.[65] What was originally light-hearted, celebratory dancing became a point of serious contention.

Dances that simultaneously express light-hearted humor and generate conflict are reflected in playwright and actress Anna Deveare Smith's seminal essay on the concept of "play," in black theater, which Smith purposefully refers to as "play" in quotation marks to signify its broad and fluid theoretical application. For Smith, "play" is a theatrical concept prevalent throughout African American culture that utilizes "planned spontaneity" as an important aspect of black "plays," both on and off the stage.[66] She states that an "important ingredient in a black 'play' is that it should wittingly, or unwittingly, raise social questions and controversies" and that "it should bring to the fore that which is unspoken. We should be forced to speak about the things we only mean to keep in the problematic area of innuendo."[67] When we closely consider the cultural meanings inherent in end zone dances and the controversies they incite (The

Bernie Lean, for example), it becomes clear that the restrictions enforced on NFL players' bodies intersect with the fundamental racial and economic politics present in the NFL. These dances give individual black men a voice and create visibility for players who historically and professionally are entrenched in a country and a game where white men continue to dominate positions of power. Football players' dancing bodies inhabit a space outside the controlled movements and prescribed bodily actions of the game that supports multibillion-dollar corporations (in 2012 the total NFL revenue amounted to 9.5 billion dollars).[68] As NFL leadership enforced end zone regulations, touchdown dances by players became an ironic statement by athletes who, despite being champions, lacked a personal, on-field ownership of their own bodies. Touchdown dances, then, become sites of agency where players can move in celebration of their accomplishments. As Smith explains, "Whether it is intended or not, black 'plays,' like the black church, have social and political significance."[69] For black athletes in professional sports, the political significance of "play" in a touchdown dance is a pointed statement about both a shared African American cultural expression and individual agency.

However subtle or fleeting these victorious dancing expressions are in American football, they push against histories of domination and oppression in one of the most iconic of American sports traditions. As fans cheer for the touchdown, the athlete takes a handful of seconds to strut his stuff. He speaks for and of himself with his body. These dances are moments of rupture in the well-oiled, wealthy NFL machine. In the fleeting moments after a touchdown, end zone dances not only celebrate victory for the athlete, the team, and the fans, but also utilize dance as a way for athletes to mitigate boundaries of race, ethnicity, geography, and spirituality.

Perhaps we are drawn to these public moments of dance performance because they transcend differences and create collective understanding. When we see a professional football player dance or symbolically gesture with his body during a game, we understand that these movements communicate multiple meanings simultaneously to millions of people. As Americans tune in to watch their favorite teams, we know there are thousands of others doing the same thing. The athlete's dance connects us to each other in celebration, hope, and victory across many metaphoric boundaries. Whether we watch touchdown dances live in the stadium, or mediated through television or the Internet, we can experience a kinetic connection to the performers as they physically express the present moment, their individual regional identities, the American spirit, and the victory of many challenges overcome. A sportscaster can only use verbal descriptions to indicate what is happening on the field, but the dancing body moves us, together, in a way that words alone cannot.

Notes

1. "The First Lambeau Leap," *G Packers*, accessed October 10, 2014, http://www.packers.com/media-center/videos/The-first-Lambeau-Leap/699633a1-344f-4a01-9fb1-d0b86ddcf761.

2. Madison Gray, "Social Dancing," *First Amendment Center*, July 20, 2004, accessed October 2016, http://www.firstamendmentcenter.org/social-dancing.

3. Lori Aratani, "Dancers Shimmy at the Jefferson Memorial," *Washington Post*, June 4, 2011, 4.

4. "Funniest Commercial by Visa—Julio Jones," *YouTube*, accessed October 10, 2016, https://www.youtube.com/watch?v=DBW4XvJkGro.

5. "Aaron Rodgers, State of Imitation, Aaron Rodgers Touchdown Dance—State Farm," *YouTube*, November 8, 2012, accessed October 10, 2014, http://www.youtube.com/watch?v=rvQtn2oytZQ.

6. Alex Gelhar, "Dancing with the Stars: Ranking the NFL Contestants," *NFLblog.com*, February 25, 2013.

7. Jon Greenberg, "Shuffling Down Memory Lane," *ESPN Chicago*, January 2010, accessed October 2016, http://www.espn.com/chicago/nfl/columns/story?id=4827883&columnist=greenberg_jon.

8. I grew up in a family of die-hard Chicago Bears fans. When my parents moved us across the Illinois state border into Wisconsin, we became strangers in enemy territory. Every time the Bears beat their rivals, the Green Bay Packers, my father would take over the PA system at his Milwaukee workplace and rebelliously play the Chicago Bears fight song—much to the annoyance of his coworkers—throughout the entire building. As a family we marked the cement sidewalks of the city's northern Rogers Park neighborhood as our inherited family stone. My great-grandmother knew every street of every intersection from the loop to the western suburbs. The seventeen cousins of my generation all seem to identify Chicago as our home despite the fact that none of us grew up in the city's limits. We, as mostly white Catholics, were taught to revere the ivy of Wrigley Field and fear the black neighborhoods of the South Side, which confused us as children when we met my father's black cousins. We listened to our elders speak of the illustrious El Train and heard thinly veiled, racist urban ghost legends of the crime in Cabrini Green. Chicago's sports teams are a crucial thread in the fabric of our familial identity. Sundays were important not so much because we went to church, but because the Bears were on TV. And during my childhood years,

no moment embodied this more than the 1985 ultimate super fan homage to the City of Chicago, the Super Bowl Shuffle. I began to absorb being "American" through the performance of race in the Shuffle.

9. Greenberg, "Shuffling down Memory Lane."

10. Jake Austen, "An Oral History of the Super Bowl Shuffle," *Grantland*, January 31, 2013, http://grantland.com/features/an-oral-history-super-bowl-shuffle-1985-chicago-bears-iconic-music-video/.

11. Richard Meyer, "The Super Bowl Shuffle," Red Label Music Publishing (1985).

12. Brenda Dixon Gottschild, *The Black Dancing Body: A Geography from Coon to Cool* (New York: Palgrave Macmillan, 2003).

13. NFL athletes identified as African American number 66.3 percent. Richard Lapchick, "The 2013 Racial and Gender Report Card, The National Football League," Institute for Diversity and Ethics in Sports, University of Central Florida, October 22, 2013.

14. Bill Pennington, "Catching On after a Last Chance; Giants' Cruz Defied Odds at UMass," *New York Times*, February 4, 2012.

15. Maria Burns Ortiz, "Opening Day: Latinos and Baseball—By the Numbers," Fox News Latino, March 31, 2011.

16. Kelsey O'Donnell, "Philadelphia: Birthplace of the Salsa . . . Victor Cruz Style," *SB Nation*, September 29, 2012.

17. Ibid.

18. Jorge Castillo, "Victor Cruz, Tony Gonzalez highlight growth of Hispanic players in the NFL," *Star Ledger*, January 8, 2012.

19. David Leonard, "NY GIANT Victor Cruz: Salsa, Sadness and the American Dream," *Ebony*, February 3, 2012.

20. Ibid.

21. Bel Hernandez Castillo, "Beyond Stereotypes," *Latino Magazine* (Summer), 2012.

22. Eduardo Vilaro, "Diversity Mambo—Fighting Stereotype through Dance," *Huffington Post*, October 22, 2013, http://www.huffingtonpost.com/eduardo-vilaro/hispanic-heritage-month_1_b_4138742.html.

23. "What Race is Victor Cruz?" *Yahoo Answers*, accessed October 10, 2014, https://answers.yahoo.com/question/index?qid=20111225181548AAH3s3W.

24. Sam Borden, "Giants' Cruz Mixing Cultures, Scoring Touchdowns," *New York Times*, November 5, 2011.

25. Vernon W. Boggs, *Salsiology: Afro-Cuban Music and the Evolution of Salsa in New York City* (New York: Greenwood Press, 1992).

26. Julio Pabon, "Victor Cruz and His Boricua Self," *Huffington Post Blog*, January 30, 2012, accessed January 30, 2014, http://www.huffingtonpost.com/julio-pabon/victor-cruz-and-his-boric_b_1239676.html.

27. U.S. Department of Commerce, State and County Quickfacts, 2011, accessed September 10, 2012, http://quickfacts.census.gov/qfd/states/00000.html.

28. Lisa de Moraes, "Super Bowl XLVI: Biggest TV audience ever," *Washington Post*, February 6, 2012.

29. Sonia G. Collazo, Camille L. Ryan, Kurt J. Bauman, "Profile of the Puerto Rican Population in United States and Puerto Rico: 2008" (paper presented at the Annual Meeting of the Population Association of America, Dallas, TX, April 15–17, 2010).

30. "What Race is Victor Cruz?" Accessed October 10, 2014, https://answers.yahoo.com/question/index?qid=20111225181548AAH3s3W.

31. "Tebowing Accepted into English Language," *Global Language Monitor*, December 12, 2011, accessed October 10, 2016, http://www.languagemonitor.com/new-words/tebowing-accepted-into-english-language/.

32. Brinda Adhikari, "Tim Tebow Super Bowl Ad: Anti-Abortion Commercial to Air," *ABC News*, January 26, 2012, http://abcnews.go.com/WN/tim-tebow-super-bowl-ad-cbs-air-controversial/story?id=9667638.

33. Patton Dodd, "Tim Tebow: God's Quarterback," *Wall Street Journal*, December 10, 2011.

34. Mike Klis, "Tim Tebow Leads Comeback, Broncos Beat Dolphins 18–15 in OT," *Denver Post*, October 23, 2011, http://www.denverpost.com/2011/10/23/tim-tebow-leads-late-comeback-broncos-beat-dolphins-18-15-in-ot/.

35. Patton Dodd, "Tim Tebow: God's Quarterback."

36. In retrospect, the media storm and pop-culture hype that surrounded Tim Tebow did not help his professional football career. He was released from the New York Jets after only one season. The same day he lost his job with the team, he tweeted, "Proverbs 3:5–6: Trust in the Lord with all your heart and do not lean on your own understanding . . . in all your ways acknowledge Him, and He will make your paths straight." David Leonard and James Braxton Peterson, "The Tim Tebow Affect or Celebrating Whiteness," *Loop 21*, December 28, 2011, https://drdavidjleonard.com/2011/12/28/the-tim-tebow-affect-or-celebrating-whiteness-loop21/.

37. This argument seeks to prove that historically privileged religious groups are now victims of liberalism in post–civil rights America. See Leonard and Peterson, "The Tim Tebow Affect."

38. Dan Barry, "He's a Quarterback, He's a Winner, He's a TV Draw, He's a Verb," *New York Times*, January 13, 2012.

39. "Tim Tebow praying LP field," *YouTube*, accessed October 2014, https://www.youtube.com/watch?v=goBxh1tl4Vs.

40. The Ickey Shuffle consists of three hops to the left, three to the right, three hops back, a spike of the ball, and twirling a finger to finish it off.

41. Michael David Smith, NBC Sports, "Pro Football Talk," April 2011.

42. "Chad OchoCinco's Best Celebration," accessed October 2014, http://www.rankopedia.com/Chad-OchoCinco's-Best-Celebration/Step1/17424/.htm.

43. "Ochocinco—T.O. AKA Batman & Robin. . . . R U Ready," *YouTube*, July 28, 2010, accessed January 2014, http://www.youtube.com/watch?v=PpR7w53t-Uc.

44. Kim Myers, "No Fun League, why the NFL is cracking down on touchdown celebrations," *Fansided*, August 7, 2013, accessed August 16, 2013, http://fansided.com/2013/08/16/no-fun-league-why-the-nfl-is-cracking-down-on-touchdown-celebrations/.

45. "Evolution of End Zone Dancing (w/Jimmy Fallon & Justin Timberlake) (*Late Night with Jimmy Fallon*), YouTube, September 10, 2013, accessed January 2014, https://www.youtube.com/watch?v=S4gW7veUPDg.

46. Kim Myers, "No Fun League."

47. Ibid.

48. "From juba to jitterbug to jookin; Black dance in America," October 5, 2014, accessed October 2016, http://www.dailykos.com/story/2014/10/5/1331124/-From-juba-to-jitterbug-to-jookin-Black-dance-in-America.

49. Richard Lapchick, "The 2013 Racial and Gender Report Card, The National Football League."

50. Ibid.

51. "The Black Quarterback: Episode Preview—60 MINUTES SPORTS–SHOWTIME," *YouTube*, August 1, 2013, accessed January 2014, https://www.youtube.com/watch?v=3FAZcuJ1Ai8.

52. Ibid.

53. Ibid.

54. Richard Lapchick, "The 2013 Racial and Gender Report Card, The National Football League."

55. "Why Is Terrell Owens Being Black-Balled by the NFL and the Media?" *Huffington Post*, July 16, 2010, accessed October 2014, http://www.huffingtonpost.com/dexter-rogers/why-is-terrell-owens-bein_b_649441.html.

56. Todd Boyd, *Am I Black Enough for You? Popular Culture from the 'Hood and Beyond* (Bloomington: Indiana University Press, 1997).

57. Ibid.

58. Brenda Dixon Gottschild, "Stripping the Emperor, The Africanist Presence in American Concert Dance," in *Moving History/Dancing Cultures*, ed. Ann Dils and Ann Cooper Albright (Middletown, CT: Wesleyan University Press, 2001).

59. Gerald Jonas, *Dancing: The Power, Pleasure and Art of Movement* (New York: Harry N. Abrams, 1992).

60. "Funny Touchdown Celebration Dances," *YouTube*, March 2, 2012, accessed January 2014, http://www.youtube.com/watch?v=aAufsbOoQws.

61. "Hot New DANCE CRAZE Hits the South It's Based on the 1980s Movie WEEKEND AT BERNIE'S!!!," *YouTube*, updated October 19, 2010, accessed January 2014, http://www.youtube.com/watch?v=TRBLm0gRL4c#t=89.

62. "Isa, Moving Like Berney," *YouTube*, November 10, 2011, accessed January 2014, https://www.youtube.com/watch?v=IjvbKaFeVak.

63. "Bernie Lean," *YouTube*, April 5, 2012, accessed January 2014, http://m.mlb.com/video/topic/8877514/v24739917/check-out-the-bernie-lean-music-video.

64. "Daddy Daughter Dance Off," *YouTube*, July 20, 2014, accessed October 2014, https://www.youtube.com/watch?v=2NFFOUFpmyA.

65. "Soccer team dance ends season," accessed January 2014, http://www.abc2news.com/dpp/news/region/baltimore_county/soccer-teams-dance-ends-season. This light-hearted celebratory dance was deemed inappropriate even though the high school athletes had been doing the dance all year. It is hard to tell whether or not this sudden disapproval and ensuing controversy resulted from disgruntled, sore losers, the nature of the dance's forward pelvic action, or the dance's origins in black American culture. For another video example of the Bernie Lean's dissemination, see www.youtube.com/watch?v=TRBLmogRL4c#t=89.

66. Anna Deveare Smith, "A Forum on Black Theatre: The Questions: What Is a Black Play? and/or What Is Playing Black?" *Theatre Journal* (December 2005): 571–76.

67. Ibid.

68. Daniel Kaplan, "The road to $25 billion," *Sports Business Journal*, January 28, 2013, accessed January 2014, http://www.sportsbusinessdaily.com/Journal/Issues/2013/01/28/In-Depth/NFL-revenue-streams.aspx.

69. Ibid.

4

Displays of Disruption

A Decade of Flash Mobs

KATE MATTINGLY

At 7:18 p.m. on Thursday, August 7, 2003, on the 2nd floor of the Manhattan location of Toys "R" Us, more than 500 people clustered around a massive Tyrannosaurus rex. Its wrinkly skin and chiseled teeth glistened in the store's bright lights. Growling and feinting "with a Hollywood-class lifelikeness," the animatronic creature attracted people like magnets to metal.[1] This was a flash mob, and its participants had been given the following instructions: "Fill in all around it. It is like a terrible god to you."[2] Within a couple of minutes of arriving at the location, the mob morphed into worshipers of the massive dinosaur, acting as if they were simultaneously awed and terrified by the creature. Bill Wasik, creator of this event, recalls that they were on their knees "moaning and cowering at the beast behind outstretched hands." Employees of the store were also frightened, not by the dinosaur but by the mob's bizarre disruption, and called the police. This flash mob not only enacted but reversed the purpose of the dinosaur: rather than being fascinated by the massive machine and purchasing toys, the mob prevented the sale of merchandise. Wasik adds: "We repaid this spectacle, which clearly was the product of not only untold expenditure but many man-months of *imagineering*, with an en masse enactment of the very emotions—visceral fright and infantile fealty—that it obviously had been designed to evoke."[3] Wasik reports that the staff was stymied as "cash registers were cocooned behind the moaning, kneeling bodies pressed together."[4] In spite of critique from bloggers, who were the most prominent reporters and commentators on the phenomenon of flash mobs in general in this pre-YouTube era, Wasik contends that the Toys "R" Us mob was the most political and most effective.[5] It demonstrated how people could infiltrate and contaminate modes of capitalism, and generated a "fundamental joy at seeing society overtaken."[6]

Flash mobbing introduces a distinct approach to collectivity and serves as a type of embodied epistemology, a form of knowledge-production that transpires through movement and kinesthetic sensation. In 2003, when Wasik created improvised gatherings in public spaces, he used these events to call attention to urban environments and our roles as citizens. Since then, numerous dancers and choreographers, as well as corporate interests, have transformed the genre of the flash mob into a tightly planned display used in advertisements, television shows, and films. Flash mobbing may be viewed by many as a vapid fad due to its appearances in these commercial contexts, but I argue that flash mobs can serve multifaceted roles, from intervention to activism to the exhibition of refined dance techniques. The flash mob is now largely depoliticized, viewed as "pure pleasure," as kitschy fun, rather than as intervention or demonstration. During the course of this ten-year evolution, as relations between aesthetics and activism shifted and were manipulated by commercial agendas, the term "flash mob" became drained of political associations.

This analysis traces the history of the phenomenon from 2003 to 2013 and provides a framework that draws from two theorists, Carrie Noland and Rita Raley, to understand the flash mob's varied intentions and interventions. In *Agency and Embodiment*, Noland writes, "kinesthetic sensations are neither inventions of discourse nor prereflexive 'affections' forever unavailable to consciousness. They are in short tools for understanding the properties of self, other, and world."[7] In Wasik's events, mobbers' improvised and unpredictable actions triggered sensations that called attention to social codes in public spaces, particularly when a person was behaving normatively or when their actions disrupted movement patterns and expectations. A mob's transformations and outcomes can be tracked through both participant and observer responses, as well as through organizers' stated intentions. As mobs spread from New York City to San Francisco as well as to international cities, they became associated with games and playful interruptions. In 2009, when choreographers of advertisements and films adopted mobs as a gimmick to draw attention to products, the flash mob became tightly rehearsed patterns of movement using Tayloristic actions that have since become the defining component of the flash mob formula.

Rita Raley's concept of tactical media offers a useful framework for considering the multiple valences and transformations of these events. Raley describes how activists critique structures or orders through small interventions that generate large-scale repercussions. She defines these projects as "not oriented towards the grand, sweeping revolutionary event; rather they engage in a micropolitics of disruption, intervention, and education."[8] In Wasik's hands, flash mobs were a kind of tactical media that commented on the hegemony of consumer cultures and highlighted the value of uncertainty and distraction. This analysis follows Raley's proposal, "the right question to ask is not whether tactical media works or not, whether it succeeds or fails in spectacular fashion to effect structural transformation; rather we should be asking to what extent it strengthens social relations and to what extent its activities are virtuosic... [Paolo] Virno explains that virtuosity is "activity which finds its own fulfillment (that is, its own purpose) in itself." Virtuosity exists as performance or in the traces of performance it leaves.[9]

If Raley's theory of tactical media proposes that such events operate on the level of momentary encounters and individual interactions, the flash mob offers an ideal site for its application. Wasik's events depended on spontaneous and improvised actions that collected people in public spaces. Unlike a political demonstration with explicit complaints or slogans, Wasik's mobs lacked literal statements, but suggested what he called "a vague feeling" of people being unhappy with things as they were.[10] In the case of the Toys "R" Us mob, the political component of disrupting consumer cultures emerged through and after the mob's actions: the number of participants who showed up and the store's decision to call police were neither anticipated nor organized.

Many of the early, between 2003 and 2004, flash mobs are virtuosic because their processes become their outcomes: the experience of being in the mob generates the kinetic and kinesthetic sensations that strengthen social bonds, foster collectivities, and linger even after the event is completed. When Wasik wrote about the August 7, 2003, Toys "R" Us event, he asked, "Did these dark impulses remain with the participants, I wondered, or did they dissipate with the mob?"[11] The "dark impulses" that Wasik referred to could point to many aspects of the Toys "R" Us action: mobbers' desire to see capitalism obstructed, the abilities of a mob to shift societal patterns and modes of exchange, or even the individuals' decisions to set aside inhibitions and to enact chaotic behaviors collectively. Each of these intents generates a basic form of disobedience in the midst of disciplining environments. As flash mobs evolved into movie scenes and commercials, their improvisatory and threatening elements vanished.

In both commercial and noncommercial events, three elements distinguish a flash mob from other types of gatherings: spontaneity, disruption, and corporeal sensation. Another three aspects are considered essential to its felicitous enactment. First, its crux lies in bypassing verbal communication and generating connections collectively through embodied languages. Second, the events occur in public spaces and reconfigure ways in which people interact with strangers in these environments. In other words, they generate temporary bonds between people and trigger questions about public spaces and codes of behavior. In Wasik's words: "I think one of the reasons why flash mobs were so powerful for people especially here in the United States is that we've lost so much of our tradition of public space in this country, you know, that today in the sorts of suburbs where most people grow up or even here in New York City or in cities around the country, what passes for public space might be a shopping mall . . . try to express yourself in that kind of space and you'll quickly find out just how nonpublic that space is . . ."[12] Third, the events blur the line between who watches and who performs, meaning some people begin the event as spectators, but then join into the action. In tightly choreographed flash mobs very few spectators can join the complex patterns of movement, making these events more planned and staged than flash mobs that are improvised and inclusive. Blurring also occurs between the mob's planning, the event, and its dissemination; each of these phases relies on networked technologies rather than an identifiable leader. Taken together, these elements show how movement can rearrange social spaces, how kinesthetic sensation can generate knowledges, and how collective experiences can be accessed kinesthetically as well as through digital technologies.

Early Years of Flash Mobs

In June 2003, Bill Wasik organized his first mob: a group of people were convened through e-mail to converge at the Claire's Accessories store at Astor Place in Manhattan, but their plans were thwarted. Minutes before the event was to begin, Wasik received a call from his friend Eugene:

> "Is the mob supposed to be at Claire's Accessories?" Eugene asked.
> "Yes," I said.
> "There's six cops standing guard in front of it," he said. "And a paddywagon." . . . Despite the police, my single email had generated enough steam to power a respectable spectacle.[13]

This first attempt was followed by another initiated by Wasik on June 17, 2003, when two hundred people congregated in the rug department at Macy's to buy a "love rug" for their Long Island City commune.[14] This time an e-mail message instructed participants to meet at four local bars close to the Herald Square store where Wasik distributed slips of paper with plans for the mob. Cognizant of the speed with which police could interfere with their activities, Wasik kept the Macy's event brief. Participants clustered around a single rug in the Rugs department for ten minutes, between 7:27 and 7:37 p.m.[15]

Newspapers and bloggers picked up the mob's Macy's activity. A graduate student in Berkeley, Sean Savage, gave the event the name "flash mob" in his blog.[16] Wasik did not identify himself as the organizer and for years kept his role hidden. Soon after the love rug mob, Wasik organized another event by telling participants, via e-mail, to find people reading the *New York Review of Books* in Grand Central Station's food court. These readers gave mobbers the itinerary for the third flash mob, which took place in the Grand Hyatt Hotel's mezzanine. A participant responded: "I was pretty apprehensive beforehand . . . the mob itself was slightly bizarre. There were about 200 of us standing at the balcony railings on the mezzanine floor of the Hyatt hotel, next to Grand Central Station. At the appointed time we burst into applause for 15 seconds as instructed. The look of joy on people's faces was incredible. And even though I'd felt somewhat detached from the proceedings, I couldn't help but smile and join. I knew it was something I wanted to do again."[17] It is unclear if the looks of joy were coming from flash mobbers or unsuspecting bystanders, yet the response indicates that the participatory experience trumped the speaker's initial uncertainty about the event. Here again is evidence of differences between earlier versions of the flash mob that contained such elements of uncertainty and later iterations of flash mobbing that became tightly choreographed spectacles meant to manifest joy instead of disturbance. Wasik's events teetered between exciting eruptions, defiant behavior, absurdist theater, and strategic commentary.

His mobs, as well as others that occurred in 2003 and 2004, engaged participants at sites of disruption as well as through traces of the event left in photographs, blog posts, and videos. With the increase in social media use and creation of YouTube in 2005, these modes of documentation influenced changes in flash mobs themselves, as they evolved from improvisatory and unpredictable eruptions to spectacular displays of unison movement created by entertainment cultures. In noncommercial forms, the mobs continued to function as tactical media, calling attention to codes of interaction in public spaces and knowledge generated through kinesthetic sensation. As flash mobs' modes and intentions expanded, the label "flash mob" attracted misunderstandings and disagreement.

Flash Mobs and Commercial Cultures

More than a year before Wasik's mobs, a group called Improv Everywhere staged pranks in New York City that similarly spotlighted sociality and absurdity but contained essential differences. One of their first events, which they call "missions," was the "No Pants Subway Ride" that occurred in January 2002 when Charlie Todd boarded a subway car in Manhattan without wearing pants. He had on a jacket, hat, scarf, and underwear. At each of the next six stops on the subway another pantless man boarded. By the third stop a passenger observing this incongruous accumulation made eye contact with other passengers and smiled. This is what inspired Todd to continue the "No Pants Subway Ride." Eleven years later, in its twelfth incarnation in 2013, more than four thousand New Yorkers participated in the city with tens of thousands more in sixty cities and twenty-five countries around the world.[18] Todd, founder of Improv Everywhere, says the point of these events is to cause a scene in a public place that's a positive experience, a prank that gives people a great story to tell.[19]

Improv Everywhere (IE) insists that they are distinct from flash mobs. Todd says about the label "flash mob": "It's become a lazy, catch-all term to describe things as varied as people dancing at a Black Eyed Peas concert to surprise Oprah Winfrey to teens meeting up to commit crimes in Chicago. I'm not sure what it even means anymore, and I don't really care to use it to describe what we do."[20] The confusion and tension surrounding the term flash mob emanates in part from its co-optation by commercial cultures. In an upcoming section I describe two commercials: one for T-Mobile created in January of 2009 and another, created three months later, for a Belgian television show; both commercials dominated conversations about the flash mob form. Their aesthetics and intentions are markedly different from initial gatherings in 2003 that were defined by the *New York Times* in that year: "Called into being on short notice by Web sites and e-mail distribution lists, flash mobs meet at an appointed time, engage in some organized spontaneity for a few minutes, then rapidly disperse. The activities are innocent, if mysterious, and tend to bring together loose groupings of surprisingly conventional looking young adults."[21] This definition appeared in an article describing a mob that erupted in Berlin during which about forty people pulled out cell phones on a crowded street, shouted "yes! yes!," and began clapping at 6:01 p.m. Like Wasik's mobs it featured no choreography but championed an absurd intervention that called attention to public space and social relations.

Similar to IE's "No Pants Subway Ride," flash mobs grew from local experiment to international phenomenon, and reporters and academics continue to confuse Improv Everywhere missions with flash mobbing, as John Muse does in a *Theater* journal article titled "Flash Mobs and the Diffusion of Audience," which describes IE missions.[22] Unlike IE missions, flash mobs became platforms for protests, performances, and advertisements, thereby transforming their subcultural capital as well as their ability to illuminate corporeal experiences that situate the body as a site of social collectivity.[23] Another difference between IE missions and flash mobs is their duration: some IE missions last much longer than the ten-minute limit set by Wasik.[24]

Environments that nurtured and supported flash mobs were key to their development and sustainability: New York's flash mobs (and Improv Everywhere missions) emerged in a city that was fractured and suspicious after September 11, 2001. I vividly recall increased police presence in subways and train stations, authorities carrying weapons, and hearing announcements for commuters to stay alert for unusual activity. Making eye contact was a risky gesture because it could be interpreted as surveillance or distrust. Resisting this pressure to behave like docile subjects, Improv Everywhere agents, like Wasik's mobbers, performed spontaneous, defamiliarizing interactions. This was such a priority in Todd's events that he and other IE agents[25] went undercover as unsuspecting bystanders in missions like "Frozen Grand Central" where they can be seen as supposedly surprised observers interacting with the frozen agents and modeling for the people who are truly surprised and confused by what they could be thinking or doing.[26]

Wasik's flash mobs were improvised rituals in commercial spaces (stores and hotels), but on the West Coast, in the summer of 2003 in San Francisco, performance scholar and game theorist Jane McGonigal organized activities, often outdoors, that emphasized participants' involvement, connections forged among strangers, and kinesthesia. Two events that exemplify her ability to create playful, interactive mobs were the cross-whirl, her first San Francisco flash mob in July 2003, then the children's games in Dolores Park in August. Different from Wasik's events, McGonigal's mobs used ilinx,[27] a visceral and bodily experience that discombobulates and is often associated with the popularity of roller-coasters and aerial performances that highlight the thresholds of a body's relation to gravity and balance. Like Wasik's mobs, McGonigal's actions shared his commitment to sociality and spontaneity. Reporting on a flash mob in Dolores Park, the *San Francisco Chronicle* interviewed organizers who insisted on remaining anonymous, going by the names, "Jane" and "The Other Jane." The Other Jane said: "I like the idea that we can get out of our houses and offices and movie theaters and go out and play together. We want to push the silly, fun angle. We want the people who show up to have a good time and be happy. That's the No. 1 priority. The point is the people, not the activity."[28] For those who are technologically tethered, the events had particular appeal, as stated in the same article: "It becomes a habit. It's fun to see other people who usually sit behind their computers, longing for some strange, random thing to occur."[29] In McGonigal's own words, "the ultimate meaning lies in the lingering traces flash mob play has left in shared spaces." As Raley explains in "Tactical Media," such traces can be a form of resistance because they taunt and disturb dominant orders or behaviors. Raley writes that these endeavors and their actants "shift the weight of emphasis slightly to the audience, which does not simply complete the signifying field of the work but records a memory of the performance."[30] More than two years after the "cross-whirl," where mobbers spun across an intersection, McGonigal has witnessed someone else whirling through the crosswalk.[31]

Watching mobbers move in unexpected ways triggers interoceptive responses, a type of kinesthetic awareness that shows us, to use Carrie Noland's phrase: "the body one *is* is not entirely one's own."[32] Herein lies the political efficacy of the events: uncertainty produced in these encounters not only transforms relationships with physical environments, but also produces, as Noland writes, "knowledge through kinesthesia that is constitutive of—not tangential to—the process of individuation."[33] In other words, when we encounter an event that disorients our sense of space and movement, we may gain understanding of the codes that shape our behavior, actions, and interactions. Moments of uncertainty set in motion awarenesses of interactions with environments, as well as shifting patterns of behaviors. As commercials and films usurped the flash mob form, these defamiliarizing and destabilizing elements faded.

Within six years flash mobs transformed radically: instead of improvised gatherings of strangers, they became associated with performances of unison choreography in public spaces. The moment flash mobs were usurped by commercial culture, the collective structure that allowed for individual differences and improvisation evolved into highly regimented and unison sequences.[34] Two commercials accelerated this shift: one in January 2009 by T-Mobile that was filmed in the Liverpool train station and one in March 2009 when two hundred people performed a dance routine to "Do Re Mi" in a train station in Antwerp.[35] It was a promotional stunt for a Belgian television show looking to cast their lead for their reboot of *The Sound of Music*. The British T-mobile and Antwerp TV show commercials share several elements with earlier flash mobs: their location in public space (both were filmed in train stations that corralled unsuspecting audiences), the rupture of ordinary routine, the slippage between participants and observers—people who initially seem surprised, then join the routine and dance along in unison with others—and the spontaneous performance shared by people both watching and dancing. What makes them different from earlier flash mobs is their emphasis on control, uniformity, and homogeneity.

Although a sense of play and absurdity remains, commercialized versions of flash mobs in advertisements, television shows, and films feature trained dancers or singers/musicians and polished routines, resulting in the event's unpredictability and participants' diversity being replaced by conformity. These mobs recall synchronized movements as performed by the Tiller Girls and seen in choreography by Busby Berkeley, who directed early sound musicals in the 1930s.[36] Siegfried Kracauer has linked an aesthetic of precise, efficient dancing to technologies of factory production in his theory of "mass ornament": "The structure of the mass ornament reflects that of the entire contemporary situation . . . The hands in the factory correspond to the legs of the Tiller Girls. Going beyond manual capacities, psychotechnical aptitude tests attempt to calculate dispositions of the soul as well. The mass ornament is the aesthetic reflex of the rationality to which the prevailing economic system aspires."[37] Kracauer articulates aesthetic preferences for synchronized bodies with regulation systems of labor and skills assessment, drawing connections between culture industries, education, and economics. Today's flash mobs can be seen as a new installation of this mass ornament aesthetic with rigid, predetermined routines recalling Kracauer's description, reproduced in sites that span from the States to South Africa, and from India to Israel.

The two commercials made in 2009 also marked the beginning of the transformation of the flash mob from social disruption to marketing tool; following

Figure 4.1. Screen capture from YouTube of T-Mobile commercial flash mob. Liverpool Street Station, January 15, 2009. YouTube video uploaded January 16, 2009.

these two ads, flash mobs were incorporated into, and disseminated through, popular culture at an accelerated rate. Although it began as a subcultural phenomenon, an event that called attention to normative behaviors and the dominance of consumer spaces, the flash mob format became disseminated through its commercial forms as choreographed spectacle. Prior to their placement in advertisements, flash mobs were covered by blogs and occasional newspaper articles. Their presence on the Internet was facilitated by the creation of YouTube in 2005. Mobs that have garnered the most views,[38] indicated in parentheses, include: *Christmas Food Court Flash Mob, Hallelujah Chorus* 11/17/2010 (42,439,278), *The T-Mobile Dance in Liverpool Station* 1/16/2009 (38,627,120), *Sound of Music in Central Station Antwerp* 3/23/2009 (27,722,542), *Jamin's Downtown Disney Flashmob Proposal* 9/26/2011 (9,155,447), *Opera Company of Philadelphia "Hallelujah!" Random Act of Culture* 11/1/2010 (8,315,392), *Flash mob at Copenhagen Central Station* 5/27/2011 (6,886,153), and *Flash Mob at Ohio Union* 5/3/2010 (5,362,723). The popularity of these YouTube versions of mobs calls into question the appeal of the flash mob as a subversive form. In "The Social Logic of Subcultural Capital," Sarah Thornton examines tensions between subcultures and mainstream media. "A critical difference between subcultural capital (as I explore it) and cultural capital (as Bourdieu develops it) is that the media are a primary factor governing the circulation of the former . . . within the economy of subcultural capital the media is not simply another symbolic good or marker of distinction (which is the way Bourdieu describes films and newspapers *vis-à-vis* cultural capital), but a network crucial to the definition and distribution of cultural knowledge. In other words the difference between being in and out of fashion, high or low in subcultural capital, correlates in complex ways with degrees of media coverage, creation and exposure."[39]

To have subcultural capital, a phenomenon must be situated outside of the mainstream. Once the mainstream, or "crowd" in Thornton's analysis, is associated with a set of subcultural practices, these practices are widely perceived (by the members of the originating subculture) as unhip and unsophisticated. It was only after the flash mob was incorporated into advertisement schemes that it featured unison choreography. In fact, on the Fox television show *Modern Family*, season 2 episode 8, Mitchell stages a flash mob to show his love for—and spontaneity to—his partner, Cam, who responds despondently, "you cheated on me with Choreography." Ironically, choreography became part of the flash mob with its co-optation by consumer culture. Since then, each appearance in commercial culture—on the Fox television series *Mobbed*, the Castle Rock Entertainment film *Friends with Benefits*, and the Summit Entertainment movie *Step Up Revolution*—features this highly choreographed version of flash mobbing. What happens when a subcultural phenomenon moves into the mainstream? The film *This Is the End* closes with a celebration that looks like a flash mob:

> Seth Rogen: They got weed in heaven?
> Craig Robinson: You tell me. *A joint appears on Seth Rogen's lips, which he lights by pressing it against his halo.*
> Rogen: That's insane man!
> Robinson: No no no. That's heaven. Anything you can think of is yours.
> *A Segway appears, with Rogen positioned as its driver.*
> Robinson: Go ahead Jay. Make a wish. Anything you can think of.
> *Jay Baruchel looks pensive, then "Everybody (Backstreet's Back)" grows in volume.*
> *The band appears, sending the crowd into a dancing frenzy that involves bboying ciphers and a flash mob as Baruchel, Robinson, and Rogen join the accumulating lines of people replicating the band's choreographed motions.*[40]

A question emerges: when a flash mob ends a blockbuster film,[41] has the form been drained of all political potential or subversive possibilities?

Although a sense of play, uncertainty, and absurdity remains, commercialized versions of flash mobs in advertisements, television shows, and films feature trained dancers and celebrities doing predetermined routines, draining the event's unpredictability and participants' anonymity. Although Improv Everywhere continued to comment on behavioral codes through its missions using subway cars and consumer environments (two of its most popular missions in stores were the one hundred and eleven shirtless agents in Abercrombie & Fitch and a crowd of blue polo, beige khaki-wearing agents in Best Buy), flash mobs became associated with choreographed scenes in films and commercials. These mobs feature similar regulatory patterns of Tayloristic actions: regimented, precise, and efficient. They also incorporate professional production teams to film and edit the action. Flash mobs in movies easily align with histories of choreographed scenes in musical theater that develop the plot or provide light entertainment.

Whereas earlier iterations of the flash mob championed spontaneity and ephemerality, the commercial versions, though meticulously planned and managed, try to conceal their preparations. The director of T-Mobile's commercial, Michael Gracey, says in the YouTube video about the making of the event: "As soon as the general public spots a camera, game over."[42] Ten thousand people auditioned to be part of this commercial; four hundred were selected. The director is heard telling the cast: "the real magic exists in you being able to convince members of the general public to join in and do what you are doing." Rather than featuring unusual and subversive elements as seen in earlier flash mobs and Improv Everywhere missions, the aim of the commercial is to lure spectators into buying a product: the music and choreography are a mix of pop songs, ballroom dancing, and easily recognized steps that accompany certain lyrics.

Friends with Benefits offers a particularly informative site for examining the evolution of the flash mob since these eruptions serve as markers of shifts in the characters' relationships throughout the film. The first flash mob takes place when Jamie, an executive recruiter played by Mila Kunis, needs to convince Dylan, an art director from Los Angeles (played by Justin Timberlake) to take a job with *GQ* magazine in Manhattan. During his tour of the city, designed by Jamie to show Dylan why New York is a fantastic place, a massive flash mob erupts in Times Square, just after they've emerged from the subway station. They are immersed in the phenomenon, almost trapped in the hundreds of dancing bodies, generating a feeling of being transported somewhere else.[43] The muscular bonding of the mob, coordinated activity used to create a sense of togetherness as seen in military exercises and patriotic parades,[44] transforms hundreds of dancers into a euphoric display, one that teeters between intimidating and exhilarating. This mob is deployed to convince Dylan to become part of the city. Like its appearance in T-Mobile advertisements, this flash mob sells a product: New York as desirable home. Unlike the mobs conceived by Wasik or McGonigal, the film's version spotlights the actors. Timberlake and Kunis cannot blend into the crowd and their recognizability as celebrities draws attention away from the collective activity of the group. Cameras zooming into them pull focus away from the crowd, detracting from the mob's ability to build a sense of camaraderie, and their conversation, rather than embodied experience, dominates the moment.

If we see flash mobs as places of possibility for interaction and collectivity, the filming and deployment of this scene eradicates these possibilities: the mobs are staged, carefully edited, absorbed into the plot rather than destabilizing norms, and audiences in movie theaters remain passive. Following this first mob, Dylan decides to turn flash mobs into promotional material—"guerilla advertising"—for GQ, causing Jamie to respond that he is "taking something so pure and commercializing it." Although this conversation seems to acknowledge the irony of a consumerist use of flash mobbing, there's no recognition of the differences between this already co-opted form with its unison choreography, and the improvised rituals of Wasik's and McGonigal's earlier versions. Even the dialogue during the Times Square mob has Dylan referring to Oprah as a generator of the phenomenon, erasing prior flash mobs that fostered greater interactivity and chance encounter:

> Dylan: What is this?
> Jamie: It's a flash mob!
> Dylan: Oh, like on Oprah... Should we get out of the way?
> Jamie: No! Enjoy it! Take it in...
> Dylan: Pretty damn cool... Do these people get paid for this?
> Jamie: No, they kind of just do it for fun. It's nice to feel like you're a part of something. New York can be lonely at times...
> Dylan: And you're trying to sell me on it.
> Jamie: Every place can be a little lonely at times...
> Dylan: I'm in... You sold me.[45]

Differences between this scene and a later flash mob illuminate the ways mobs are staged to advance the plot of *Friends with Benefits*. One of the last scenes of the film features Dylan using a mob in Grand Central Station to convince Jamie to begin a sincere relationship with him. The songs are now a soundtrack of their friendship, recalling certain scenes and conversations. Grand Central, familiar to audiences of flash mobs and urban pranks, was the site of the AT&T commercial mocking flash mobbing and the Improv Everywhere mission "Frozen Grand Central." The choreography here uses stillness in prominent ways, citing this earlier Improv Everywhere mission. But again, like the Times Square mob in the film, the essence of flash mobbing as spontaneous interruption dissipates: this event features unison choreography to advance the plot, like a dance routine in a musical.

In spite of its superficial use of flash mobs, *Friends with Benefits* provides commentary on factors that contribute to flash mobbing as a cultural phenomenon: technological innovation impacts and frequently deters face-to-face communication. Flash mobbing, like the Improv Everywhere urban pranks, emerged as ways to connect physically, affectively, and kinesthetically, particularly for people who found themselves in isolating, alienating, and virtual worlds. In other words, even though the film fails to examine flash mobbing as a kind of tactical medium, it elucidates the conditions that nurture mobbing's popularity, starting with the title, which refers to the arrangement Dylan and Jamie create to have sex without any attachment or emotional support. In spite of numerous ways to connect with their devices, characters in the film struggle with intimacy and commitment; their conversations involve, depend on, and revolve around technology. When Dylan gets an offer from *GQ*, Jamie texts him the news even though she will be meeting up with him in minutes. Dylan gets the text when they are together and asks why she opted for texting instead of telling him. Jamie replies, "because it's more dramatic." When Dylan is surprised that Jamie knows his father was an accomplished journalist, Jamie replies, "I have this thing at work called Google." The quantity of information available at one's fingertips seems to preclude the ability to engage more personally, more intimately.

In spite of its skewed versions of flash mobs, the film includes scenes that highlight disruption, challenge codes of behavior, and promote physical and emotional connections, operating much like the initial flash mobs designed by Wasik and McGonigal. To give one example, Dylan's father has Alzheimer's and prefers to go pantless, a habit that initially embarrasses Dylan. Toward the end of the film, Dylan arrives at a table in a restaurant and sees that his father removed his slacks. The father asks his son: "Are you going to join me?" and Dylan replies, "Absolutely," taking off his jeans. The scene evokes the disobedient and infectious rebellion of Improv Everywhere's "No Pants Subway Ride." Dylan and his father then pursue a conversation that serves as the climax of the movie: his father reveals the relationship that transformed his life and encourages Dylan to repair the damage he has done to his friendship with Jamie. As clichéd as these formulaic conversations and characters are, *Friends with Benefits* reveals a message that aligns with McGonigal and even the creators of Improv Everywhere: notice and appreciate the people around you, savor contact and communication.

A year after *Friends with Benefits* appeared in theaters, Summit Entertainment released *Step Up Revolution*, a film that makes flash mobs its focal point. A preprofessional dancer, Emily (played by Kathryn McCormick) falls in love with Sean (played by Ryan Guzman), a dancer who organizes choreographed interruptions by The Mob into Miami's streets and buildings. On the surface its narrative aligns with flash mobbing's interest in challenging conformity and homogeneity, but the film itself is a predictable series of scenes with flashy special effects. Camera angles heighten the seemingly impossible feats: cars that bounce as they carry dancers like surfers on their hoods and dancers who turn the tables of a fancy restaurant into their stages to shock the clientele and make a viral video.

A massive dance scene by The Mob occurs midfilm when sixty-five performers dressed in black business suits, hats, and briefcases transform an office building into their performance space, using its escalators, café tables, and atrium.[46] Highly choreographed, unison, and precise movement distance their actions from the spontaneous, improvised scenes of early flash mobs by Wasik and McGonigal. Choreographed by Christopher Scott, this scene calls to mind the vocabularies seen on reality shows like *So You Think You Can Dance*, which featured McCormick and has used some of the film's choreographers, namely Travis Wall. In spite of the diversity of dancers and movement genres included in the film, there is a flattening effect in this scene as all performers subscribe to the same regimented actions. Each mob scene in *Step Up Revolution* incorporates a similar vocabulary, obliterating the idea that flash mobs use movement to call attention to social codes or public spaces, like the cross-whirl, children's games in Dolores Park, or dinosaur worship in Toys "R" Us. Their steps in the business plaza are a series of stop-and-go poses, angular shapes, and unison

Figure 4.2. Screen capture from YouTube of a flash mob in *Step Up Revolution*. A dancer's parkour-like flip is visible in the upper right corner. (2012 Summit Entertainment).

marching patterns that weave columns of dancers through one another. Acrobatic feats abound: in one moment, slow motion is used to show a dancer executing a parkour-like flip off the atrium walls.

Ironically, in the behind-the-scenes videos for *Step Up Revolution*, dancers play and improvise together, but such spontaneity and camaraderie are erased from the final product.[47] Dialogue consists of trite one-liners: in case it isn't clear that Sean uses The Mob as a way of vying for recognition, he explains to Emily, "It's like us saying, 'Listen up. We exist.'" Emily exclaims just before the flash mob in the business plaza: "Enough with performance art. It's time for protest art!" Her statement conflicts with the notion that momentary encounters and kinesthetic awareness shape cultural and political understandings. As The Mob's popularity builds through YouTube hits she states: "You have four million people listening but you are not saying anything that actually matters! You know it's not okay to make art for fun anymore, and it's not okay to make trouble either."[48] The film's dialogue, like that in *Friends with Benefits*, erases the history of flash-mobbing as social intervention with political potential because Emily assumes that mobs must further a specific agenda in order to be considered worthwhile.

As Wasik made clear in 2003, disrupting behaviors unattached to particular causes triggered awareness of societal codes and prescribed interactions. Emily's line not only dismisses this concept, rendering invisible the early years of the flash mob, but also describes performance art as lacking political possibilities. Her statements disregard Raley's theory of tactical media that favors small-scale intervention rather than orchestrated demonstrations. *Step Up Revolution* distorts the flash mob, making the commercial version of unison, complex choreography into statements with political messages. Although the film acknowledges the importance of the Internet in creating an audience for flash mobs, *Step Up Revolution*'s mob scenes are uncannily similar to dance sequences in the other *Step Up* films. Flash mobs appear to have entered the *Step Up* franchise as a way of staying relevant with current trends and appealing to wider audiences. The film does little to further the phenomenon's ability to challenge norms, encourage participation, defy expectation, and reconfigure public spaces. Director Scott Speer admits to changing the nature of flash mobs for the film: he told the *Hollywood Reporter* he wanted to amplify their action-packed characteristics, "to boost these flash mobs into heist-style takeovers."[49]

The outrageousness of these scenes distances the film from flash mob's intent of connecting people and generating a sense of collectivity. Transformed by cinematic techniques, the flash mob becomes a choreographed musical number with intricate camera work rather than a site of corporeal experiences and momentary engagement. Although the film professes to use flash mobs to call attention to social and economic inequalities, the mobs' movements reinforce the separation of performers and observers, negating opportunities for interoceptive responses or corporeal collectivity. In the final mob scene, only the Miami mayor gets caught up in the movement and starts to mimic the performers' actions. Perhaps these scenes are more accurately considered "flash casts" since they are composed of carefully selected, uniformly dressed performers, unlike a "mob" that retains a sense of spontaneity and improvisation. In the movie's closing dialogue, The Mob willingly agrees to advertise products by Nike, a massive corporation that has historically created sweatshops and used child labor.[50] Not only does the film eradicate the history of mobs as eruptions of improvisatory dancing or playful behaviors, it also equates achievement with working for a multibillion dollar corporation. While the Nike endorsement may be read as success to certain audiences because it offers financial security, there are artists and performers who consider the means they use to make their products more important than their salaries.

To complicate Thornton's defining of subcultural capital, the explosion of the flash mob as unison choreography did not negate its ability to provoke and to resist hegemonic structures. In 2012 women in Israel used a flash mob to expose a vital facet of their lives: the ability to move and dance freely. As

Figure 4.3. Screen capture from YouTube of the Official Beit Shemesh Women's flash mob. January 6, 2012. YouTube video uploaded January 8, 2012.

organizer Brenda Ganot explained, it was designed "to show another face of Beit Shemesh" as well as to oppose media depictions of their region: "Beit Shemesh is not just the extremists you see in the news . . . we are not afraid to express ourselves publicly: If you spit at us when we walk down the street, then we'll dance down the street. This was about cooperation between all different types of women from different backgrounds, showing that we can get together and do something fun and empowering. We are free to dance in our own city."[51] As a form that locates the site of social collectivity in corporeal experience, flash mobbing possesses a particular adaptability as its impact resonates not only visually, but also physically, personally, and kinesthetically.

Raley addresses experiential aspects of participatory events in her article "Walk This Way": "artists self-consciously position themselves as 'tactical' media practitioners working within a tradition of experimental cartography and protest against the organizational rationality of urban design. This is not naive idealizing of resistance, but resistance situated at the level of the ordinary and the experiential."[52] The Beit Shemesh flash mob exemplifies ways in which movement by participants challenges spatial and cultural obstacles placed on women. Their performance is situated in the realm of the everyday, literally on the streets of their city, and challenges barriers to movement and expression by defying these strictures and performing together, collectively, in these spaces.

The question is whether it is possible to reconcile flash mobs' past as a form of resistance to consumer cultures with its current role in advertisements and Hollywood spectacles that promote products and commercialism. A historical precedent informs this evolution: dance scholar Susan Manning posed a similar question about movement choirs (*Bewegungschöre*) before their co-optation by the Third Reich as spectacle and propaganda. For Rudolf Laban, in the pre-Nazi period, the movement choir was experiential rather than presentational, manifesting Laban's interest in movement that stirs profound consciousness, a "spiritual attitude that deepens the sense of mutuality and the appreciation of the personal identity of each individual."[53] Manning describes how the form was transformed:

> When redeployed as part of the *Thingspiel* the movement choir became the basis for a large-scale spectacle that reinstated the separation of performer and spectator. In the open-air theaters specially built for *Thingspiel*, several thousand spectators would watch the precision patterns executed by the hundred or more members of the movement choir. Thus the form dramatized the individuals' subordination to the group. As the political and performative contexts for the movement choir changed, so too did the form and its ideological import. Thus, my model conceptualizes form as variously mutable across time and space and as deceptively mobile from one ideological context to another.[54]

Does the adaptability of the movement choir indicate that flash mobbing can also be "mutable across time and space," and if so what are methodologies that can track its evolution and efficacy? Are there developments of flash mobbing that, counter to their appearances in films like *Friends with Benefits* and *Step Up Revolution*, offer possibilities for social change? One example is the organization of the first Cash Mob in 2011, which was inspired by flash mobbing and encouraged people to go into local businesses and spend their money en masse, giving business owners an economic stimulus.[55]

Another question remains: how to construct an analysis that acknowledges flash mobbing's mutability of form? Earlier iterations responded to corporate and biopolitical structures of control, revealing how a suspension of norms—going pantless, freezing in place, whirling through crosswalks—exposed techniques of regulation and privileged participatory structures and sensorial experiences. Responses of participants reveal mobs' impact: when Wasik described

MOB #4 as a crowd of hundreds pretending to be tourists in a shoe store in SoHo, he wrote "all [were] feigning awe—an awe I myself truly felt—to be not merely in New York, but so close to the center of something so big." Ten years later in San Francisco, Bryan Goebel described his participation in a flash mob that performed Janet Jackson's choreography: "One of the best experiences of my life (really!) was taking the Rhythm Nation dance class (my first dance class ever!) and then participating in the flash mob Sunday. Even though the choreography was simplified so that more people of all ages and abilities could take part..."[56]

Separated by a decade, their responses indicate uncanny similarities, particularly the significance of uncertainty. Not only are the spectators who happen upon a flash mob surprised, but participants themselves don't anticipate their own affective and kinesthetic responses. Herein lies the political potential of the phenomenon: flash mobbing jars the passersby with its disruption of movement and nonsensical interaction as it sparks awareness of their own skeptical states prior to participating in or viewing the event.

One way of tracking participant and viewer engagement is through comments on YouTubes of flash mobs. These are from a 2010 flash mob at Ohio State University: "i cried...i dont know why...maybe I just want to see happy people...its very hard to see one nowadays.... *weezurd.*" D Malichi47 in reply to *weezurd*: "Maybe it's just a powerful thing to see and you just didn't know it. The same thing happened to me."[57] Comments posted about the T-Mobile flash mob include this one from Leviwosc: "The lady at the end said she was in a bad mood and after the flash mob she was in a good mood. That's the whole idea of a flash mob. To surprise regular people in their every day lives with something special which makes you feel good. And I'm certain it had the same effect on more people."[58] Other comments appear to have been left by people who did not realize the T-Mobile mob was a commercial. Leigh McGee posted four years ago, "This was a wonderful idea, and flawlessly executed. Who could resist such fun! I wish I'd been there. I would have loved it!" One of the dancers in the T-Mobile commercial says afterwards: "I felt a moment of love. It was connective like. For five minutes there, everyone was just relaxed for a second and was happy. It was nice."[59]

Antwerp's Do Re Mi mob inspired organizers in the States to gather participants for noncommercial experiences.[60] Occasionally there are comments that critique the nonsensical, as this person wrote about Charlie Todd's TEDTalk on March 15, 2012: "The luxury of privileged people to be completely inane."[61] This statement is a crucial reminder of ways in which access to mobs as both participants and observers is foreclosed to certain populations.

While there are examples of mobs used to address economic hardship, as in the Cash Mob, and discrimination, as in Beit Shemesh's action, it is still a form that depends on access to public spaces, the ability to move freely without being policed or surveilled, and digital technologies to record and disseminate events. Tensions exist between bodies that are made visible through these activities and those that are excluded from these representations. Furthermore, it is a type of intervention that spotlights an atmosphere of uncertainty and instability, as neither participants nor observers can predict how it will evolve. A problem surfaces when we consider how a similar sense of precarity characterizes political-economic landscapes under neoliberal policies. Are mobs validating short-term quick fixes that add fun and creativity to individuals' lives but do nothing to address long-term insecurity?[62] The flash mob form leaves open the possibility for participants and observers to rethink social interaction, public space, and disrupting behaviors.

Most of today's mobs are used to surprise a girlfriend with a marriage proposal or to perform in public space with a preplanned routine, as the U.S. Air Force Band did recently in a museum in Washington, D.C.[63] At the same time, there are events that provoke critical thinking about commodification cultures as well as agency and embodiment. Although a flash mob to honor Nelson Mandela appeared on December 7, 2013, in a food store in Johannesburg, responses to the event highlight the way it triggered reflection of the country's sociopolitical histories.[64] Traces of such mobs, left in personal memories and public spaces themselves, open ways of considering alternative perspectives.

Flash mobbing emerged as technologies of mobile communication and social media made it possible to connect to more people, more frequently, and more easily with less person-to-person contact. Today pedestrians and commuters are frequently tethered, situated in multiple sensorial spheres: visually on a street or subway, acoustically on an iPod or iPhone, and mentally planning a get-together or rehashing a conversation. Flash mobs are corporeal experiences: alluring, disorienting, and captivating, these fleeting eruptions remind spectators and viewers of connectivity and difference, of the value of defamiliarizing experiences. As kinesthetic experiences they place pressure on social conditioning and leave traces. Carrie Noland writes: "gestural routines of inscription yield kinesthetic experience that is a resource in its own right, a resource of sensation capable of subverting the institutions of inscription by promising new, unmarked material to record. In short my wager is that the interoception provided by movement can be productive of new cultural meanings."[65] A flash mob's ingredients—participatory design, corporeal sensation, and jarring unpredictability—engender events that bypass language, engage viewers, and trigger kinetic and kinesthetic knowledges.

McGonigal acknowledged contributions Wasik made to the phenomenon as well as the malleability of the form when she wrote: "Wasik invented the bones, the structure, of flash mobs—yes. But independent organizers in their own cities put their own flesh and blood on top of that skeleton."[66] Although its structure has traveled across countries and continents, each location where a flash mob has appeared has inserted its own adaptations, its own participants, its own organizing "flesh." These aspects are modifiable and adaptable. They physically disintegrate after the event, but are traced in the memories of participants and observers. McGonigal writes that she has been "enchanted and delighted by Capetown's, Bogota's, Montreal's, and Warsaw's interpretations of the flash mob, none of which looked like each other's and each of which captured the imagination of local residents in their own site-specific, community-specific ways."[67] Participants activate modes of engaging with one another as well as transforming public spaces. Flash mobs exist as both vehicles of consumerism and actions that resist dominant structures or pressures to conform and consume. Flash mobs show how disruption and collectivity can evolve in mutually beneficial ways, and their range of intentions and outcomes makes evident the spectrum and powerful attraction of embodied epistemologies.

* * *

Thanks to Professor Abigail De Kosnik for her many generative suggestions and consistent encouragement as well as for her graduate seminar at UC Berkeley, NWMEDIA 290/THEATER 266: New Media Research Seminar.

Notes

1. Bill Wasik, *And Then There's This* (New York: Viking, 2009), 34.
2. Ibid.
3. Ibid., 35.
4. Ibid.
5. One example of critique of the Toys "R" Us mob from the blog *Satan's Laundromat*: "A cute idea, but not public enough; again, it was in a store, with limited means

of ingress and egress; I'd still like to see one outdoors in a heavily trafficked public place, where the mob can form from all directions and disperse in all directions as well, and where there are more spectators to bewilder. Once again, people jumped the gun, starting each phase too early and dispersing too early," http://www.satanslaundromat.com/sl/archives/000108.html, accessed December 21, 2013.

6. Bill Wasik, "My Crowd: Or, Phase 5," *Harper's*, March 2006, 2016, http://harpers.org/archive/2006/03/my-crowd/, accessed December 21, 2013.

7. Carrie Noland, *Agency and Embodiment* (Cambridge, MA: Harvard University Press, 2009), 13.

8. Rita Raley *Tactical Media* (Minneapolis: University of Minnesota Press, 2009), 1.

9. Ibid., 29.

10. Bill Wasik, interview by Francis Heaney, *Stay Free!* magazine, http://www.stayfreemagazine.org/archives/24/flash-mobs-history.html, accessed December 21, 2013.

11. Wasik, "My Crowd," *Harper's*, http://harpers.org/archive/2006/03/my-crowd/9/, accessed December 21, 2013.

12. Bill Wasik, interview, June 3, 2009, *Big Think*, http://bigthink.com/videos/bill-wasik-introduces-flash-mobs, accessed December 21, 2013.

13. Bill Wasik, *And Then There's This*, 20.

14. Ibid., 21.

15. This temporal dimension is important because it distances flash mobs from Improv Everywhere missions that sometimes last for hours.

16. Sean Savage, "Flash Mob Takes Manhattan," *cheesebikini.com*, June 16, 2003, http://www.cheesebikini.com/archives/000271.html, accessed December 21, 2013.

17. Diana Kendall, *Sociology in Our Times* (Boston: Cengage Learning, 2007), 672.

18. "No Pants Subway Ride 2013," *Improv Everywhere*, January 14, 2013, http://improveverywhere.com/2013/01/14/no-pants-subway-ride-2013/, accessed December 21, 2013.

19. "Charlie Todd: The shared experience of absurdity," *TEDTalk*, posted November 2011, http://www.ted.com/talks/charlie_todd_the_shared_experience_of_absurdity.html, accessed December 21, 2013.

20. Charlie Todd, "Frequently Asked Questions," *Improv Everywhere*, http://improveverywhere.com/faq/, accessed December 21, 2013.

21. Otto Pohl, "What: Mob Scene. Who: Strangers. Point: None," *New York Times*, August 4, 2003, http://www.nytimes.com/2003/08/04/international/europe/04BERL.html, accessed December 21, 2013.

22. John H. Muse, "Flash Mobs and the Diffusion of Audience," *Theater* 40, no. 3 (2010): 9–23.

23. "Audience as Subject," an exhibit at Yerba Buena Center for the Arts, posed questions about corporeal experiences as sites of social collectivity, exchange, and potential that influenced this paper.

24. "A lot of the fun of the flash mobs is that because they were 10 minutes or less usually the police would show up just at the point that everyone was leaving." Bill Wa-

sik, *BigThink.com*, June 3, 2009, http://bigthink.com/videos/bill-wasik-introduces-flash-mobs, accessed December 21, 2013.

25. Thanks to Jen Atkins for pointing out that "*Mad Men* actor Rich Sommer (also known for his improv work) is another plant in the crowd!"

26. "Frozen Grand Central," *YouTube*, January 31, 2008, http://www.youtube.com/watch?v=jwMj3PJDxuo, accessed December 21, 2013.

27. Roger Caillois, *Man, Play, and Games* (Urbana: University of Illinois Press, 2001).

28. Neva Chonin, "Anarchy Rules!" *San Francisco Chronicle*, August 11, 2003, http://www.sfgate.com/entertainment/article/Anarchy-rules-Flash-mobs-big-spontaneous-2574910.php, accessed December 21, 2013.

29. Ibid.

30. Raley, 12.

31. Jane McGonigal, *Avant Game*, February 26, 2006, http://blog.avantgame.com/2006/02/maybe-i-take-play-too-seriously.html, accessed December 21, 2013.

32. Noland, 47.

33. Ibid., 4.

34. Other corporations had used flash mobbing in advertisements, particularly Ford and Swatch, but not with the unison choreography introduced in 2009. Information on the Ford and Swatch campaigns is available here: http://harpers.org/archive/2006/03/my-crowd/, accessed December 21, 2013.

35. T-Mobile Liverpool YouTube viewed 38,769,973 times as of December 18, 2013; Antwerp YouTube viewed 27,944,189 times as of December 18, 2013. Accessed December 18, 2013.

36. Flash mob choreographer Ashley Wallen cites Busby Berkeley as an inspiration in "Ashley Wallen, choreographer," July 3, 2011, http://www.ideastap.com/IdeasMag/all-articles/ashley-wallen-choreographer, accessed December 21, 2013.

37. Siegfried Kracauer, *The Mass Ornament* (Cambridge, MA: Harvard University Press, 1995), 78–79.

38. All view totals as of November 12, 2013. These are imprecise calculations since some videos have been posted by different accounts, meaning more than once, but this collection indicates that several traits are important to the spread of the flash mob: events occur in public spaces (train stations, food courts, public parks), and it's difficult to tell the difference between grassroots and commercial versions.

39. Sarah Thornton, "Social Logic," *The Subcultures Reader* (New York: Routledge, 1997), 203.

40. *This is the End*, directed by Seth Rogen and Evan Goldberg. 2013. Columbia Pictures. DVD.

41. As of October 18, 2013, *This Is the End* has grossed $101,470,202 in North America, and $21,796,250 in other countries.

42. "Making of T-Mobile Dance," *YouTube*, January 24, 2009, 2016, http://www.youtube.com/watch?v=uVFNM8f9WnI, accessed December 21, 2013.

43. Sherry Turkle writes in *Simulation and Its Discontents*: "Simulation demands immersion and immersion makes it hard to doubt simulation. The more powerful our tools become, the harder it is to imagine the world without them." *Simulation and Its Discontents* (Cambridge, MA: MIT Press, 2009), 8.

44. William McNeill, *Keeping Together in Time: Dance and Drill in Human History* (Cambridge, MA: Harvard University Press, 1997).

45. *Friends with Benefits*, directed by Will Gluck. 2011. Castle Rock Entertainment. DVD.

46. Ashley Lee, "Step Up Revolution Director, Choreographers Talk Flash Mob Attraction and Former Martial Artist Ryan Guzman Debut," *Hollywood Reporter*, July 26, 2012, http://www.hollywoodreporter.com/news/step-up-revolution-kathryn-mccormick-ryan-guzman-355033, accessed December 21, 2013.

47. "Step Up Revolution: Fun on the Set," *YouTube*, July 16, 2012, http://www.youtube.com/watch?v=qP1yatLcBxo, accessed December 21, 2013.

48. *Step Up Revolution*, directed by Scott Speer, 2012, Summit Entertainment. DVD.

49. Ashley Lee, "Step Up Revolution Director, Choreographers Talk Flash Mob Attraction and Former Martial Artist Ryan Guzman Debut," *Hollywood Reporter*, July 26, 2012.

50. John Cushman, "Nike Pledges to End Child Labor and Apply U.S. Rules Abroad," *New York Times*, May 13, 1998, http://www.nytimes.com/1998/05/13/business/international-business-nike-pledges-to-end-child-labor-and-apply-us-rules-abroad.html, accessed December 21, 2013.

51. Yoni Kempinski, "Beit Shemesh Women Protest with Flash Mob," *Israel National News*, January 8, 2012, http://www.israelnationalnews.com/News/News.aspx/151499#.UrDLsJiWfap, accessed December 21, 2013.

52. Rita Raley, "Walk This Way: Mobile Narratives as Composed Experience," *Beyond the Screen* (Bielefeld: Verlag, 2010), 208.

53. Nancy Reynolds quotes Laban's "A Life for Dance" (1935) in *No Fixed Points* (New Haven, CT: Yale University Press, 2003), 79.

54. Susan Manning, "Modern Dance in the Third Reich," *Choreographing Histories* (Bloomington: Indiana University Press, 1995), 165–76.

55. "About Us," *Cash-Mobs,* http://cash-mobs.com, accessed December 21, 2013.

56. "Janet Jackson Flash Mob," *MuniDiaries.com*, April 3, 2012, http://www.munidiaries.com/2012/04/03/janet-jackson-flash-mob-on-the-f-market/, accessed December 21, 2013.

57. "Flash Mob at the Ohio Union," *YouTube*, May 3, 2010, http://www.youtube.com/watch?v=HDNOB6TnHSI&, accessed December 21, 2013.

58. "The Public's Reaction to the T-Mobile Dance," *YouTube*, January 15, 2009, http://www.youtube.com/watch?v=9Jv6rHJiNhQ&, accessed December 21, 2013.

59. "Making of T-Mobile Dance," *YouTube*, January 24, 2009, http://www.youtube.com/watch?v=uVFNM8f9WnI, accessed December 21, 2013.

60. Connie Bergstein Dow, "Dance, Pop Culture and Community: A Tale of Two Flash Mobs," *Journal of Dance Education* 11, no. 4 (2011): 140–42.

61. Comment posted March 15, 2012, "Charlie Todd: The shared experience of absurdity," *TED*, http://www.ted.com/talks/charlie_todd_the_shared_experience_of_absurdity.html, accessed December 21, 2013.

62. For more on associations between aesthetics and political economic conditions, see Shannon Jackson, "Just-in-Time: Performance and the Aesthetics of Precarity," *TDR: The Drama Review* 56, no. 4 (2012): 10–31.

63. Sarah Barness, "US Air Force Band Surprises Museum Goers," *Huffington Post*, December 6, 2013, http://www.huffingtonpost.com/2013/12/06/usaf-holiday-flash-mob_n_4398667.html, accessed December 21, 2013.

64. "Woolies and Soweto Gospel Choir: Madiba Tribute," *YouTube*, December 9, 2013, http://www.youtube.com/watch?v=MHHjP7XrBqo. Comments include the Sunpilots: "Beautiful and heart-warming performance. But the fact that it was a coordinated stunt designed to get Woolies some publicity on the back of such a great man's death makes it a little distasteful too." Ana di Lupis responds to The Sunpilots, "I cried, it touched me and that's what counts, because my tears were for Madiba . . . out of joy and sadness alike. The fact that it was "only" a publicity-seeking action doesn't minimize the artistic skill . . . and the energy of everyone listening to it and feeling touched, will be entirely going towards Madiba . . . I couldn't care less for Woolworth at that moment . . . and I think, the shoppers didn't either." Accessed December 21, 2013.

65. Noland, *Agency and Embodiment*, 215.

66. Jane McGonigal, "Maybe I take play too seriously," *Avant Game*.

67. Ibid.

II
Intimate Spaces, Staged Subversions

5

(Post) Pious and Porn Spectacles

Frontier Choreographies of the U.S. Jewess

HANNAH SCHWADRON

A rabbi and a porn star walk into a (*fill in the blank*) somewhere between the JCC on Olympic Blvd and downtown LA's nightclub scene... and any number of punch lines that might follow could easily run the risk of several oversights: the porn star I mean is Joanna Angel, an ex-orthodox Jewish "punk princess" and founding director of her own adult film company; the rabbi is Sharon Brous, my own nondenominational spiritual leader and arguably the baddest woman with a full-time pulpit position I've yet to encounter. Incidentally, they're both thirty-something-year-old leaders of their own "best of" businesses with too much at stake for the same garish jokes.[1]

No doubt, Brous and Angel would do better scripting their own sacred-profane send-ups and regularly do. Funny, savvy bosses in their respective domains, the reputations of these two antitraditionalists loom larger than their five-foot frames. Were the religious maven and porn directress ever to actually converse, I could imagine the two agreeing on at least a few things: today's Jewish progressive bounds are edging forward in real and virtual space, mobilizing forces of progressive thought and embodied action that should be tweeted, blogged, e-mailed, podcasted, sold as merch, made in LA, sent home to New York networks, and posted onto voters' favorite lists of hot and hotter Jewish frontiers.

"Hot" in this case relates to the undeniable success of both figures. Both women sustain spotlights in current top-five lists of breakthrough businesses: Rabbi Sharon Brous of LA's Jewish spiritual community, Ikar, on *Newsweek*'s Top Rabbis of 2012,[2] and director-model Joanna Angel for Adult Video News Awards 2011 Best Porn Site and Best Solo Sex Scene.[3] Also hot is the humor of matching company slogans and the flirtatious tenor of their rhetorical tease. Respective mantras promise that one is "Not Your Bubbe's Synagogue" and the other, "Not Your Daddy's Porn."[4] The "not your" sensibility is a tongue-in-cheek refusal of two American Jewish generations underlining a promise to entice audiences in ways more relevant to a contemporary 18–35-year-old demographic. As both mottos envision a next step for Jewish progressivism, they tie that thinking directly, if distinctly, to a sexier Jewishness and its performative potential. Likewise, in both cases, the marketing ploy features its female lead—her edginess, her exceptional ideas, and her ability to move bodies beyond boundaries set by previous generations, and en masse.

As spectacular icons on the progressive fringes of Jewish America, Brous and Angel offer their respective stances of Jewish and female authority as funny, even "sexy," alternatives to patriarchal conservatism in both fields. While Angel invests in an explicit, bodily sexiness by trade, Rabbi Brous heads a Jewish spiritual community that, while liberal in its sexual politics (among other progressive platforms), cultivates its sexiness through the success of a practice-based religiosity and its emphasis on embodied action.

When viewed through a dance studies approach, it appears that both Brous and Angel lead Jewish movements through embodied means: Angel, through the raunch of hard-core porn, and Brous, through a heightened physical approach to prayer. Where Angel's physicality may be more typical of her genre, Brous's revitalized mobilization of liturgy and social practice directly intervenes in the disembodied personifications of the "bookish" religious Jew, as well as the growing disinterest in synagogue participation noted of an "unaffiliated" Jewish generation today.[5]

In what follows, I outline Rabbi Brous's goal to envelop a disenchanted Jewish generation and Joanna Angel's agenda to revive a (Jewish) progressive edge in the ever-expanding genre of alternative porn.[6] In the name of the Jewish new, the newly hip, and the reaffiliated, both leading women position themselves, ideologically and physically, in relation to a "post" world no longer consumed with the concerns of their fathers and grandmothers. As each pushes against generational borders, they motion away from "traditional" forms of authority in frontierist choreographies led and modeled by Jewish women.

Borrowing from Sander Gilman's notion of the "Jewish Frontier" as a symbolic space in real time and always under construction, I look to how these seemingly opposed organizations—one religious and one punk-porn—work together to choreograph related frontiers of revisionist Jewish discourse, as literal embodiments of LA's westwardness and figurative pioneers of unorthodox cultural campaigns. For live and virtual networks (both Jewish and not), both organizations enact socio-spatial performances of contemporary Jewish identity politics. Congregations in both contexts help sharpen the edge of today's Jewish women in the spotlight, as Angel and Brous move in and across male-ordered parameters of religiosity and pornography alike.

Frontier Femininities

Jewish cultural studies scholar Sander Gilman defines the "Jewish Frontier" as "the conceptual and physical space where groups in motion meet, confront, alter, destroy, and build."[7] Gilman's postmodern definition constructs a symbolic space linked to a variety of concrete locations and histories. He writes that "authentic" Jewishness exists at the frontier of fantasy and reality.[8] A "narrative" best understood as "superimposed on a landscape," Gilman explains that the frontier "is a means of organizing the world, rather than the world itself."[9] It is this organization of "the world in which Jews not only live," but where they "more importantly self-define," that defines Gilman's notion of Jewish collective identity.

I add progressive porn and piety to Gilman's theory of the Jewish frontier as elements in creating and re-creating Jewish identity within the symbolic and concrete spaces of cultural fantasy and reality. It is on such a Jewish frontier, or at least in motion toward one, that both pious and porn subcultures transgress traditional boundaries in the name of transcending them. As Gilman reminds us, such transcendence of boundaries through their violation is inherent to the very construction of a frontier phenomenon. My emphasis on porn and pious women attends to the ways their material and symbolic violations animate, inspire, or otherwise encourage Jewish and non-Jewish bodies to move in new ways, and "not" those designed for daddy or bubbe.

Still, a frontier phenomenon and its generational break risks any number of problems. As Gilman admits, the concept is abstract and ahistorical, stretching across contexts as a model for the creation of Jewish history at large.[10] But as a "material" concept that must be understood "symbolically," the frontier imagines such slippages between the real and the representational, or history and its abstraction, as prime opportunities to track the construction and deployment of bodies as also both *material* and *symbolic*. It is this ability of a frontier fantasy to project the symbolic space of the new and give it physical shape through the deployment of bodies that lends itself well to a movement-oriented analysis.

Surprisingly, though, how bodies enter Gilman's model is less than fully fleshed out. In fact, without disclosing a particular rationale for the subjects he selects, Gilman's examples of Jewish frontiers dwell almost entirely on male authors, filmmakers, and representations. Proust, Kafka, and the first (male) film directors to make funny movies about the holocaust figure for example prominently in Gilman's manuscript as bodies branded by the literary, philosophical, psychosocial borders they cross. When the body is addressed, it is to outline studies of male or nongender-specific Jewish illnesses, physical inferiorities, and various perceived insufficiencies.[11] This essay revises Gilman's Jewish frontier in at least two fundamental ways: first, through a focus on mass choreographies in distinctly defined (Jewish) domains; and second, as a space centered on women-led practices that propel zones of feminist discourses into being and into the body.

In claiming the import of a Jewish female leadership in the creation of new collective identities, I acknowledge up front how slippery it can be to craft a cohesive or singular American Jewish self-image. Jewish discourse has increasingly acknowledged the demographic diversity of American Jewries. That said, an overwhelming amount of popular and scholarly attention still circulates the portrait of the Jewish subject and the question of (his) layered postmodern identity politics.[12] The interplays of femininity and Jewishness outlined in this essay investigate the most recent fears and fantasies inherent in this ongoing, but newly iterated "Jewish question" alongside an equally nebulous contemporary "Woman question." By privileging these pious and porn femininities as sexy examples of today's new Jewishness, such a project would seem to necessarily invert longstanding stereotypes of the effeminate male *schlemiel*, arguably still at play in mainstream depictions of Jews and Jewishness.[13] But instead of a simple binary that would merely flip one fiction for the other, masculinizing Jewish female leaders, I position spectacular roles of real women alongside and against misrepresentations of womanly male Jews in pop culture.

The central pairing of Brous and Angel likewise contends with a U.S. pop cultural imagination of porn and pious opposites. As opposed to any virgin-whore imaginary, and its Christian point of view, the combination of contemporary spectacles of sex and synagogue femininities as part of a shared progressive discourse reflects a Jewish American stance more open to sex and plays with sexiness. To partner their leading female figures here, however, requires readers to suspend moral judgment around either genre in order to see the ways each emboldens the position of Jewish women in cultural practices oriented around movement and ideas.

Moreover, to foreground frontierist movements with reference to California poses yet another set of problems. It risks the potential forgetting of colonialist histories critical to any analysis of the American West and its pathologies of progress.[14] While Gilman's Jewish frontiers make explicit claim to a symbolic site of enacting culture, this essay's West Coast phenomenon quite unsymbolically extends a history of Jewish participation in a dream of land-mined riches and white settlement. Even as the Jewish story of western expansion is beyond the bounds of this essay, I invoke its legacy of wealth and mobility to suggest a knotted sense of today's Jewish progress as still entangled in assimilatory aspirations and upwardly, or westwardly mobile fantasies.[15]

Brous's and Angel's online activity likewise furthers a frontier imagination of "free space" that renders the frontier an Internet phenomenon as well as a geographic one. The web relevance of a Jewish virtual frontier is especially significant in an age identified by the decline in organized religious affiliation, an anxiety over the increase in interracial/interethnic marriage, and the fear-factor of American Jewish secularization overall.[16] That Jewish or Jewish-aspiring individuals are congregating on Jewish sites is significant for this reason. A whole host of Internet communities presumably allow those turned off by temple dynamics to be virtually Jewish and, perhaps, more truthfully so because of it. Slipping between material and symbolic selves, droves of online audiences are drawn to sexually explicit sites. Popular examples like KinkyJews.com blur the lines of sex and self-discovery, while other sites, like Second Life synagogues, promise visitors can play hard and pray harder.

As frontier theories situate a new Jewishness both tied to place and in transcendence of it, a bodily reading of the frontier as both female-led and expressly feminized inevitably approaches its own limits. That is, the social and spatial reference to the female body conjures up less intentional ethnic and gender connotations of various sorts.[17] To centralize bodily femininity in a discussion of the Jewish future foregrounds the obsessive tensions around Jewish continuation and its pressures on woman and their reproductive organs. In a moment when both progressive rabbis and porn stars, including but not limited to Brous and Angel, are deliberately resisting heterosexual, patriarchal traditions in either domain, the problems of their femininity are ever present.

Any discussion of Jewish futurity is still tethered to the most ancient of Jewish dictums: more Jews, not less. The Jewish woman, no matter her field, is always inherently a Bubbe in training.

In spite of these flaws of a frontier formulation, and more likely because of them, I reconsider the frontier as model for contemporary Jewish history in the context of today's new Jewishness. The rerouting of typical borders between pious and porn spectacles unveils a shared strategy of Jewish movement in an era when many bemoan a religious logic with diminished relevance to current, pressing issues.[18] When put in conversation together, best-in-show businesses and their Jewish female bosses make possible a consideration of mutually informing movements of Jewish sex and synagogue femininities. Without reducing my discussions of the pious and porn as veritably good or bad, what follows theorizes the roles of Jewish rabbi and porn star at the "sexy" edges of contemporary Jewish America.

Holy *Chutzpah*: "Not Your Bubbe's Synagogue"

Walking into Ikar's High Holiday services in Los Angeles, I breathed in the festival curtains, the rented chair covers, the light sheen of the borrowed yarmulkes, and the fashionable cotton basics combined sensibly with see-through linens, muslins, and khakis. Finding my seat against the rhythmic soundscape of hand-drummed songs without words, I thought: "Here they are, my frontier Jews," a group of neo-Jewish experimentalists donning white ritual attire per the rabbi's unique request in multipart harmony. I convened among them in ritual costumed reference to the priestly robes of way back when, and joined in the improvised song with ease. These were the thirty- and forty-somethings, pro-peace in Israel/Palestine and proud of it, projecting beyond the backward logics of a billion years of culture wars, digging deep into the Old Testament to wake up the crowd of comic writers, young lawyers, and nonprofit art educators from the guilty nap of whiteness that plagues our Jewish generation.[19]

Core organizers of Ikar's extensive social action committees came with interlocked arms up to the *bima* to read from the Torah. Active members spoke of a garden project in Boyle Heights, advancements in the community's education and immigration reform, progress in food justice, and a global partnership with a school in Uganda. Throughout the long day of prayer, the crowd of straight and same-sex couples, interracial pairs and happy singles, seasoned and first-time Jews sat and stood and swayed on cue as unchained children roamed freely through the makeshift pews. This was the portrait of today's newest Jews, politically alive and working for good.

On this holiest day of the year, the rabbi's cue for unison choreography translated a visceral zeal in the gym-sanctuary into a wave of bows across the sea of all white. At a pinnacle moment of the Yom Kippur service, Brous asked all present to take off our shoes and drop down to hands and knees in genuine and generous surrender. Akin to the Muslim full prostration, and the same movement directives as the yoga child's pose, Rabbi Brous's plea to prayerfulness prostrated more fully than any Day of Atonement I had previously experienced. Calling for a new authenticity in a return to the ancient embodiments, Rabbi Brous's yearly High Holiday sermon is well known for this retake on the biblical bowing before God. In all other services I've attended elsewhere, this collective bow occurs only as a gentle hinge at the waist. The difference was striking. Generations of old and young knelt down to the ground and folded in full flexion at the knees and hips with practiced ease. When the ocean of to-the-floor bows reappeared at the midday restorative yoga session, I began to understand that these forward-folds effectively mobilized a newly animated, spiritual body, more willing to get down with ritual practice and go all the way.

Ikar is not the only congregation to link yoga and Jewish spirituality. Diverse congregations across the country and around the Jewish world are increasingly adding yoga to Saturday morning Torah service, religious retreats, and adult and family education programming.[20] While yoga is gaining visibility and practitioners worldwide far beyond a Jewish demographic, it may be possible to draw conclusions about the body's unique capacity to activate a restorative spiritual need within a progressive Jewish context. In thinking through the restorative relevance of yoga to the enhanced embodiment of Jewish prayer, alongside the bow's resemblance to the Muslim full prostration, multiple somatic and social significances of the shape and its movement emerge. Beyond its physical qualities, which soften the body, massage the hip joints, and extend the spinal column to encourage slowed, steadied breath, the associations of an iconic prayer pose known across faiths suggests a growing Jewish desire to connect across contexts.

Beyond this illuminating repetition of full bows, Brous made any number of other gestures toward an expanded lens of religious obligation that might be conceived as universalist in its politics. In the sermon Brous offered in the same service, she recalled reactions to the previous year's High Holiday message: she had been thanked profusely by one temple member for "not talking about Israel," while profusely questioned by another why she stayed quiet on the matter. The congregation laughed in recognition. The split vote is funny enough within the Ikar community, whose diversity on all matters from religious practice to rationale for its revitalization are reflective of its openness toward a range of leftist perspectives. And yet, to talk about Israel is precisely what gets Brous and her deep-bowing congregation in trouble.

In response to the fall 2012 bombing in Israel/Palestine, for instance, Brous circulated an e-mail to members calling for a balance of perspectives based on the dignity of Israeli and Palestinian lives alike. For her position against a one-sided defense of Israel, another Los Angeles rabbi accused Brous of ultimate betrayal and abandonment.[21] Blaming Brous for her "universalized" Jewishness, the rabbi publicly denounced Brous for having surrendered all sense of Jewish particularity (and its need to defend Israel in all cases). A more "universalized" Jewishness, however, may be the goal Brous is reshaping through the multisignifying bowing down. However, the criticism by other rabbis, while familiar enough within the Jewish community, especially concerning matters of Jewish statehood, preys on Brous's increasingly vulnerable position in the limelight. Her position is vulnerable precisely because of the power a female rabbi both wields and never can.[22]

For the reader less familiar with female participation in the rabbinate, it may be helpful to explain that the place of women in positions of religious leadership extends a longstanding feminist vision of progressive Jewish synagogue practice. Jewish second-wave feminists were famous in the 1960s and '70s for their revisions of the traditional scripts. Their aim was to open up a woman's role in temple affairs, especially in Reform and Renewal movements, including where she sat in the sanctuary in relation to men, new allowances to read from the Torah, when and how she could adopt leadership roles, and the adoption of gender neutral pronouns for God. Despite their immense progress, the growing presence of female rabbis across the country still divides the Jewish religious community along lines delineated by age and gender demands for rabbi roles.[23]

If unwelcome by the religiously strict, however, Brous's huge popularity as a rabbi of the year, known for her unique vision of re-embraced religious observancy and advocacy of progressive local and global politics, garnered her national attention as the official rabbi presiding over President Obama's Inaugural reelection ceremony.[24] While her position as a female rabbi is likely to appeal to an effort to balance genders of clergy invited in this capacity, Brous's growing public recognition as an exceptional character would appear to exceed her gender, or the problem of it. The constant in-flow of young rabbis in training who come to study with Brous (mostly women) suggests as much.

But Brous's serious Torah study, countless accolades, and tireless human rights advocacy—while they win her Presidential recognition—are sadly not the featured storylines of even those well-intentioned articles meaning to celebrate Ikar's spiritual renaissance. In a piece posted just one month before the Inaugural Prayer Service on *The Jewish Daily Forward*, reporter Rex Weiner writes first of male rabbis in LA synagogues nearby before poking fun at Brous's casual hairstyle in that "little science experiment called Ikar." Weiner's critique of Brous's tousled "hippie look" and "whatever spiritual approach" emboldens a familiar patriarchal condescension naturalized on and of the body in discussions of female leaders, religious or not.[25] To be clear, Weiner includes no discussion of what the male rabbis are doing with *their* hair. The loosening of a grip on orthodox religious observance thus accompanies a fear and fantasy of the rebel woman who transgresses patriarchal boundaries of an old Jewish boys club still monitoring each toss of Brous's "hippie" hair. This fatherly flippancy that judges the teenage behaviors of good Jewish girls gone bad speaks for the unfortunate flipside of the same progressive rhetoric Brous and staff select for their move away from traditional authority. A revitalized religious connection undermined as a "whatever spiritual approach" only barely veils a longstanding rejection of Jewish women speaking out on such a large scale.

Brous's speaking out, together with her restorative and globally minded neo-Jewish physicality, no doubt butts heads with a longstanding threat of the feminine. While it would be misguided to call the Ikar full bow or Brous's stance on Israel/Palestine especially "sexy," however, the embodied and sociocultural animation of Jewish practices and philosophies, as well as their criticism, expose the stakes of a shape-shifting, gender friendly new Jewishness.

If such moves reveal a productive violation of boundaries, Brous and team bring other kinds of Jewish sexy back, too. Take Ikar's 2013 annual adult-themed Purim Party, for instance.[26] I paid entrance for myself and an ethnographic team of four friends, fitted in the best of my polyester collection. My own costume invoked a disco-take on the biblical queen in a spandex pink onesie with a paisley pattern. Game booths, popcorn, and prizes rendered the "Jewishness" of the event illegible to my friends, until a swarm of attention rushed to Rabbi Brous. Claiming her rightful place at the center of the dance floor and dressed as Princess Leia (note the pun on Leah, an Old Testament foremother), Brous was uninhibited, dancing with enthusiasm beside a female congregant who was costumed as a stripper (complete with an attending metal pole on wheels). At least I thought she was a temple member. I wondered whether she, like the stilt walker and two DJ-dancers in rainbow wigs and "afro-circus" T-shirts, might be help hired for the evening. The uncertain terms of who was there and in what capacity added to the masquerade theme. Had this dancing lady in fishnets been a devout temple member, her stripper alter ego would be unmotivated by financial concerns. If she was a hired party pumper, however, the pole-dancing persona would assume a role among the event's for-profit entertainers and their enhancement of this not-for-profit spiritual scene. The difference seemed significant in its ability to classify (and draw class-based conclusions about) the kinds of incentives provided for sexy figures and their erotic dancing amidst the carnival theme. If paid by the planning committee to work the pole, the pole dancer could be seen as a Purim festival job akin to a clown or DJ. If unpaid, the personage would have merely won personal favorite of the evening, and maybe bragging rights among familiar faces of fellow Ikarites. In either case, the woman's grinding undulations against the pole, as she wheeled it awkwardly from spot to spot, set an adult tone of the evening, if only in jokish reference.

The dancing reached its peak with the "Harlem Shake," the crowd exploding with enthusiasm for the latest craze in viral dance video culture.[27] At first recognition of Baauer's hit song and its collective response in the room, a non-Jewish friend of mine immediately picked up on the vibe. He rushed for the trash can right behind the mobile pole, hoisting the oversized prop overhead to pump as musical accent in the style of the ever-expanding dance video uploads amassing each day. I watched the rabbi watching him, not stopping the even pulse of her extended arms as she worked them interchangeably up and down, a bit more go-go than in the video dance style. Still, partying just as fully, and with liberal permissibility, our sci-fi Princess Rabbi presided over this ritual day of dance and debauchery.[28]

It was not until some time later, when I bought my two tickets for the motorized bull ride, that I realized Brous was gone. Though Brous had exited, I remained immersed in the experience. For me, riding the bull translated as my attempt at playing into the sexy humor of the evening. How easily I had transformed from the modest onlooker to the eager ethnographer-performer, suddenly finding myself playing up my Jewish insider status. On the barrel chest of a would-be bull, I winked at strangers standing in line for turns at the edges of an inflatable rodeo ring. I acted as if staying on top took no effort, denying the strain of squeezing my thighs for dear life. When, for a split second, I could spare to loosen my grip, I gestured toward the scattered onlookers with a limp-affected hand, scrunching my nose and tightening my lips in some mock-invocation of Fran Drescher from *The Nanny*. Bucking, I exaggerated the girlish oohing of my mouth and lift of the eyebrows. Playing to the crowd of strangers outfitted in angel wings, Luchador masks, Frida Kahlo unibrows, and Pregnant Nun habits, I found myself strangely zealous. Suspended beyond a desire to entertain and elicit laughs, I had entered a realm of Jewish reconnection, acting "Jewish" in the newest old ways I knew how.

My participation in temple embodiments at the edges of the sacred (High Holiday prayer services) and the jokishly profane (riding the bull at Purim's adult-themed party) offered convincing evidence of Ikar's wide range of renewed Jewish cultural practices. The energized celebration of spiritualism effectively hooked me as Brous and team reached to my generation of unaffiliated Jews with a "holy chutzpah" as funny and "hip" as it was earnest in its efforts to do humanistic good. As Ikar throws into perpetual motion tired synagogue models reflective of patriarchal controls over Jewish piety, Brous's leadership gestures toward the spiritually and politically authentic with new emphasis on the expressly embodied and woman led.

Punk Princesses in Pink and Black: "Not Your Daddy's Porn"

Manipulating (Jewish) boundaries in entirely different ways, the award-winning Burning Angel Studios website (http://www.burningangel.com) prominently features the company founder herself among the 200 pierced and tattooed female models she calls her "army of hot punk chicks." As the "original home of hard-core punk rock emo porn," the site boasts infinite pages of video and photo content, event and blog posts, and interactive chat forums against a mostly Metal soundscape. The sex itself looks and sounds "punk" in commercial ways, as the imagination of cursing, hyper-coiffed, inked up bodies in straight, same-sex, and group combinations together with band interviews and black Burning Angel tank tops for sale assumes a familiar antiestablishment image with magenta-accented graphic design.

What distinguishes Angel's site from the mainstream pornography the company's byline calls "daddy's porn" is the ways in which Burning Angel presumes to empower all involved through a focus on its raunchy girl power. From the direction of the camera, to subcategories of video content like "Goth," "Horror," and "Glasses," to the "Words" page profiles of models and musicians, young women appear to run the show and like every part of what they do. The impression is a focus on women as both pleasurers and pleasure-seekers. While the sheer emphasis on hyper-sexualized women arguably perpetuates mainstream hetero-male interest among "alternative" gazes, the site promises postfeminist freedoms unfettered by masculinist expectations of how women should act or behave.

Projecting an image of female empowerment outward to its online audiences, Angel's main webpage invites female site visitors who are "having way too much good sex . . . behind closed doors, for no pay" to "help take over the world." The "world" that Angel wishes to take over, while left perhaps deliberately unspecified, may be understood in any number of ways. It offers a kind of fill-in-the-blank that likely attracts a younger generation (or two or three) that seeks to undercut or otherwise disassociate with normative structures of power and patriarchy. Whether it be through musical tastes, sexual fetishes featured on the site, or female interest in enlisting in Angel's army of hot punk chicks, the site boasts an ever-expanding space of sex-positive egalitarianism that breaks all rules and promises the same to you. Encouraging male and female viewers to dialogue with models and one another through user profiles in addition to buying memberships and merchandise, Angel directs and stars in an interactive world whose takeover talk and choreographies advance a frontier theme.

Even as the company continues to expand in size and scale, models and online users report feeling "at home" at Burning Angel.[29] While some would argue that this is a marketing ploy to bolster user numbers through strategically welcoming, happy rhetoric in an otherwise entirely for-profit agenda, the sentiment offers insight into the ways Angel constructs a girl-next-door image for herself and her compatriots. This feeling of being "at home" with Angel and her friends juxtaposed against the hard-core porn they collectively stage creates a softer space in ways mainstream porn may not. That site-users may in fact be at home while posting from bedroom computers and devices only enhances the "realness" of a growing alt porn genre and the accessibility of its appeal.

Angel invokes this kind of "realness" with an additional website especially devoted to getting to know her. Clickable from any Burning Angel page, Angel's own site, (http://www.Joannaangel.com) offers a running dialogue with her visitors: "This website is for my special fans who want to know the REAL me ... It's the next best thing to carrying me around in your pocket." Promising full accessibility to those fans that carry her around presumably through downloadable Apps on smart phones, Angel and her virtual body propose a fantasy of authenticity and its ability to function as an erotic stimulant. This in-your-pocket intimacy, together with Angel's professions of being known and wanting to be known by her fans, blurs Angel's status as porn celebrity icon. Net-porn theorist Niels van Doorn writes that the desire for "real" authentic sexual practices is a response to the increasingly spectacular, silicon-enhanced artificiality of commercial feature-length pornography. In opposition to big-budget productions, alternative porn that blurs the distinction between pro and amateur evokes a sense that the bodies onscreen could be your neighbors.[30]

Even as Angel invites fans to know the "real" her, there is little to nothing written on her personal site that indicates her Jewish background. Those unfamiliar with Eastern European Jewish looks may not even recognize the Jewishness of the nose and deep-set eyes that distinguish her facial features. And yet it is the conversation that she has stirred among Jewish online communities (as a leading Jewish female porn director and "Punk Princess") and the particular jokishness of her porn persona in deliberately funny acts that make her such an important Jewish figure.

Angel does out her Jewishness in one holiday-inspired spoof video that stars herself and a cast of eight men meant to signify the eight nights of Hanukkah. The video opens with a Point-of-View camera angle as the male voice behind the camera identifies a sexual gift he'd like to give Joanna for Christmas. She replies with a flirtatious laugh, "But I'm Jewish and you're Jewish, so why not celebrate Hanukkah instead." The voice behind the camera admits that it's a great idea, and suggests they go downstairs where the rest of the men are waiting. Downstairs, Angel makes a show of counting only seven men and asks into the camera about the missing eighth. The voice answers, "What am I, chopped liver?" Angel laughs freely at her hidden boyfriend behind the camera, and his gender-bending reference to the quintessential Jewish Mother's refrain. As the group sex scene begins, Angel directs the "menorah of men" to circle her. She lowers to her knees and invites the camera in on her face, now eye level with the eight anonymous penises. Sustaining at center frame of all that happens next, Angel spends time with each of the men, whose faces are rarely seen. Camera edits move the short film along, cutting from Angel's seductions of one male performer to the next.

As in typical heterosexist imagination, the men do not touch each other, but only themselves as they wait for Angel's individual attention. Untypically, however, it is Angel in total control of this "gang bang" scene. Directing the thirteen-minute movie from inside of it, Angel calls the shots as the action progresses. She issues all movement directives of male counterparts and camera, indicating with vocal and physical cues where the camera focuses and what audiences see next. Shifting her gaze between camera and male pelvis in front of her, Angel's director's eyes work attention of audience, cast, and crew. However impossible it may be to assess the pleasure she gleans, it is Angel's physical and vocal expression of enjoyment that carries the action across the spliced encounters. As compared to the largely silent male cast and their contained movements, Angel accentuates the pleasure of pleasuring through creative, expressive control, and gives it in excess to the group.

Playing both director and star roles simultaneously evidences Angel's capacity to empower both parts as female roles, while considering them part and parcel of her alternative approach to porn. When seen through a Jewish lens, the entanglement of director–porn star roles position Angel in ways that directly invert expectations of the Jewish woman: namely, her reproductive role in Jewish marriage. The scene stages Angel in total control over sex, as her Jewish boyfriend's gift is initially his body and "whatever [she] wants to do with it." When multiplied by eight lovers, the plotline exaggerates Angel's sexual desire. The holiday porn parody directly upturns stereotypical expectations of the Jewish woman bored with sex so common to Jewish male joking, and its basis on traditionalist assumptions of monogamy and reproduction.

No matter her conspicuous play with stereotypes, Angel's Jewishness meets the most expected of meathead comments. "Everything's hot except her huge nose," one viewer comments below on an unaffiliated porn site that reposted the video.[31] This kind of response, while nowhere found on Angel's own sites, is familiar enough of Jewish female noses on camera. Even as it indicates the kinds of criticism her distinctly "Jewish" face may raise for those outside the in-crowd of her online world, however, the comment raises no issue of the video's Jewish content and its Hanukkah theme. Mediating her variously conceived Jewish parts in ways in and out of her control, Angel's holiday-reel thus spoofs on her Jewishness to mixed reviews. It may be argued that in joking about Jewishness, Angel invites this kind of laughter "at" in addition to any laughter "with." But so long as her own "huge nose" cannot be "hot" the way her body underneath it can be, the stakes of Jewish (looking) women in porn are less than entirely embracing.

Angel's "real" thus always returns to the issue of her simultaneous Jewish female difference/sameness and the criticism its sex and sex appeal invites. But no matter how much Angel makes light of her Jewish identity, passing it off in spoof films at key points on the Jewish calendar, the idea of a Jewish female pornographer looms large for Jewish and gentile viewers alike. In his online article from December 2009 titled "The Rise of the Hot Jewish Girl: Why American Men are Lusting after Women of the Tribe," *Details* reporter Christopher Noxon comments that Jewish pornographers have only just begun to actively "out" their Jewishness. He cites Angel: "I never thought my Jewishness would be an asset." That being the case for Angel, Noxon's article still moralizes the porn starlet's Jewishness over anything else. Of her ethico-religious boundaries, he notes that she rejected offers to perform in a holiday-themed adult fair called "Dr. Suzy's Porn and Purim DVD Bacchanal," which mixes group sex with *hamantaschen* (triangular cookies shaped like the three-pointed hat of Purim's antagonist, Haman). "I've desecrated Christian traditions before," said Angel. "In one video, I put a cross-shaped dildo inside me, but I'd never do that with a menorah—that's just creepy." As evidenced in the Hanukkah video described earlier, references to menorahs versus actual menorahs would appear to make all the difference from Angel's point of view.

Even when viewed through Angel's punk rock hard-core aesthetic, the Jewish female body may never achieve what cultural and media critic Laura Kipnis has called the "Hustler body"—one that rails against the establishment with hyper-sexualized images of pregnant women, amputees, transvestites, and the like, all meant to shock or scandalize bourgeois sensibilities in some way.[32] As Kipnis explains (while invoking the familiar second-wave feminist slogan), the porn star's body is always a "battleground." In Kipnis's understanding, opposing sexual and cultural forms such as religious morality, class pretensions, and feminist consciousness, duke it out with the armies of bodily vulgarity, kinky fantasy, and "unromanticized fucking."[33] But whereas Angel's own armies of vulgarity may market a commercial aesthetic of punk's antiestablishment sensibility made popular by a decade of the music industry's commoditization of porn, her reported confession of Jewish ethics sterilizes any serious attempt at hard-core sacrilege. A subtext of Jewish self-reflection thus mediates her hypersexuality, taming it through self-restriction. Angel's prudish testimony not to desecrate ritual paraphernalia stand out among her own hot punk chicks who need not assume such moral Jewish responsibility.

But, then, give or take a few holiday spoofs, how Jewish is she really? Or, more important, how Jewish is her porn? As often as Angel posts Hanukkah films, she also readily dresses up in candy cane costumes for annual Christmas photo shoots. As mentioned earlier, the particular Jewishness of her pornography has been noted most by Jewish communities invested in the anomalous possibility of a Jewish female pornographer, and one with such high visibility. Gracing the cover of *Heeb Magazine* in spring 2005, Angel blew up, so to speak, after the magazine published an article on Angel and a new blow-up doll fashioned in Angel's image, complete with an online link to Angel's website. Also posted was a two-minute cash prize video contest announcement and a punning "dry" review of the sex toy.

One of the magazine's male interns, who looks twenty-one at most, speaks candidly to the viewer as he holds the blow-up doll next to him. He wears a typical Israeli-tourist's T-shirt that replaces the Superman logo with the Hebrew letter lexicon for "S," as he discusses his antiheroic sexual encounter (not of his own doing, of course) with the inflatable prop. The intern stifles laughter at the admission of difficulty with the toy. While seemingly all for laughs, the intern's humor makes clear that the failure of the plastic Joanna is precisely what's so fun about it; a one-sided sexual pleasure uncharacteristic of sex with "real" girls, especially Jewish ones who are expected to be stereotypically uninterested in sex in real life.[34] The joke of this fake Jewish girlfriend undermines the very possibility of sexy Jewish femininity, and renders the experience entirely unsexual. But rather than blaming himself for his awkward attempts with the doll, the intern faults his inanimate Jewish sex partner that, for Jewish audiences familiar with this stereotype, is at once too demanding in sex and not enough, making her, once again, the root cause of his problems.

Heeb's simultaneous promotion of Angel and demotion of her doll offers significant insight into the ways that the Jewish female pornographer actually threatens Jewish men. As the magazine celebrates the humor of the artificial body that teases with some semblance of a sexy object, it likewise deflates the possibility of the actual Jewish woman's sexual wants, directions, and desires. How Angel reroutes these assumptions through Burning Angel by positioning herself as the desiring subject rather than merely the object of desire, however, is where her alternative potential may carry transgressive power.

Angel's own play with the doll may illuminate this transgressive promise. The sample video reel shows the two side by side in a poolside montage, making light of the product and its source with shots of sunbathing, floating on rafts, and—for even more laughs—a moment of attempting (not very well) to play catch. That Angel creatively personifies the prop beyond its intended usage encourages the same kind of laughter as might greet the male intern but directs it from her own position of directorial authority.

Constructed as a "Jewishness without an agenda," sites like *Heeb* target a Jewish demographic through technologies that don't require the memberships of synagogue or Jewish organization. Performance studies scholar Barbara Kirshenblatt-Gimblett calls this population the "unaffiliated" and "hardest to reach."[35] In this vein, the Brooklyn-based magazine started in 2001 self-identifies "as a take-no-prisoners zine for the plugged in and preached out," that "has become a multi-media magnet to the young, urban and influential."[36] Reaching out to these jaded Jews appears to come with a price, however. Kirshenblatt-Gimblett accounts for an "anything goes for a lost cause" clause that allows *Heeb Magazine* (underwritten by mainstream Jewish philanthropy) to "bite the hand that feeds it."[37] The generational gap, understood in this way, offers significant insight into Joanna Angel's popularity among *Heeb* audiences.

An interview with Joanna Angel's mother reveals as much. Blogger Arye Dworken asked Angel's Jewish mother if she was ashamed of her daughter's life work. "A long time ago, she knew she was doing something not nice," Angel's mother responded. "And she did whatever she could to not embarrass me, like change her name." Proud of her daughter for having worried about her mother, Angel's mom insists finally that Angel betrayed a Jewish familial loyalty. Offering the Hebrew word "*arzut metzach*" as explanation, which means—in the mother's own words—that "you steal but you're proud of it," the justification for taking pride in doing something without embarrassment "is not nice."[38] The upset of a Jewish mother at her daughter exemplifies the gap Kirshenblatt-Gimblett describes between Jewish generations. The degree to which Angel appears to steal with pride, or "bite the hand" that fed her, sheds light on her lead role as head of the *Heeb*-generation pack.

If generation-wars over boundaries of appropriate behavior are nothing new, according to Kirshenblatt-Gimblett, the so-called New Jews are "new by virtue of the edge that they define and occupy." In her estimation, "they espouse an ethics and aesthetics of edge," which, she argues, "is *not* the same as margin or periphery." Clarifying that positions along the margin/periphery "suggest an involuntary disadvantage among those striving for the center," Kirshenblatt-Gimblett argues instead that this "is about the cutting edge, an edge in constant need of sharpening, a moving—a leading, even a bleeding—edge that resists the center."[39] Such an edge that is not the margin or periphery sounds strikingly similar to Gilman's frontier, particularly in its reconceptualization of Diaspora as a center-periphery model. This break with Diaspora thinking is precisely where Kirshenblatt-Gimblett's New Jews take off. She writes: "If the historical edge, the outsider and marginal status of Diaspora Jews has dissipated, the New Jews have turned elsewhere for the energy—the stimulus—that comes from the margin: they have turned to subculture and counterculture, and to experimental contemporary art. They may have been born Jewish, but they consider themselves native to Hip Hop or reggae or punk, among others."[40]

The ever-adjusting edge outlined here articulates a similar postmodern culture-in-motion that Gilman calls the Jewish frontier. However, in a significant way, the nonaffiliation of today's New Jews breaks with any model that would claim a Jewish futurity of any kind. This so-called "Jewishness without an agenda"—like Angel's world takeover that posits no stated mission in particular—poses the greatest generational threat of all. That its "ethics and aesthetics of edge" cut across models of Jewish marginality is crucial. Moreover, that such ruthless slashing necessitates an edge in "constant need of sharpening," indicates a complex understanding not only of the New Jew Kirshenblatt-Gimblett describes and the mechanisms through which it sharpens its tools, but also why the edges are so sharp.

Angel's contributions to a Jewish hard-core help sharpen the tools and the edges of contemporary Jewish identity. Its female pornographer's perspective, directed from inside and outside the camera frame, choreograph the ways that the raunchy female body moves and how. The degree to which she may mediate her own Jewishness on camera, however, is less than totally clear, as it necessarily entangles intentional and less intentional aspects of bodily and narrative components. As her public persona likewise invites attention of all kinds on the subject of the convincingly sexy Jewish woman, Angel contends with any number of competing views that must confront, encourage, or criticize her position at the forefront of distinct and overlapping frontiers.

Progressive Pioneers (?)

What is this obsession with the new, the frontier, and the moving, slicing blade of Jewish becoming? Gilman explains that the struggle lives in the impossibility of Jewish self-definition. "Who are the Jews?" he asks, to which he replies:

"Those who understood themselves as Jews at specific moments in time."[41] Insisting that the definition is constantly changing, he adds that "The less possible a definition is, the more rigid it appears ... Over and over, one group comes to be defined as the authentic Jews."[42] As Brous and Angel lead droves in distinct domains, they define the bounds of New Jewishness through progressive ideals and bodily expressivity.

While magazines like *Heeb* might be loath to concern themselves with anything called "authentic Jews," (an epithet that Angel's renounced religiosity also breaks with), how might the cutting and undercutting of these New Jew/esses be best understood in using Jewishness to undo itself? It is clear that *Heeb's* chauvinist tenor sharpens a weapon against depictions of a wimpier Jewish (male) past while simultaneously reacting against Jewish women and the very sex appeal (read as success) they stage and sabotage. Angel's own role in this, as we have seen, is an example of the complications of post-Jewish femininity; her work entangles itself in debates surrounding both pornography and the ambivalence of any feminist promise, Jewish or not. Having left religious life behind, but claiming still that her best gift was "getting 8 guys for Hanukkah,"[43] Angel's unorthodox play with sexy Jewishness at once reveals the playful allure of Ikar's holy chutzpah and unhooks her (only partially) from it. Significantly, we could contend that Angel is the poster child/sexy pin up of the trend of new generation Jews that synagogues like Ikar both emulate and excuse. Indulging and also complicating feminist freedoms in an era arguably fully Americanized and convincingly assimilated, the pioneering of Jewish women in positions of Jewish and not-so-Jewish authority forges into uncertain terrain still threatened by female corporeality.

By partnering Brous and Angel as co-choreographers of a Jewish frontier through expansive notions of the feminine and the feminist, critical distinctions in their respective projects cannot be overlooked—the version of feminism and prospect of its "post" function differently in porn and pious realms. The frameworks employed here thus cannot mean to contain women with labels indicated by their positions of authority, especially since this would easily fall back on the binary thinking that opposes a rabbi and a porn star. The ability of such a project to expose the ruse of finite lines of identification (religious/secular, sacred/profane, good/bad and even pious/porn) presents a spectrum of progressive Jewish and gender discourses whose blurriness is its power and its limitation. While Brous and Angel update diminutive stereotypes of the desiring Jewish woman by playing Star Wars and Punk-Porn (Jewish American)

Princess roles, meant to illustrate, perhaps, a strong female influence over their respective domains, these women perform two models of today's Sexy Jewess. Brought together as founding Jewish anti/mothers of a conceptual Jewish new, the pairing actualizes a spectrum of Jewish, female positions-in-excess via "sexy" movements on both frontiers.

And yet, as "sexy" has come to stand in for the revamped self-image of a new and improved Jewishness, a certain appropriation of a hotter, hipper Jewish femininity inevitably reestablishes the binary modes it wishes to move beyond. That is, sexiness and the efforts to embody it through post-feminist and post-assimilationist embodiments of various kinds may be precisely the trap these women are working against. While Sexy Jewess evocations of the frontier cut across boundaries of Jew and Woman alike, they also necessarily recontain those categories in order to differently capitalize on their excessive Jewish, female thing-ness in the name of new freedoms. So long as sexy is mediated by the marketability of femininity and its hetero approval and consumption, such rhetoric of empowerment may still too easily fold in on itself. Is the Jewish "edge" sharp enough to cut through its patriarchal ropes? As both "Woman" and "Jew" are reappropriated by frameworks that refeminize the Jewish frontier (or resist its feminization), razor edges of either category would appear to cut themselves open. What bleeds in this conceptual cutting—this metaphorical castration even—of the Jewish femme body? The messy possibility of a convincingly powerful Jewish woman, all jokes aside, for instance?

Turned around as a frontier feminization in flux, if still on the "edge," a critical focus on the roles of women in the sexualization of today's New Jew/ess remaps a contemporary, urban American promise in bodily terms. Ikar's holy chutzpah is predicated on the bold charge of Brous's female lead and her physicalization of spiritual life. Burning Angel's antiestablishment ethos is premised on her nice (Jewish) girl gone bad persona and her embodiment of a directorial girl power. By emphasizing the ways both leading figures are able to mobilize groups of people across boundaries, a dance studies analysis allows the focus to foreground the various choreographies of new frontier ideologies. However, inherent in the boundary-crossing (bodily) movements of the progressive pious and porn spectacle alike may be the threat of the female body. Meaning, as these approaches trade in the tired old "Jewish Question" for a fantastic something else, that something else can too readily regress to an equally worn-out "Woman Question." While seeming to make space for a new emblem of Jewishness, such moves may more or less intentionally appropriate the funny "thing" about Jewishness and womanness that can't be separated from the gendered body. What can never be reconciled in each case are the tensions between the liberatory potential of reappropriative power and the reductive reference of the age-old inferior logics it relies on.

As efforts to mobilize subcultures of contemporary Jewish self-representation, both Ikar and Burning Angel share any number of intentions aligned with empowering people in and out of Jewishness. And yet, even the comparison of sex and synagogue femininities in the context of fun, newly feminized frontiers runs the risk of objectifying women, relying on artificial constructions of the sacred/profane and its polar imagination of good girls versus bad ones. Even in my intentions to "rescue" female agency in both pious and porn realms, the theoretical pairing itself proves problematic. For those invested in the real power of spectacular Jewish femininity and its bearings on the survival of porn or pious subcultures alike, it is clear that the transgressive work of religious parody, powerful in its sexy ruse, may be much easier to enact than challenge, in Brous's case, against a Jewish state. It is clear enough that Angel can more easily push against the patriarchal bounds of Jewish female sexuality through sexy ruse than Brous can. It is a core part of Angel's work, after all. But finally, what Angel achieves through sexy ruse reveals more about the restrictions of patriarchal traditions than something that looks especially liberated or free.

How to make sense of these inevitable limitations that ultimately compete with themes of forward movement, of intended progress, and of Jewish pioneering? Answer: The frontier logic is flawed, and thankfully so. In fact, I'd argue that the very premise of Brous's and Angel's cultural projects rely on and reconstitute a flawed frontier logic as part of their acts. Among my visits to both ends of the sexy scale, Rabbi Brous admits to a crowd of the religiously recommitted that she returned from Jerusalem with the hope to be one day accredited by male colleagues and Angel wishes on camera that she possessed a penis to make it all easier. Underlining these expressions are the various distinctions that influence Brous's or Angel's position at the top of their respective fields. In other words, the limitations themselves offer concrete and motivating causes for change. For Brous, this is the hyperobservant sector of the Jewish community in the United States and Israel that refuses her rabbinic authority. For Angel, this is the prospect that her director-performer agency may not, or cannot, challenge patriarchy or misogyny. However flawed those frontier fantasies may be in terms of patriarchal controls in either field, both women embody forward-movement schemes along distinct trajectories with increasing momentum. In doing so, each physicalizes real possibilities of subtle subversions for growing numbers of devotees.

Notes

1. Such jokes spoof rabbi roles in combination with other religious or ethnic figures and most often return to the failures of effeminate Jewish masculinity. To begin the joke with a rabbi and a porn star would seem to assume the same in an explicit heterosexual encounter, but for the twist of their unsuspecting roles as women.

2. Abigail Pogrebin, "America's Top 50 Rabbis for 2012," *The Daily Beast*, April 2, 2012, http://www.thedailybeast.com/articles/2012/04/02/america-s-top-50-rabbis-for-2012.html. Voted fifth of the top rabbis of 2012, Brous's organization Ikar has been described as the "gold standard for captivating young, unaffiliated American Jews."

3. "AVN Announces the Winners of the 2011 AVN Awards," *AVN Media Network*, posted January 9, 2011, http://business.avn.com/articles/video/AVN-Announces-the-Winners-of-the-2011-AVN-Awards-421782.html.

4. *Bubbe* is Yiddish for "grandmother." Used in this context, *Bubbe* connotes a generation of Jewish immigrants, and a certain coming-to-America outsider identity.

5. Barbara Kirshenblatt-Gimblett, "The 'New Jews': Reflections on Emerging Cultural Practices" (paper presented at Re-thinking Jewish Communities and Networks in an Age of Looser Connections Conference, Wurzweiler School of Social Work, Yeshiva University and Institute for Advanced Studies, Hebrew University, New York City, December 6–7, 2005), 1.

6. Alternative porn, also known as Altporn, refers to online and print pornography that emerged in the 1990s oriented toward alternative subcultures like punk, goth, and ravers and has grown increasingly popular ever since. While many argue that Altporn is premised on an alternative view of mainstream pornography and its hypermasculinist content, others disagree that the growing for-profit niche has succeeded or truly aimed to succeed at this mission.

7. Sander Gilman, *Jewish Frontiers: Essays on Bodies, Histories and Identities* (New York: Palgrave Macmillan, 2003), 15.

8. Ibid., 19.

9. Ibid., 28.

10. Ibid., 16.

11. See also Sander Gilman's *The Jew's Body* (New York: Routledge, 1991).

12. For more on Jewish studies as a majority male discourse, see Daniel Boyarin, *Unheroic Conduct: The Rise of Heterosexuality and the Invention of the Jewish Man* (Berkeley: University of California Press, 1997); and Joyce Antler, *Talking Back: Images of Jewish Women in Popular Culture* (Hanover, NH: Brandeis University Press, 1998).

13. *Schlemiel* is a Yiddish term used to describe a widely popular archetype of the anxious, effeminate Jewish male. Many have cited Woody Allen as one of the most

famous performers to embody this stereotype, though the trope has been arguably personified in Hollywood to such a degree that scholars cite the Schlemiel role as responsible for a "Jewification" of American media. For more on this subject, see Daniel Itzkowitz's "They Are All Jews" in *You Should See Yourself: Jewish Identity and Postmodern American Culture*, ed. Vincent Brook (New Brunswick, NJ: Rutgers University Press, 2006); and Jon Stratton's "*Seinfeld* is a Jewish Sitcom, Isn't It?" in *Coming Out Jewish: Constructing Ambivalent Identities* (London: Routledge, 2000).

14. Gilman himself makes reference to Frederick Jackson Turner's seminal study on the Frontier mythology, which is less about expansion into Western America and more the fantasy of the frontier wherein "one imagines oneself teleologically as the center and end of history and where one understands one's own physical position in the world as that cutting edge of (divine) history," *Jewish Frontiers*, 27. Gilman's reference is to Frederick Jackson Turner's "The Significance of the Frontier in American History," presented at a meeting of the American Historical Association at the World's Columbian Exposition in Chicago, Illinois, 1893, accessed February 4, 2011, http://www.library.csi.cuny.edu/dept/history/lavender/frontierthesis.html.

15. For reading on this subject, see Jeanne E. Abrams, *Jewish Women Pioneering the Frontier Trail: A History in the American West* (New York: NYU Press, 2007); Ava F. Kahn, *Jewish Life in the American West* (Berkeley: Heydey, 2004); and Moses Rischin and John Rivington, eds. *Jews of the American West* (Detroit: Wayne State University Press, 1991).

16. Kirshenblatt-Gimblett, "The New Jews," 7.

17. It is worth considering that the "not," which departs from the patriarchal holds of the past in exchange for something new, vast, and yet unfulfilled, suggests the movement into, or the penetration of empty space that implicates the vagina itself. The material and symbolic frontier of female anatomy itself implies logics of lack, as well as libidinal social desire.

18. Any number of scholars, bloggers, and activists criticize the tendency of Jewish lobbyists to support causes only in so far as they defend pro-Israel Jewish interests. See, for example, Joelle Novey, "Climate Change Means: Enough Already with What's Good for the Jews," *Huffington Post*, posted December 9, 2011, http://www.huffingtonpost.com/joelle-novey/climate-change-and-jewish-activism_b_1137888.html.

19. This "guilty nap of whiteness" names the economic and racial aspirations of Jewish American assimilation and the psychological ramifications of having (nearly) achieved it. It articulates the effects of majoritarian acceptance that render Jewish organizations less relevant for younger Jews. See Internet forums like *Reform Judaism Magazine* for discussions of the twenty- and thirty-year-old Jewish engagement and the basis of its distrust of big institutions, including big Jewish institutions. ReformJudaismMag.com, accessed October 4, 2012, http://reformjudismmag.org/Articles/index.cfm?id=3130.

20. New York's Upper West Side Ramemu's offers "Shabbatasana" before Saturday Torah study. See adult education courses and podcasts on the connections between

Judaism and Yogic tradition at Romemu.org, Torahyoga.com, Jewishtorahnetwork.org, and "Bibliyoga" on the "Kosher Sutras," thenextbigjewishidea.com. The growing popularity of yoga in Israel, among even the strict Orthodox, is noted in Michal Chlebin's photojournalistic article, "Yoga Poses in Israel," *NYTimes.com*, accessed March 9, 2014, http://www.nytimes.com/2014/03/09/magazine/yoga-poses-in-Israel.html.

21. Daniel Gordis, "When Balance Becomes Betrayal," *Times of Israel*, November 18, 2012, http://blogs.timesofisrael.com/when-balance-becomes-betrayel/.

22. Brous is one of the few women to occupy a full-time pulpit position in a nondenominational Jewish congregation and the only one I know of to start a "best-of" synagogue from scratch. See Steward Ain, "JTS Women Grads Struggling for Pulpits," *The Jewish Week*, May 31, 2011, http://www.thejewishweek.com/news/new_york/jts_women_grads_struggling_pulpits.

23. While female rabbis are regular fixtures of Reform synagogues, religiously Conservative congregations are less likely than they were even a decade ago to hire a female rabbi. Uriel Heilman, "Gender Gap for Rabbis," *JTA*, November 30, 1999. The possibility of a female rabbi is still forbidden in Orthodox practice, where the particular case of Sara Hurwitz, an Orthodox woman ordained as Maharat (rabbi by any other name), caused major scandal in the Orthodox community. Hilary Krieger, "A woman rabbi (by any other name)," *Jewish Chronicle*, New York, June 3, 2009. Furthermore, a study headed by Rabbi Suzanne Singer of (Reform) Temple Beth El in Riverside, California, on Second Career Rabbis shows that age discrimination bars men and women from new pulpit positions. Rabbi Suzanne Singer, chair, "Report From the CCAR Task Force on The Second Career Rabbinate," May 2005. Though Singer regularly sports a T-shirt that reads, "This is what a Rabbi Looks Like," her own experience of gender and age bias adds the distinctions of sub/urbanity to the list of tensions raised by Gilman's frontier concept. For a clear outline of who can become a female rabbi and how in the various sects of Judaism, see Avi Hein, "Women in Judaism: A History of Women's Ordination as Rabbis," *JewishVirtualLibrary.org*, accessed October 4, 2014, http://www.jewishvirtuallibrary.org/jsource/Judaism/femalerabbi.html.

24. A video of Rabbi Sharon Brous reciting a blessing at the 57th Presidential Inaugural Prayer Service, held at Washington National Cathedral on January 13, 2013, can be viewed at http://www.youtube.com/watch?v=2LLGkY1vmhE.

25. Rex Weiner, "Ikar Looks to Build Without Losing Magic," *Jewish Daily Forward*, December 30, 2012, http://forward.com/articles/168454/Ikar-looks-to-build-without-losing-magic/?p=all.

26. The Purim festival revolves around the participatory recitation of the Megillah, or Book of Esther. Chosen by King Ahasuerus to be his bride, Queen Esther learns of an evil plot to kill the Jews. Being Jewish herself, she appeals to the king not to be so cruel to her people. Having not known previously of her heritage but being in love with her, he immediately reverses his plans and orders his advisor, Haman, to be hung for the creation of such a horrible death plot. Esther's saving of the Jews is regularly commemorated with outlandish costume parties and merriment all around. Ikar's Pu-

rim parties are known for being a particularly good time. Readers may be interested to note that feminist Jewish scholars have taken issue with the narrative retelling of the plot in this way, reminding that Esther was selected as queen in a beauty contest, an offense no less degrading after the previous Queen Vashti refused to dance naked at the king's banquet. See Eve Kosofsky Sedgwick's queer questioning of her own Queen Esther costume around age 5 in *Epistemology of the Closet* (New York: Harvester Wheatsheaf, 1990), 82.

27. With nearly 10,000 video uploads a day by the end of February 2013 and several with millions of views, the Internet dance craze known as the "Harlem Shake" redefined "viral" in the month the recorded song by Brooklyn DJ and producer, Baauer came out. Tom Heyden, "Harlem Shake: Tracking a Meme Over a Month," *BBC News Magazine*, March 1, 2013, http://www.bbc.co.uk/news/magazine-21624109. Ann Power argues that like any dance craze, the "Harlem Shake" combines the double phenomena of hilarity and sexuality in "Long before the Harlem Shake, We Did the Shimmy," *National Public Radio*, February 21, 2013, http://www.npr.org/blogs/therecord/2013/02/20/172517323/long-before-the-harlem-shake-we-did-the-shimmy. The Harlem Shake Internet meme should not be confused with the original Harlem Shake, also known as the funky monkey of dances, which came out of Harlem in the early 1980s and claims to reflect the shaking movements of ancient Egyptian mummies. See Harlem-based dance group called World Star Hip Hop who call themselves the "Original Harlem Shakers" on *KissCasper.com*, accessed October 16, 2016, http://kisscasper.com/the-real-harlem-shake-is-taking-back-the-throne/.

28. The costumed Purim affair with its blend of adult themed mayhem and zany religiosity added live biblical flair to the online cache of videos competing for more absurd setting and bizarre costumes. Adding an ironic religio-twist to an already ironic dance, dancers played up a "holy chutzpah." [translates as shameless audacity; impudence].

29. Many such comments appear on the website's "Forum" pages. BellaVendetta wrote on April 5, 2010, that "I've formed some really intense, lasting relationships with some of the girls and I am proud to call them my friends." A member named Cody wrote that among many reasons why Burning Angel rules, "they don't treat new people like crap or put them through humiliating games like [Suicide Girls] chat did to [him]," http://www.burningangel.com/forum/thread/2022/why-burning-angel-rules.

30. Niels van Doorn, "Keeping it Real: User-generated Pornography, Gender Reification, and Visual Pleasure," *Convergence: The International Journal of Research into New Media Technologies* 16, no. 4 (2010): 414. See also Susanna Paasonen, "Labors of Love: Netporn, Web 2.0 and the meanings of amateurism," *New Media & Society* 12, no. 8 (2010): 1297–1312.

31. Comment from Ballzdeep21, *PornHub.com*, accessed October 16, 2016, http://www.pornhub.com/view_video.php?viewkey=1696556116.

32. Laura Kipnis, *Bound and Gagged: Pornography and the Politics of Fantasy in America* (New York: Grove Press, 1996), 128.

33. Ibid., 129.

34. Such jokes often refer to the Jewish American Princess, too busy on the phone with her mother to be interested in sex.

35. Kirshenblatt-Gimblett, "The 'New Jews,'" 2.

36. "About Heeb," *Heeb Magazine*, accessed October 16, 2016, http://heebmagazine.com/about/.

37. Kirshenblatt-Gimblett, "The 'New Jews,'" 2.

38. Arye Dworken, "Kiss Your Mother with That Mouth? PART 1" *Jewcy Magazine*, November 15, 2006, http://www.jewcy.com/post/kiss_your_mother_mouth_part_1#sthash.ioXgW97g.dpuf.

39. Kirshenblatt-Gimblett, "The 'New Jews,'" 3.

40. Ibid., 3.

41. Gilman, *Jewish Frontiers*, 25.

42. Ibid., 25.

43. Joanna Angel, "Profile," *BurningAngel.com*, accessed October 16, 2016, http://www.burningangel.com/en/user/Joanna-Angel/127.

6

Pole Dancing for Jesus

Healthy Bodies, Healthy Souls

MICHELLE T. SUMMERS

While I was conducting a Google search for keywords "Christian" and "Dance" in 2011, my browser was suddenly inundated with hundreds of articles about a woman named Crystal Deans and a small dance class that she had begun in Spring, Texas. Her Best Shape of Your Life pole studio had somehow sparked a national media frenzy when she began offering "Pole Dancing for Jesus" classes. Reporters from the *Hollywood Gossip* to *ABC News* scrambled to produce the most sensational headlines, from the tame "Pole Dancing for Jesus: Texas Girl Lives the Dream" to the playfully ironic "Pole Dancing for Jesus Shakes up Spring: Bearing the Cross Gets Sexy."[1] Tongue-in-cheek comments from bloggers also exploded in response. Rick Chandler of NBC Sports quipped: "And the Lord saw the pole dancing, and knew that it was good. Jesus did not, however, have any singles. And so They summoned a cab."[2] This media attention created an atmosphere of intense scrutiny, which invited anyone to comment on the life, work, and faith of Crystal Deans.

Despite this barrage of witty media remarks, Deans's life is anything but a sound bite. Instead, her complex experiences as a daughter, mother, stripper, wife, and teacher inform the ambivalent ways white Christian women are able to conjoin their sexuality and spirituality through an embodied rhetoric of the "healthy." In order to understand the media fascination with Deans's class and the eventual failure of "Pole Dancing for Jesus" to survive the onslaught of attention, this essay explicates the larger historical discourses on health in the United States, including an evolving, and often overlooked, Christian dance fitness industry. The trajectory of twentieth-century secular fitness reveals a moralizing narrative enmeshed within Protestant Christian prerogatives.

Dance comes to play a central role in this moral health agenda by providing a gendered outlet for Christian women to explore embodied religious practice.

This article chronicles the rise and fall of "Pole Dancing for Jesus" as documented through the life of its founder, Crystal Deans. Referencing the videos, photos, and comments made about Deans's class, I argue that two strategies arise for legitimizing this practice as Christian worship. First, the class is framed as part of the Christian diet and fitness industry's spiritual war on excessive fat. This war revolves around an ethic of bodily care that equates healthy bodies with healthy souls, while the sexual connotations of pole dancing are largely disavowed. A second strategy also arises, however, rooted in reclaiming the sexual as sacred through female empowerment. In this configuration, a healthy sexuality is the primary pursuit, so pole dancing's ties to the sex industry are embraced rather than denied. These two seemingly contradictory strategies alternate as justifications that are invoked by Deans, her students, and the secular pole fitness community, as these women make tactical choices in order to pole dance. This discussion of strategy reveals the class-based power that the predominately white female practitioners accrue through their ability to "try on" pole dancing during these classes without having to become strippers. A language of empowerment and choice often emerges, rooted in the practitioner's class, gender, and race. This chapter, "Pole Dancing for Jesus," reveals the oscillatory pockets of power that these women are able to inhabit through their avowal of pole dancing as a healthy, Christian pursuit.

Dance, Fitness, and Christianity in the United States

"Pole Dancing for Jesus" developed alongside the emerging Christian dance fitness industry over the course of the twentieth and twenty-first centuries, sharing a dominant narrative that focused on the "healthy" body. Health became aligned with a physically fit body and, as a female-dominated genre, dance allowed women an active voice in discourses on fitness. This conception of fitness surfaced primarily in response to the detrimental effects of industrial labor on the stationary bodies of America's nineteenth-century manufacturing class.[3] At a time when women were actively seeking greater agency in their personal and public lives, dance offered both a corrective to urban living conditions and a pleasurable venue for personal expression. The growing preoccupation with bodily cultivation relied fundamentally on the body as an "organism striving for erectness whose musculature contributed centrally to that effort."[4]

Training regimes that disciplined the body into a physically fit musculature emerged as viable methods for developing a healthy body. These changes ushered in an era that emphasized fitness, exercise, and training as a necessary part of American physical education, health, and well-being.

In particular, the inclusion of physical training in educational systems consolidated the important role that fitness would play in the development of female morality and corporeality. Historian Dominick Cavallo argues that organized play reformers assumed that "a link existed between carefully organized physical exercise and both moral vitality and cognitive alertness."[5] Particularly directed toward urban immigrants, the organization of physical activity targeted children as the primary demographic, training them to be "good" American citizens through the moral and ethical discipline brought about by play and sport. This concept of metamorphosis through physical training presented a mixed message for women, who were called upon to possess muscular strength while retaining an expected "female" softness. As women's roles began to be redefined at the turn of the twentieth century, the consignment of women to the domestic, private sphere was contested, and women began to negotiate their newfound access to the public sphere through physical exercise.[6] Cavallo's account of pioneer social worker Jane Addams and the Hull-House Social Settlement elucidates how the reform of play led to the redefinition of women's social roles. Addams advocated for sport, play, and athletics for both boys and girls because she felt that "Young people who work long hours at sedentary occupations, factories, and offices, need perhaps more than anything else the freedom and ease to be acquired from a symmetrical muscular development and are quick to respond to that fellowship which athletics apparently afford more easily than anything else."[7] Cavallo argues that the idea of the "team" perpetuated through Addams's organized recreation programs for children served as an ideal metaphor—women could participate in the public realm while still retaining the moral and ethical qualities that constituted femininity, precisely because a good teammate demanded a blend of masculine and feminine traits.[8]

Other early feminists also echoed Addams's support for fitness as a women's health issue. Dance scholar Susan Foster notes that the movement of men into exclusive sports clubs quickly gave rise to feminist advocates who "protested the constricted conditions of women promoted by corsets deforming the body and by public policies and medical practice that denied women the opportunity to exercise more freely."[9] These historical demands helped lay the groundwork for women's increasing access to the fitness world through a narrative of health. However, while fitness regimes such as weight training or sports such as football are recognized as primarily masculine undertakings, dance and its associations with femininity may account for its popularity with women, who could participate in the fitness craze without abandoning "appropriate" gender identifiers.

Additionally, government initiatives in the mid-twentieth century explicitly linked citizenship with moral health and fitness. The President's Council on Youth Fitness (established in 1956) took the responsibility of physical training—and its moral imperatives—out of the hands of parents and reformers and placed it squarely within a growing government agenda. President John F. Kennedy's famous essay "The Soft American" appeared in *Sports Illustrated* magazine in 1960 and declared a similar purpose to that of the Progressive Era playground organizers. He encouraged military might born out of physical strength that would also create strong moral and intellectual Americans. Yet, as Foster argues, this political articulation of fitness, meant to combat a perceived communist proclivity toward homosexuality, perpetuated a fear of effeminacy or the "soft," thought to be combatted through methodical physical fitness and training.[10] Thus, muscular hardness was asserted as a sign of heterosexual masculinity, morality, intellect, and democratic ideals.

This emphasis on muscularity relied on a narrative of health as a moral initiative, partially rooted in religious ideals about the training of the good *Christian* citizen. One example that emerged alongside the nineteenth-century physical culture movement was an ideology known as "Muscular Christianity," perpetuated primarily through the Young Men's Christian Association's (YMCA) desire to spread the new gospel that "physical exercise in all forms can become a mighty factor in the development of the highest type of Christian character."[11] Muscular Christianity became particularly popular because it sought to train both the Christian body and soul. Originally a response to a perceived feminization of spirituality, the YMCA's adoption of its "Red Triangle" in 1891 established an idealized unity between "body, mind, and spirit."[12] In its early stages, the YMCA targeted men as muscular Christianity enthusiasts, but, with increasing female membership in the 1930s, the organization took a more familial bent.[13] Although intended to reinforce masculinity, some Christian women embraced the health-oriented aspects of the Muscular Christianity movement and integrated the concepts into groups such as the Girl Scouts, the Camp Fire Girls, and the YWCA.[14] Women's increasing participation in the YMCA, embrace of Muscular Christianity, and growing involvement in the sporting world demonstrates an emerging negotiation of femininity and fitness with the ideas of normative Christian masculinity.

As religious scholar Sydney Ahlstrom argues, a developing sense of "patriotic piety" resulted in a "triple melting pot" of Protestantism, Judaism, and Catholicism in the mid-twentieth century.[15] Christian fitness grew in tandem with this emerging religious plurality and was based on a generalized, cultural morality. During the McCarthy era "being a church member and speaking favorably of religion became a means of affirming the 'American way of life,'" particularly in response to the atheism perpetuated by communist regimes.[16] For example, by the 1950s, the YMCA was no longer a retreat exclusively for Protestant Christian men; Catholics and Jews actually comprised two-fifths of the association.[17] By broadening its identity as a religious institution, YMCA fitness activities became a productive use of leisure time.[18] Organizations such as the YMCA entered an emerging American marketplace where people could "purchase 'culture' as a means of self-improvement and relaxation," according to R. Laurence Moore.[19] He argues: "No one dares suggest that neon signs blinking the message that 'Jesus Saves' may be false advertising."[20] Thus, marketing phrases such as "for Jesus" access a commodified religious discourse that makes any action under this heading difficult to contest, as exemplified by groups such as Goths for Jesus, Jews for Jesus, and Hookers for Jesus. This increasing commodification of Christianity continued into the 1960s in what Ahlstrom identifies as a "Post-Puritan America," where a plurality of religions, practices, and beliefs came to dominate the American religious landscape. In the wake of this plurality, Protestant culture began to absorb aspects of other religious and secular practices in order to remain current in the commercial market. These adoptions, I argue, included the integration of dance fitness into Protestant practices.

Dance classes such as zumba, cardio ballet, and Latin heat are currently proliferating in American fitness culture, with a particular marketing focus on women. A predecessor to these trends, Jazzercise (popularized by fitness gurus such as Jane Fonda) was one of the first to meld fitness culture with dance in order to create a hybrid form in the 1980s.[21] While these forms draw on dance techniques such as ballet, jazz, hip hop, and ballroom, they follow the conventions of exercise and sports training rather than those more typical of dance instruction. The official Zumba website promotes the form as an "exhilarating, effective, easy-to-follow, Latin-inspired, calorie-burning dance fitness-party that's moving millions of people toward joy and health."[22] The allure of fun is combined with the benefit of fitness to promote commercial enterprises aimed at developing bodies that are healthy physically, mentally, and emotionally. Another more recent example is First Lady Michelle Obama's fitness and health initiative "Let's Move," which utilizes dance fitness to combat childhood obesity.[23]

The commodification of religious culture, combined with the increasing popularity of dance fitness programs, paved the way for the emergence of Christian dance fitness crazes. Today, everything from "Devoted Fitness" to "MIRA! Christian Fitness with a Latin Beat!" and "PraiseMoves: The Christian Alternative to Yoga!" populate the scene. Programs such as Devoted Fitness describe their intentions in marketing campaigns: "worship and workout! Dance your way to a healthy body and soul . . . Burn an average of 650–800 calories per workout. Christian dance aerobics created to get down and lift HIM up!"[24] Studios have popped up across the United States with the intention of getting women fit for the Lord by invoking a "Jesus as Lover" mentality that suggests a love relationship between women and Jesus. YouTube channels and DVD sales proliferate with trained aerobics instructors who are using their skills and talents to connect working out with worshiping. Advertising fun moves, modestly dressed instructors, and clean lyrics, these videos reach a Christian market niche that has taken up the moral mandate to craft a physically fit body.

Christian dance workouts have also cropped up in the churches themselves. When I attended a local Christian dance fitness class in Albuquerque, New Mexico, in December of 2011, I found myself in a Lutheran church gymnasium surrounded primarily by older white people in workout clothes, "sweating it out" to Christian music. The teacher, a former Jazzercise instructor, utilized repetitive movements such as *chassé* step, ball change. While the steps were from the familiar aerobics canon, arm movements and upper body positions were uplifted, toward the imagined location of the Judeo-Christian God, reminiscent of liturgical dance choreography that employs the high release of the chest as a symbol of divine interaction. The class structure was based on the aerobic precept of "just keep moving," but halfway into the class the traditional frontal orientation morphed into a counterclockwise circle of improvisational dancing. This element of improvisation, not common in most aerobics settings but common in modern dance idioms, bridged these two forms. The experience incorporated a diverse range of dance genres, merging modern dance improvisation, liturgical dance high releases, Jazzercise aerobic movements, and strength-based circuit training, with yoga-like stretching and breath awareness. The elements that made it "Christian" were the music, the setting, the assumed intention behind each of the dancers' movements, and the general consensus that everyone could have an embodied Christian experience while getting fit. The two worlds of dance fitness and Christian worship were able, in this contemporary moment, to coalesce in the church gymnasium, and practitioners were able to "get healthy" by dancing in a Christian-sanctioned environment.

"Pole Dancing for Jesus"

The original interview of Deans by Fox News in 2011 occurred in her pastel-purple studio and featured Deans teaching a "Pole Dancing for Jesus" class to two students. The opening visual sequence shifts abruptly between the class demonstration and the interview, with contemporary Christian music fading in and out of the audio. It begins with Deans gripping the metal pole with an outstretched arm and demonstrating a swiveling, high kick. The camera cuts to Deans explaining her past. As she speaks, the metal pole is foregrounded, partially blocking our view of her. The video segment returns to the class with a series of fetishized shots: silver stiletto heels slide down a pole . . . two thighs grip it . . . now an upper body is upside down in a "look-no-hands" stunt . . . hands with blue fingernails grasp the gleaming metal . . . a full body is seen, but it is only a mirrored reflection. Deans's face and voice constantly interrupt the dance shots—always with the pole in the foreground and the person in the background.

Crystal Deans was twenty-eight years old when this interview went viral. Though a number of media outlets picked up the story, very few actually interviewed Deans,[25] looked into additional details about the story, or researched the history of pole dancing. Instead, they reposted snippets from the original news report, inviting commentary by the reading public on the morality of her practice. Predictably, responses were largely negative. Some bloggers went so far as to post vicious verbal attacks and heap ridicule on Deans and her studio, openly questioning her intentions. The cultural and religious weight that the phrase "Pole Dancing for Jesus" represented (a phrase largely utilized by media outlets—Deans called the class "Pole *Fitness* for Jesus") created a loaded opportunity for outsiders to comment on what they saw as a gimmick that capitalized on controversy rather than a sincere approach to embodied Christian worship.[26] Deans soon retreated from the public eye, giving up her studio and eventually even her career as a pole fitness teacher. Deans, however, did agree to two additional interviews with the *New York Times* and the *Cindy Davis Show* after the original commentary aired on Fox News. These responses to the media scrutiny provide a closer, more in-depth look at the struggles Deans faced both before and after "Pole Dancing for Jesus" went viral.

Deans was acquainted with the exotic dance industry from a very young age. When she was a child, her mother was a stripper who struggled with drug abuse. Deans became pregnant at the age of fourteen, and, after her daughter was born, she fought to make ends meet. She managed to finish high school and a year of college, but eventually turned to exotic dancing as a way to overcome her financial troubles. According to Deans, "I know there are other jobs, but it is hard to support a child on your own with other jobs. So I did what I did, and then as soon as I was able to, I got out of it."[27] Deans states that she was a stripper for three years (2002–4), approximately seven years before the "Pole Dancing for Jesus" saga erupted. On the *Cindy Davis Show*, she explains that she really only knew how to do three dance moves while she was in the business.[28] It was only after she quit stripping professionally and began to teach that she learned the more difficult moves associated with pole fitness.

Deans's Christian conversion experience occurred around the time she stopped stripping in 2004 (by this time, she was married). According to the *New York Times* interview, Deans remembers: "Something came into my head and said, 'You need God. You need Jesus. You need a church.' A beloved great aunt, near death from pulmonary fibrosis, suggested she try the church 'over there by the Y.M.C.A., Houston Northwest Church.'"

"I went to church all by myself that day, . . . I came home and I spoke to my husband, because during that church service that day, they had mentioned they do family counseling. I said to my husband, 'I am going to marriage counseling Wednesday evening.' We started marriage counseling once a week for two and a half years." This conversion not only helped Deans's marriage; it also motivated her to quit the stripping industry for good and eventually open her own business.

Deans's studio, Best Shape of Your Life, opened in North Houston in the summer of 2010 and relocated to Old Town Spring in early 2011.[29] The classes regularly offered by the studio were primarily secular and not advertised as Christian. In March of 2011, after the move to Spring, Deans began to offer "Pole Fitness for Jesus" classes, advertising on the company's Facebook page: "Best Shape of Your Life proudly introduces POLE FITNESS FOR JESUS!

The first 11 women that bring in their church program every second Sunday of the month at 2pm get in FREE! We will be playing upbeat contemporary Christian music! Come in and take care of the body the Lord gave you!"[30]

Deans made good on her offer regardless of denomination. But the class was short-lived. Almost immediately after Deans's first interview, she was inundated with denouncements of her new class. On March 27, 2011, ten days after that first interview, Deans declared on the Best Shape of Your Life Facebook page: "To all of God's children: Whether you have made nasty comments or positive ones, believers or not, God and I love you all!"[31] In a later interview, Deans revealed, "I have had a lot of people say that I'm going to burn in hell, I'm Satan, or using Satan's ways, things like that, but that's just not how it is, and I'm confident about that."[32] Deans sought out her local pastor to help her better understand the situation, and while she acknowledges that she did not consult him before starting the class, he did tell her afterward that "God knows what was in your heart" and "good for you for not squandering your gifts that God gave you."[33]

In late 2011, Deans announced her decision to sell her studio in order to spend more time with her kids. While she did not teach any Christian-focused pole dance classes during this time, she did teach online lessons before she and her husband moved the family to Auburn, Maine, in 2012. Deans attempted to open a new Best Shape of Your Life studio in Maine, but it did not prosper, and so in 2013 she closed it due to financial difficulties. Deans is now the owner of a repurposed home décor and gift business called the Same as Never.[34]

The Perfectible Body

The rhetoric surrounding "Pole Dancing for Jesus" largely seeks to disavow pole dancing's associations with the sex industry and instead align it with the pursuit of a fit Christian body. First, both secular and Christian pole fitness dancers tend to frame their practice in terms of "fun" in order to circumnavigate the seriousness of pole dancing as a job. Second, practitioners place pole dancing alongside other dance fitness forms to prove that it is just another kind of workout. Its equivocation with more mundane, less controversial styles helps to desensationalize its sexualized roots. Dancers and studio owners enact this by referencing historical lineages that do not attribute the history of pole dancing to the sex industry alone but also align it with sports practiced by men in various cultures. Finally, pole dancers claim the homosocial environment as a means by which the male gaze is avoided; therefore, sexuality becomes a nonissue. I argue that these three strategies invoke the Christian ideal of the "perfectible body," developed by religious scholar R. Marie Griffith, as pole dancing becomes part of a larger discourse in the Christian fitness industry's spiritual war on excessive fat.

In her book *Born Again Bodies*, Griffith examines devotional fitness culture and asserts that the pervasiveness of Protestantism plays an essential part in the dialogue surrounding the creation of the perfectible American body. Griffith defines contemporary devotional diet culture in America as "the addition of expressive relationships with sacred figures such as God or Jesus, accompanied by the belief that the human body's fitness affects such relationships in direct and indirect ways."[35] Stemming from a Protestant history of disdain for and regulation of the body in service of the soul, Griffith argues that religious diet culture longs for an *embodied* religion and so promises authentic discovery of the self through body reformation.[36] Capitalizing on an ethic of bodily care, Christians in the United States came to imagine a well-maintained body as the marker for a well-maintained soul. Advocating the ideal of "mind over matter," self-realization is achieved through perseverance, dedication, and self-control, all objective projects in the making of the perfectible body. We can clearly see this in the way Crystal Deans chooses to frame her class: "I help these women get fit. I hope it makes them feel good about themselves because a person who is in good health physically and mentally is definitely in a better position to be, I believe, open to Jesus and what he did for us."[37] Deans's philosophy relies on a specific understanding of the relationship between body and soul, dovetailing with Griffith's argument that Christian embodiment capitalizes on the body as an instrument of salvation and asks visible bodies to display invisible souls.[38]

One of the primary strategies that secular and religious pole dancers employ in the making of this perfectible body is the tactical disavowal of pole fitness as a sexual pursuit, reframing it instead as a fitness regimen that is "fun." In a study conducted by psychologists Kally Whitehead and Tim Kurz, interview responses from members of an Australian secular pole dance fitness class were analyzed from a feminist, poststructuralist perspective in order to determine the discursive construction of pole dancing as a recreational activity.[39] One participant in the study stated that there is "nothing wrong with having fun," a rhetorical framing that allows these dancers to sidestep denigrating associations the form might elicit.[40] Getting fit, being healthy, is fun. Words like "fun" in this setting (or "joy" in the case of Zumba) work to remove the dance forms from hypersexualized associations and instead place them squarely within the moral imperatives established by the educational, social, and governmental precursors previously mentioned. Similarly, two female students of Crystal Deans, when interviewed by Cindy Davis, repeatedly state that pole dancing is both "fun" and "challenging."[41] By linking pole dancing to dance fitness, the participants claim a positive moral imperative, aligned with Protestant dictums instead of a working-class body that *must* dance on a pole for a living. The element of "fun" constitutes pole dancing as a leisure activity rather than an economic necessity.

Another reframing strategy declares that the class is just one of many workout genres. In the original interview on Fox News, one of Deans's students—a redheaded, twenty-something who identifies herself as Tiffany Booth—states: "I think it's a fabulous thing. I was raised around religion. My parents were very religious, and also it's a great way you get the stigma off . . . It's not just dancing on a pole. You have music and you have girls together working out . . . there's tons of different kinds of workouts; this just happens to be one."[42]

How can something be "unhealthy" if it is just another fitness workout? Comparing pole dancing to other dance fitness styles makes it just one choice among many within a commercialized, religious landscape that has flourished precisely because it is about self-improvement. Strategically, Booth cites her family's religious background as evidence for the authenticity of her own participation in a Christian pole dance class. This authentic Christian lineage is what allows her to invoke pole dancing as a way to "get the stigma off," a phrase insinuating that this dance form operates like Hester's scarlet letter. If the stigma of pole dancing—of the sex industry—is emblazoned on the female body, then Christianity becomes the methodology by which it is removed.

Another student of Deans, identified as Whitney during a later interview, reveals that she is a physician's assistant and has invited many of her "professional friends" to join her in the class. She says they are "willing to come but if they hear somebody else is doing it, they're like 'Oh I've always wanted to do that,' but for some reason they wouldn't break out and do it themselves because they were scared about what other people would think. But I think there's a stigma that goes along with it, that it's something dirty, but it's really not. It's a really good workout."[43] It seems likely that Deans, whose reflection you can see in the mirror during the conversation, handpicked this student for the interview. Whitney is immediately asked her occupation by the interviewer, and her class status as a physician's assistant appears to lend credibility to her endorsement, perhaps countering the images of white women in the first "Pole Dancing for Jesus" news video who wore clothing that revealed tattoos, were a bit overweight, and could be read as less "middle class." Class differentiation is iterated by words like "dirty," which separate working-class labor from middle-class respectability. Accordingly, Whitney is a very clean-cut, fit, young blonde woman who is well spoken. She states that many respectable women, just like her, attend pole dancing classes at Crystal Deans's studio. It is Whitney's own validation of the classes as "just a workout" that enables these women to overcome the "stigma" and participate.

The workout element of "Pole Dancing for Jesus" also relies on pole dancing's increasing codification. Deans describes the benefits that her lessons provide: "We average about 500 calories in an hour class . . . it builds a lot of strength. We're talking upper body, back, shoulders, chest, core, even wrists and hands."[44] Here Deans appeals to a woman's perceived need to burn calories in order to be fit. In both her original and subsequent interviews, Deans addresses the classroom attire as necessary to fitness objectives.[45] The lack of clothing—the short-shorts and tank tops—are required because a lot of skin is needed to stick to the pole, particularly in more advanced moves where you release the pole with your hands, and the body contact with metal is all that holds you up. Comparatively, the high heels that Deans and other pole dance studio instructors encourage are not worn because they are "stripper heels," but instead, Deans asserts, they are heavy and help to develop leg muscles during the leg lifts, spins, and pivots. Deans also emphasizes that pole dancing technique is becoming more and more codified; she lists many common moves in pole terminology, such as boomerangs, back leg hooks, shoulder mounts, and twisted grip handsprings.[46] She and others cite pole dance's legitimacy by pointing to the many competitions that now exist and to the widespread rumors that pole dancing may become an Olympic sport. Between its fitness objectives and its growing credibility through codification, Deans and others argue that pole fitness is a workout, not just an erotic dance.

Historical accounts cited in support of codification emphasize that pole dancing was a sport originally performed by men. Many sources identify pole dancing as an exotic dance form created during the 1970s and '80s in Vancouver, Canada, and trace its transformation into a form of recreational fitness in the 1990s.[47] However, Deans's version is quite different and worth quoting at length:

A lot of people think that pole has been taken from the strip clubs, and that's what this is, but for thousands of years the Chinese and Indian men have been competing doing it. It didn't actually become a sexual thing until the Great Depression. The men were off at war, and the women had no way to make a living. This is my understanding from doing my research. When the circus would come to town, they would have tents all around the circus during the Great Depression. The women would be out there, and one of the tents was called the pole tent. Well, it was held up in the middle by a pole. And the women would dance seductively, and the men would pay them. And that was strictly as a means to be able to get by while their husbands and even older sons were off at war. So that's where that actually started, and then some genius in the U.S. and Canada decided to put it into the adult entertainment establishment. So that's actually where it became dirty.[48]

Instead of sketching pole dancing's lineage through exotic dance, from the burlesque scene in the 1920s and '30s to the emergence of upscale gentlemen's clubs in the latter part of the twentieth century,[49] Deans cites the gymnastic sport of pole and mast climbing. This move mirrors the official history of pole dancing established by the International Pole Dance Fitness Association (IPDFA), which states that pole dancing "is a fusion of Chinese pole, Indian Pole or 'Mallakhamb,' other circus-based (e.g. Dutch and French pole), exotic dance of various international influences and pole dancing as seen in the travelling fairs of the American Depression."[50] While both Deans and the IPDFA recognize contemporary pole dancing's relationship to exotic dance, they situate it within a broader cultural and historical context to equate it with gymnastic feats, thus affiliating it with male strength. Additionally, Deans's explanation aligns with her own modern-day, working-class experience, which led to dancing on the pole due to familial needs (family need is largely absent in the IPDFA's version). She only equates pole dancing's "dirty" quotient to the form's entrance into the adult entertainment industry. Her account, while still acknowledging the impact of an exotic dance history, foregrounds physical strength, personal endurance, and dedication to family in order to absolve pole dancing of its stigma.

In the attempt to "strip" away such negative connotations, one other crucial justification remains: pole dancing's potential as a realm of homosocial bonding. At the time of the 2011 interview, Deans did not offer male pole dancing classes and acknowledges that if she did decide to offer them, men and women would remain largely separated unless the class was specifically labeled coed.[51] This maintenance of a homosocial context draws parallels with early modern dance, which also asserted a wholesome female camaraderie and sought to distance itself from the moral suspicions associated with dance.[52] Dance scholars have argued that historically homosexual subtext in modern dance was often marginalized by historians, choreographers, and dancers in order to claim space for artistic practice.[53] In the pursuit of a "nonsexual investigation of human movement," sexual implications implicit within a given dance production were denied.[54] Similarly, the construction of the "Pole Dancing for Jesus" space is highly regulated as a controlled, homosocial environment where overt sexuality can be disavowed since there is no male gaze. Deans's student Tiffany Booth makes this point when she claims that this is just a place where girls can get together and work out. Deans also reiterates homosociality when she declares that the purpose of her original interview with Fox News was to "bring Christian women, with similar beliefs, into a supportive system where they can work past the stigma and feel comfortable working out in this way."[55] And Deans functions in some sense like a counselor in this female-dominated sphere. She takes this opportunity to tell her own story and listen to the troubles of other women. One student, for example, revealed to Deans that she was physically impaired due to attempted suicide but has now rededicated her life to helping others.[56] Through this model of women gathering in a safe (and sacred) environment to work out, the fitness model enables these dancers to develop their bodies, both physically and mentally, as they disavow the sexual implications of pole dancing and rely instead on the construction of a healthy, perfectible body dedicated to Jesus.

Healthy Sexuality

While some practitioners are content for pole dancing to reside solely in the realm of the perfectible, fit body, even Deans herself sometimes complicates the rhetoric. In a *New York Times* interview Deans stated: "This has helped a lot of people . . . It's helped people with weight. It's helped people spice up their marriages."[57] Thus, in a seeming contradiction to the previous arguments for pole dancing as *just* a fitness regimen, Deans undoes this model by highlighting the potential for pole dancing to spice up your marriage. Instead of denial, her statement embraces female sexuality within the confines of the Christian heteronormative marriage model. In my own pole dance class experience, I found the ties to the sex industry to be overt and largely undeniable, but the sexiness still seemed to be conceptualized either within the framework of marriage or female sexual empowerment. Thus, the fit, perfectible body and its disavowal of sexuality is staged in tension with the assertion that pole dancing actually helps to create healthy female sexuality in terms of one's marriage, one's relationship with Christ, and one's feeling of female empowerment.

Despite a fitness focus, sexuality is never completely absent from pole dancing, so an analysis of Christian health discourses that interlink fitness and sexuality illustrate how a narrative of female empowerment operates. Religious scholar Lynne Gerber builds on Griffith's research through an examination of the First Place weight loss program, which she triangulates with sexuality through her analysis of Exodus International, an ex-gay ministry designed to eliminate homosexual desires. The overlaps between fat as transgression and nonnormative sexuality as transgression are important because both emerge as methods for talking about excess, an issue that also plagues pole dancing. Medicine and religion in the United States aspire to curb excess in order to create normalizing discourses around discipline and the body. According to Gerber, religion's adoption of the medical conception of "healthy" through groups that regulate one's diet and sexuality creates an accessible secular, yet moral, category within a theological framing.[58] Thus, boundary transgressions such as fatness (eating too much) and homosexuality (sexing inappropriately) come under the scope of the religious and medical mandate to curb bodily excess. The body becomes the locus for these disciplinary projects within U.S. culture.

Though fitness can be foregrounded, this does not explain the motive for the sensationalized media coverage—the unavoidable questions that come up about Christian sexuality and what is going "too far," that is, what is excessive. Thus, a different model emerges, explaining "Pole Dancing for Jesus" as rooted in a desire to create a healthy sexuality that conforms to the normalizing values of Christian discourse. In an interview conducted by ABC News that sought to provoke a reaction to the "Pole Dancing for Jesus" saga, religious studies professor Thomas Tweed stated: "Some people of course would say that this is not the way; that it's too vulgar, it's too crass, it's inappropriate . . . But I can imagine some Christians saying if it actually brings a husband and wife together as Christians to deepen the marriage bond, that actually it's okay."[59]

As I read Tweed's quote, I was reminded of a 7th grade girls' church retreat I attended at the home of a local Southern Baptist woman. It was intended as an opportunity to educate newly sexually awakened girls about the Christian qualities that must be maintained in romantic relationships, and I remember one story in particular. One speaker, a middle-aged white woman, attempted to assure us that embracing your sexuality was alright as long as it was in service of your husband's desire. She declared that it was not OK to sunbathe topless normally, but since her husband liked tanned boobs, she did it in the back yard when no one else was around. The message to us as young Christian girls was clear: grooming our sexual bodies was acceptable insofar as it served the needs (and confines) of the heteronormative model of Christian marriage.

In the Whitehead and Kurz interviews, a similar theme emerges in the secular community. One female participant's response declares: "they can easily objectify you and just go 'this is a body (.) . . . whereas (.) when it's someone you love (.) they're gunna see you as '*wow* (.) she cares about me this much that she's willing to do *this* and (.) oh my god (.) look at her confidence.'"[60] This example, along with Tweed's remarks, illustrates a construction of sexuality in religious and secular pole dancing that justifies participation when it serves a properly constrained sexuality within the boundaries of a heterosexual marital relationship. So the assumptions of the homosocial environment and its removal of the male gaze can be conceived, alternatively, as a space for working out sexuality, not just a space for working out. "Pole Dancing for Jesus" provides opportunities for Christian women to experiment with their sexuality and shape it for their men. Pole dancing classes are meant to "spice up your marriage," like the recently popular, self-help texts that serve as Christian sex manuals. For example, Christian sex therapist Douglas Rosenau's book, *A Celebration of Sex: A Guide to Enjoying God's Gift of Sexual Intimacy*, helps religious couples cultivate sexual techniques within married life.[61] When framed within the context of Christian marriage, proponents of "Pole Dancing for Jesus" don't deny that dance is sexual. They also don't deny that it is spiritual. Instead, sexuality and spirituality are reconciled as mutually beneficial elements within healthy marital relations. Thus, sex within the confines of Christian marriage exists as a point of agency for Christian women.

Many pole dancing students expand this conversation to include female empowerment more generally, asserting that pole dancing gives a woman "confidence." First-wave feminism reframed the white female body as a site of empowerment through suffragist language; second-wave feminism in the 1960s and '70s brought further empowerment through the discourse of civil rights. As the interviews by Whitehead and Kurz demonstrate, these movements directly influenced our contemporary understanding of female sexuality as reliant on "choice," mobilized under the auspices of female agency born out of "sexual liberation/empowerment."[62] "Pole Dancing for Jesus" also utilizes this discourse of empowerment, albeit covertly, for many conservative Christians are still largely suspicious of feminist sentiment.[63] Moreover, I would argue that an empowerment narrative in a Christian context is strongly tied to a woman's right to worship. Deans clarifies that "we do the upbeat contemporary Christian music because people have to bring their church program to get into the class, so we basically are just continuing the whole worship thing here."[64] Being able to worship in any manner deemed "from the heart" empowers women to reclaim their dancing bodies for Jesus and places worship firmly within a discourse of rights. This in many ways unites the first amendment freedom of the right to worship with neoliberal prerogatives that also demand the right to have a healthy body.

Still, the delineation of worship and matrimonial sexuality as empowerment are complicated by the phrase "for Jesus." Griffith discusses the power of Christian diet and fitness culture, which targets women by appealing to aspirations of becoming the "chosen one." This is accomplished through the practice of a woman cultivating her health and beauty in order for her relationship with God to mirror a romantic relationship with a man on earth. Griffith's examples, and my own experience growing up in a Southern Baptist church in Arkansas, illustrate how aspirations to be both sexy and modest are resolved through training Christian girls to be "the kind of girl Christ would want to marry."[65] This approach is most frequently directed at women who attempt to preserve their virginity for their future spouse by redirecting their energies and focus onto God. (This language has much in common with the Catholic consecration of nuns who become the Brides of Christ when taking their vows.) Once a woman has married, most Christian self-help narratives shift focus from a two-way relationship to a triangulated marriage with Christ as the head and the center. Even in this new configuration, divine love relationships are played out in the dedication of the body (including the sexual elements in a relationship) to Jesus, as the biblical metaphor of the body as a temple of the Holy Spirit extends to a marriage where two bodies become one in Christ.

The contradictions inherent in "Pole Dancing for Jesus" can be further explored by comparing Deans's classes with my brief participation in a secular pole dance community, comprising primarily African American women.[66] The pole dance fitness class I attended was held at a studio called Spinarella in Atlanta, Georgia. The bright lights and light purple paint of Crystal Deans's studio were definitely not the vibe in Spinarella's dimly lit warehouse. While many dance studios offer classes like Zumba, hip hop, and Jazzercize that draw on disparate cultural influences, sexually explicit or suggestive moves are often sanitized through repetition, upbeat rhythms, bright lights, and an overall feeling that you are just "working out." Such classes encourage women to dance a cleaned-up sexy. The short video class snippets the news outlets provided of "Pole Dancing for Jesus" downplayed the sexy part, and pole dancing instead became about fitness, acrobatics, flexibility, and strength. While Crystal Deans's version of pole dance fitness appeared to enable white women the privilege of choosing whether or not to be sexy, Spinarella's class seemed to encourage women, and particularly women of color, the opportunity to reclaim their sexuality. So while the elements of fitness still existed in small doses in the Spinarella pole dancing class, working out was more of a by-product of feeling sexy.

In the Spinarella class, students and instructor all wore hot shorts or thongs; the music was sexually charged; and when the dancing started, it was less about camaraderie and more about getting down to business. After participating in a short warm up, the students learned to walk and spiral using the pole, often utilizing the inner part of the leg to grip the metal. We also executed floor work and "wall" work, showcasing flexibility and suppleness with the stretch of a leg or the articulation of the spine to show off the chest and pelvis. Spinarella's website includes terminology used in class, and advocates of pole dancing in general speak of its ability to empower women. One student testimonial attests, "I was instantly hooked on the idea of finding that inner 'diva' that could do anything."[67] And as much as the homosocial space asserted a supportive environment for all women, who clapped for each other's performances, the fact that men were not in attendance did not mean that the male gaze was absent. While never said directly, the aesthetics of the situation clearly suggested that *someone* was watching. Certainly the omnipresent mirror, the instructor circling the room, and the other students standing against the wall watching you grind generated a significant audience. In determining what was "sexy," I could not help but watch what other women did and try to emulate their style, most of the time realizing that their "best" moves were closely related to a simulation of a sexual act. So even though the male gaze was physically absent, his ghost was undoubtedly present. I left the class wondering if the "for Jesus" part of Crystal Deans's pole dance fitness actually hindered any sort of feminist agenda that might emerge from the self-empowering rhetoric associated with pole dancing. Does "for Jesus" assert the omnipresent power of a white male God who is always watching?[68] How does this factor differently for white women and women of color? Does it invoke the commodified history of women dancing for men because it implies that pole dancing is *for* something, that is, someone is paying *for* it?

Yet I acknowledge that my own discomfort with the imagery of "Pole Dancing for Jesus" is rooted in a specific cultural construction of the sacred and the sexual—a barrier that Audre Lorde's reading of the erotic refuses. In her seminal essay "Uses of the Erotic: The Erotic as Power," Lorde asserts that the erotic has wrongly been vilified within Western (white) culture because it has been associated with the pornographic, and thus with the "suppression of true feeling."[69] Lorde encourages women to no longer accept the separation of the spiritual and the erotic.[70] She argues that we must not relegate the erotic to the bedroom alone, but find power in the truthful understanding of the phrase "It feels right to me."[71] And this is exactly what Crystal Deans's politics embraces: "As far as continuing the worship, any time I do anything throughout the day, I really think about, none of this would be possible without Jesus and what he did for us. So because of that, yeah I do feel that. I'm not going to guarantee that every woman that comes in here on the Sunday class is going to feel that. But that is what I feel, and so that's why I do it."[72]

Deans embraces what feels right to her. In doing so, she is able to access erotic empowerment through worship and the Christian model of marriage, leading to a danced relationship that is complicated by her racial position as a white woman dancing "for Jesus."

The Politics of Empowerment

"Pole Dancing for Jesus" exists in part because of the thriving cultural push to create a healthy body and a healthy sexuality as part of a neoliberal self-help mentality that has been codeveloped and co-opted not only by a recognized U.S. Christian contingent, but also by a pseudo-Christian secular culture that denies Protestant ties. Protestant Christianity within U.S. culture operates in much the same way that whiteness does—as an unnamed, universal force that is a driving factor in what we see and understand as "normal" or "healthy."[73] Lynne Gerber extrapolates from religious scholar Tracy Fessenden's argument that a Protestant sensibility has become an unmarked, invisibilized moralizing discourse in U.S. culture, based on a perceived universality rather than an explicit religiosity.[74] Complications emerge if we read "Pole Dancing for Jesus" through this lens because a peculiar kind of dualism unites a universalized Protestant sensibility that allows for the logical evolution of "Pole Dancing for Jesus," alongside a simultaneous denouncement of "Pole Dancing for Jesus" by a self-identified Protestant (in particular evangelical) discourse. As Gerber argues, Protestant evangelicalism has become a marker of cultural identity that demarcates a difference, a counterculture to secularism.[75] At the same time, Protestantism is a pervasive discourse within the secular world and occupies a space at the heart of American culture.[76] Protestantism can thus occupy both a marginalized and a dominant subject position—an overlapping strategy that whiteness also invokes in constructing itself as a category.

This is significant because Christian pole dancers also maintain this ambivalent position as subjects, marginalized or dominant depending on gender, race, or class. As Griffith argues, the ability to afford dance fitness classes is tied to a leisure culture of wellness that is often a particularly white luxury. Ideally, fit bodies are effective agents of devotional intimacy, particularly in a racialized doctrine of slimness.[77] Since food has become readily available, the middle class's ability to control quality and intake has become a class differentiator, especially since poorer populations are statistically associated with higher obesity risks in the United States.[78] Middle-class white women tend to have a desire to be fit and healthy; they also have the means to accomplish it. In the case of Christian women, Griffith asserts that the body of the American white middle-class woman becomes a manifestation of God's will. Fat is a disease, a sin, a transgression, and food is a temptation. In a shift from salvation to self-realization, thinness is equated with godliness.[79] The health rhetoric of "Pole Dancing for Jesus" reflects this shift as Deans tries to make pole dance part of the self-realization process.

Still, Deans's own background as a working-class woman turned business owner complicates these assumptions. Her story preaches the achievable desire of middle-class respectability, a goal that not all the women who are taking the "Pole Dancing for Jesus" class necessarily aspire to or mirror. Building on the work of Beverly Skeggs, feminist scholar Esther Bott argues in her essay "Pole Position" that a primary driver for British lap dancers in Tenerife was respectability through class disidentification.[80] Bott reveals that Tenerife exotic dancers disassociate from the working-class body of the prostitute, and likewise, I assert that "Pole Dancing for Jesus" also disassociates itself from the working-class body of the exotic dancer. Even though Deans herself was an exotic dancer, she reproduces this distancing in a story she tells about exotic dancers who came to take her pole dancing classes in order to improve their job skills: "I've had probably three or four exotic dancers actually come in. They take two to three classes, realize it's hard work, don't want to hear what I have to say about trying to better themselves and get out of the business, and they don't come back . . . I ask them, Do you enjoy what you do? Because I disliked it a lot."

Deans, in order to invoke a portrayal of upward mobility through the morality of a middle-class business owner, must distance herself from the working-class body of the exotic dancer—who does not "realize" the immoral nature of her work. Deans's Protestant work ethic also emerges as a differentiating factor: professional strippers do not want to work hard enough to "get out of the business."

Deans "owns" her personal narrative that aligns with Christian discourses about bodily training and neoliberal conceptions of self-styling. Griffith speaks to a long Christian history in which women, in particular, equate bodily suffering (fasting, abstinence, etc.) with the suffering of Christ on the cross.[81] Thus, Deans's account of pole fitness as hard work continues this Christian ideology of bodily regulation and training that overcomes sinful flesh, gains middle-class respectability, and secures a relationship with Jesus Christ. Deans's description of spiritual journey plays into the expectation of self-realization based on religious bodily fashioning. If, as Jasbir Puar argues, modern individualism and neoliberalism are predicated on who is free to style themselves,[82] then the idea of overcoming the body and resisting temptation are fundamental components of individual success. Deans and these women in the studio gather to fashion the body of Christian, white, middle-class respectability through the molding of a healthy body and healthy sexuality. While their pursuit is suspect because of their gender status and fears of sexual excess, the dancers are largely able to invoke their right to worship through pole dancing even though they are critiqued by the media, blogosphere, and local citizens.

"Pole Dancing for Jesus," then, is actually helping to reify and constitute how a normative female sexuality might be defined. Puar's notion of self-styling is built upon Michel Foucault's theories on sexuality, which posit "one had to speak of it (sex) as of a thing to not be simply condemned or tolerated but managed, inserted into systems of utility."[83] "Pole Dancing for Jesus" provides a space where sex is experimented with as a utilitarian function of health. By operating at the fringes of acceptability, the perceived deviance of "Pole Dancing for Jesus" is reinscribed into the system, enabling religious women to negotiate their own relationship to health, sexuality, and Christianity. Although it is a transgressive testing of the limits, it is also integral to understanding what constitutes a Christian, white, middle-class respectability: Deans's dance studio operates at the fringes of the American religious landscape, shaping and contending with what a normalized female religious subject looks like, and what she dances like.

At the same time, agency was temporarily reclaimed as these women worked to reconcile their sexual and spiritual selves. Deans ministered to her students, providing a safe space where everyone's story could be heard. Women were able to think about and accept their sexuality in terms of their faith and marriage. They were able to get fit and have "fun" while exercising their right to worship. While the ideals that enabled the existence of this class were short-lived, the ambivalent tension surrounding the sexual Christian female body that ignited media outrage and international attention are still operating. As for Crystal Deans, although she is no longer in the "Pole Dancing for Jesus" industry, I suspect she will continue to advocate with the fiery yet resolute determination that made her an excellent media character in the first place. Perhaps Deans's most telling comment on the situation is stated in a sympathetic review she gave to the family-business "Duck Commander," whose television show *Duck Dynasty* has been loudly criticized for its radical Christian views. Deans said, "we are praying for you and all of the people against you. I ran a pole fitness studio in Spring, Texas and ran a free class for Christian women on Sundays. Media turned it into 'Pole Dancing for Jesus' and I received death threats and hate mail. I get it."[84]

Notes

1. Free Britney, "Pole Dancing for Jesus: Texas Girl Lives the Dream," *The Hollywood Gossip*, March 23, 2011, accessed June 7, 2011, http://www.thehollywoodgossip.com/2011/03/pole-dancing-for-jesus-texas-girl-lives-the-dream/; Steven Thomson, "Pole Dancing for Jesus Shakes Up Spring: Bearing the Cross Gets Sexy," *CultureMap Houston*, March 23, 2011, accessed May 8, 2017, http://houston.culturemap.com/news/city-life/03-23-11-pole-dancing-for-jesus-shakes-up-spring-when-bearing-the-cross-gets-sexy/.

2. Rick Chandler, "'Pole Dancing for Jesus' class somehow causes controversy," NBC *Off the Bench*, March 23, 2011, accessed June 7, 2011, http://offthebench.nbcsports.com/2011/03/23/pole-dancing-for-jesus-class-somehow-causes-controversy/.

3. Linda Tomko, *Dancing Class: Gender, Ethnicity, and Social Divides in American Dance, 1890–1920* (Bloomington: Indiana University Press, 1999); and Susan Leigh Foster, *Choreographing Empathy: Kinesthesia in Performance* (New York: Routledge, 2010).

4. Foster, *Choreographing Empathy*, 102.

5. Dominick Cavallo, *Muscles and Morals: Organized Playgrounds and Urban Reform, 1880–1920* (Philadelphia: University of Pennsylvania Press, 1981), 4.

6. Tomko, *Dancing Class*, 39.

7. Jane Addams, *Twenty Years at Hull-House with Autobiographical Notes* (New York: Macmillan, 1912).

8. Ibid., 128.

9. Ibid.; Foster, *Choreographing Empathy*, 102.

10. Foster, *Choreographing Empathy*, 118.

11. As quoted in R. Laurence Moore, *Selling God: American Religion in the Marketplace of Culture* (New York: Oxford University Press, 1994), 114.

12. Clifford Putney, "From Character to Body Building: The YMCA and the Suburban Metropolis," in *Men and Women Adrift: The YMCA and the YWCA in the City*, ed. Nina Mjagkij and Margaret Spratt (New York: New York University Press, 1997), 231.

13. Ibid., 232.

14. Clifford Putney, "Muscular Women," *Muscular Christianity: Manhood and Sports in Protestant America, 1880–1920* (Cambridge, MA: Harvard University Press, 2003), 144–61.

15. Sydney Ahlstrom, *A Religious History of the American People*, 2nd ed. (New Haven, CT: Yale University Press, 2004), 954.

16. Ibid., 951.

17. Putney, "From Character to Body Building," 234.

18. Growth could also be due to a proselytizing mission.

19. Ibid., 5.

20. Ibid., 7.

21. Foster, *Choreographing Empathy*, 120.

22. Zumba Fitness, accessed May 21, 2014, www.zumba.com.

23. Let's Move, accessed May 21, 2014, www.letsmove.gov.

24. Devoted Fitness, accessed May 21, 2014, www.devotedfitness.com.

25. Deans mentions in a follow-up with Fox News that she had received more than 200 phone calls for interviews, and she was only going to choose a few that she believed might provide better coverage and cites this as evidence of the fact that she is not trying to make money/get publicity. I tried to contact Deans multiple times and did receive one voicemail, but she never returned my call. See "Pole Dancing for Jesus Goes Global," *YouTube*, posted by ksalbrecht88, March 25, 2011, accessed May 8, 2017, https://www.youtube.com/watch?v=DbZr2wJVUHY.

26. I use "Pole Dancing for Jesus" because this phrase captured the public imaginary

of femininity/sexuality in dance rather than the masculinity/utilitarianism of sport fitness.

27. "Pole Dancing for Jesus?—The Cindy Davis Show," *YouTube*, posted by Jacob Hodgson, May 9, 2011, accessed May 8, 2017, https://www.youtube.com/watch?v=Mzhy_2fDXt4.

28. Ibid.

29. Much of this information is compiled from the company's Facebook page because the company website has been shut down. Best Shape of Your Life Facebook page, accessed May 21, 2014, https://www.facebook.com/pages/Best-Shape-of-Your-Life/124028607622373. When I tried to call the Best Shape of Your Life Studio in Spring, the administrator's only comment was that they no longer offer "Pole Dancing for Jesus" classes.

30. Ibid.

31. Ibid.

32. "Pole Dancing for Jesus?—The Cindy Davis Show."

33. Ibid.

34. Information on Deans's company can be found on Etsy at http://www.pinterest.com/stephaniehansco/same-as-never-on-etsy/.

35. R. Marie Griffith, *Born Again Bodies: Flesh and Spirit in American Christianity* (Berkeley: University of California Press, 2004), 5.

36. Ibid., 7–10, 247.

37. "Pole Dancing for Jesus?—The Cindy Davis Show."

38. Griffith, *Born Again Bodies*, 23, 67.

39. Kally Whitehead and Tim Kurz, "'Empowerment' and the Pole: A Discursive Investigation of the Reinvention of Pole Dancing as a Recreational Activity," *Feminism and Psychology* 19, no. 2 (2009): 224.

40. Ibid., 234.

41. "Pole Dancing for Jesus?—The Cindy Davis Show."

42. "Pole Dancing for Jesus," *YouTube*, posted by JesusLoveUYesHeDo, March 17, 2011, accessed May 8, 2017, https://www.youtube.com/watch?v=tplfas9OIFI.

43. "Pole Dancing for Jesus?—The Cindy Davis Show."

44. Ibid.

45. See "Pole Dancing for Jesus" and "Pole Dancing for Jesus?—The Cindy Davis Show."

46. "Pole Dancing for Jesus?—The Cindy Davis Show."

47. Whitehead and Kurz, "'Empowerment' and the Pole," 226.

48. "Pole Dancing for Jesus?—The Cindy Davis Show."

49. See Katherine Liepe-Levinson, *Strip Show: Performance of Gender and Desire* (London: Routledge, 2002).

50. International Pole Dance Fitness Association, "History of Pole," accessed May 21, 2014, http://ipdfa.com/about/history-of-pole/.

51. "Pole Dancing for Jesus?—The Cindy Davis Show."

52. Many of the strategies outlined in this section also align with the strategies used by early modern dancers to legitimize their practice within theatrical dance forms. From associations with the physical culture movement to the invocation of "high art," dancers like Isadora Duncan and Ruth St. Denis enabled modern dance to become a site of agency for women. This pursuit was often framed through spirituality and expressiveness in the homosocial sphere, similar to Pole Dancing for Jesus, although the modern dancers did perform in front of mixed audiences, unlike the dancers in this example.

53. Liepe-Levinson argues that "straight strip shows" often transgressed conventional gender representations even though her project's aim was to make dominant heterosexuality "strange." My analysis examines this material within the frame of heterosexual excess/deviant sexuality, though I acknowledge the possibility of homosexual or queer subtext. Liepe-Levinson, *Strip Show*, 4.

54. Susan Foster, "Closets Full of Dances," in *Dancing Desires: Choreographing Sexualities On and Off the Stage*, ed. Jane Desmond (Madison: University of Wisconsin Press, 2001), 150.

55. "Pole Dancing for Jesus?—The Cindy Davis Show."

56. Ibid.

57. Mark Oppenheimer, "Pole Dancing with a Big Difference: The Clothes Stay," *New York Times*, April 1, 2011, accessed May 21, 2014, http://www.nytimes.com/2011/04/02/us/02beliefs.html?_r=0.

58. Lynne Gerber, *Seeking the Straight and Narrow: Weight Loss and Sexual Reorientation in Evangelical America* (Chicago: University of Chicago Press, 2011), Kindle Edition.

59. Sherisse Pham, "Hallelujah! Christians Pole Dance for Jesus in Texas," *ABC News*, March 22, 2011, accessed May 21, 2014, http://abcnews.go.com/US/hallelujah-christians-pole-dance-jesus-texas/story?id=13194891.

60. The participant here self-identifies as heterosexual. Whitehead and Kurz, "'Empowerment' and the Pole," 237.

61. Douglas Rosenau, *A Celebration of Sex: A Guide to Enjoying God's Gift of Sexual Intimacy* (Nashville: Thomas Nelson, 2002).

62. Whitehead and Kurz, "'Empowerment' and the Pole," 226.

63. Griffith, *Born Again Bodies*, 220. Griffith argues that American feminism is often constructed as antithetical to the piety of Christian womanhood. See Saba Mahmood, *The Politics of Piety: The Islamic Revival and the Feminist Subject* (Princeton, NJ: Princeton University Press, 2005) as she asserts that we need to denaturalize the normative subject of liberal feminist theory because it often marginalizes women's religious experiences.

64. Quoted in Lindsay Goldwert, "'Pole dancing for Jesus' class mixes faith and fitness; Church going women offered free class," *New York Daily News*, March 24, 2011, accessed May 21, 2014, http://www.nydailynews.com/life-style/pole-dancing-jesus-class-mixes-faith-fitness-church-women-offered-free-class-article-1.118340.

65. Griffith, *Born Again Bodies*, 198.

66. Since "Pole Dancing for Jesus" was no longer offered at the time I began this research, I took this class to get a feel for the structure of a pole dance class. I am not claiming this class as representative of all pole dance classes, but rather use this as a counterexample to the representations that were presented by the media and Crystal Deans.

67. Spinarella website, accessed May 21, 2014, http://www.spinarella.com/testimonials-section.

68. "These constructions of God, particularly as a white man, have led some black women to see themselves as the farthest from "him," which, in turn helps solidify their marginalized place in society . . . the image of God as a white man is omnipresent and feeds into oppression." Nadine George-Graves, *Urban Bush Women: Twenty Years of African American Dance Theater, Community Engagement, and Working It Out* (Madison: University of Wisconsin Press, 2010), 149.

69. Audre Lorde, "Uses of the Erotic: The Erotic as Power," *Sister Outsider: Essays and Speeches* (New York: Crossing Press, 1984), 54.

70. Ibid., 56.

71. Ibid., 56.

72. "Pole Dancing for Jesus?—The Cindy Davis Show."

73. I want to be careful not to collapse whiteness and Christianity, while still considering their interrelationship with American identity. See Rey Chow, *The Protestant Ethnic and the Spirit of Capitalism* (New York: Columbia University Press, 2002); Janet Jakobsen and Ann Pellegrini, eds., *Secularisms* (Durham, NC: Duke University Press, 2008).

74. Gerber, *Seeking the Straight and Narrow*, 76.

75. Ibid., 82.

76. Ibid., 108.

77. Griffith, *Born Again Bodies*, 161.

78. Food Research and Action Center, "Relationship between Poverty and Overweight or Obesity," accessed May 21, 2014, http://frac.org/initiatives/hunger-and-obesity/are-low-income-people-at-greater-risk-for-overweight-or-obesity/.

79. Griffith, *Born Again Bodies*, 170.

80. Esther Bott, "Pole Position: Migrant British Women Producing 'Selves' through Lap Dancing Work," *Feminist Review*, No. 83, Sexual Moralities (2006), 23–41.

81. Griffith, *Born Again Bodies*, 24–26.

82. Jasbir Puar, *Terrorist Assemblages: Homonationalism in Queer Times* (Durham, NC: Duke University Press, 2007), 23.

83. Michel Foucault, *The History of Sexuality, Volume I* (New York: Vintage Books, 1990), 24.

84. Crystal Deans's Facebook Page, accessed January 6, 2015, https://www.facebook.com/cdeans10/reviews?pnref=lhc.

7

Dancing the Brand

Striptease, Corporeality, and Corporatization

JESSICA BERSON

My first visit to a strip club was in the fall of 2004. I was there not as a patron, but to take lessons in exotic dancing from a former stripper-turned-tutor named Michelle. I had answered Michelle's ad in *The New Haven Advocate*, and had met her one previous weeknight in the parking lot of a local KFC (where I had handed over a check for $150 for five sessions). I had no idea what to expect from the club, or even if Michelle would show up. I waited for her outside the club's entrance and watched men go in. When Michelle arrived, we went in together; though I later spent a lot of time at Backstage Bill's, that was the last time I used the front door.

In the club's foyer one of the bouncers agreed to waive the ten-dollar entrance fee and we walked past the main bar to another room that was used only for feature acts. On the way we passed a woman dancing on the stage who looked about thirty-five years old, swinging her ample hips to 1970s hard rock. She was wearing a thong, six-inch platforms, and nothing else. I wasn't really sure where to look, but I settled on her eyes, and she gave me a warm, sincere smile. In a room reserved for "feature dancers," away from the mainstage, Michelle gleefully turned on the smoke machine and the lights and put in a sultry R&B CD that easily drowned out the thin wailing of Led Zeppelin from next door. I was afraid she was going to ask me to take off my clothes, but she did something even scarier: she told me to get up on the stage and "dance sexy." I put on what (at the time) I considered high heels and did my best; but no matter what I did, she just repeated, in a voice that was somehow simultaneously encouraging and disappointed, "no, sexy. No, SEXY."

I started investigating striptease in part to ask what's sexy, to ask what kinds of movements are constructed as erotic by a dance form that depends on a legible expression of sexual excitement and desire. For about a year, dancing sexy became more than an esoteric, academic inquiry; it was also how I earned my living. Performing at Backstage Bill's in New Haven, Connecticut, and at Diamonds in Hartford, I discovered that dancing sexy assumed divergent meanings depending on who was dancing and who was watching, and I was surprised by the extent of the differences between the two clubs. My research as a practitioner granted me a kinesthetic understanding of striptease dancing and a first-person, embodied experience of the sense of erotic subjectivity that this dance form can offer female performers. However, when I began this research project, I was struck by how little attention most scholars paid to the actual dancing. In the past decade a number of autobiographical, historical, and critical accounts of striptease have emerged, but these discourses have often focused on anything and everything *but* dance.[1]

Perhaps this absence stems in part from the training and perspectives of many researchers who often work within disciplines other than dance or performance studies. Watching a childhood friend perform striptease, women's studies scholar Catherine Roach even muses, "'Dance' is perhaps not quite the right word for what the women do onstage."[2] In her preface to her book *Stripped: Inside the Lives of Exotic Dancers,* sociologist Bernadette Barton wrote about her distress at the quality of the dancing she saw during her first strip club visit. "Although I was in researcher mode and avidly entranced with the space, I still felt uncomfortable. I first noticed that the dancers lacked rhythm and grace; they literally could not find the beat. This lack of skill was incredibly distracting. Nor did their acts reflect any trained aesthetic, consisting largely of random gyrations in front of men, interspersed with apathetic meandering around a pole in the middle of the dance floor."[3] It's certainly possible that the dancers at this particular club weren't very good, or that the ones who might have been were having a bad night. But I wonder if Barton, like many others who write about striptease, is simply unable to recognize the dancing taking place before her eyes.

This isn't to say that striptease dance meets the aesthetic criteria usually applied to theatrical dancing; it is similarly disingenuous to argue that the idiom operates within (or toward) another set of criteria altogether, as might be said of certain other popular or nontraditional dance forms.[4] However, as a sometimes disorienting hybrid of theatrical dance, popular dance, and sex work, striptease dancing resists easy categorization as "good" or "bad," and the "skill(s)" that Barton missed—"grace" for example—have relative meanings and relevance from one form to another. In most clubs, stage performances have multiple purposes (some, but not all, of which overlap with those typical of theatrical and popular dance): to entertain and seduce audiences; display the dancer's body; engage individual audience members visually, verbally, and often physically; and, sometimes, to advertise the dancer's availability for private dances. If one is looking only for signs of skill or virtuosity in terms of concert dance—elongated extensions of the legs, high jumps, multiple turns, and so forth, which do in fact sometimes appear in striptease dancing—one will miss the display of skills more imperative to the form itself: those that constitute "dancing sexy."

I wish to add to the growing scholarly interest in exotic dance by addressing striptease as *dance*. Analyzing the dancing I both performed and witnessed at strip clubs led me toward an understanding of *how* striptease dancing can generate possibilities for erotic agency within its performance and also how those possibilities can be undermined and subverted. This approach also allowed me to investigate the ways in which exotic dance can be a site for corporate branding and to draw connections between the management of brand identity—advertising, interior design, costume—and the manipulation of movement vocabulary. Examining striptease as a mode of expression offers new possibilities for our understanding of the social, cultural, and political debates it provokes. And striptease does provoke. As Judith Lynn Hanna, who has written extensively on exotic dance, notes, "In a unique way, the stigmatized but poorly understood exotic (also referred to as erotic, striptease, stripper, topless, titty bar, nude, go-go, and barroom) dance clubs are a lightning rod for certain cultural conflicts in the United States."[5] The conflicts Hanna alludes to involve rifts between individual freedom and community standards, church and state, expression and repression. In her book *The Naked Truth: Strip Clubs, Democracy, and a Christian Right* (2012), Hanna describes how striptease has become a battleground in right-wing Christian political organizations' pervasive theocratic agenda. The religious attack that Hanna documents reveals a quintessentially American perspective on the meanings of exotic dance. However, in the final years of the twentieth century and the early years of the twenty-first, a new American force has come to dominate discourses on art, culture, and entertainment: the corporate brand. American brand identities have overtaken many of our most fundamental experiences in the United States and beyond—the way we eat, dress, speak, move. Striptease embodies an ongoing debate about the power of corporations and brands within every facet of our cultural and personal lives. Dancing at two clubs in Connecticut and talking with dancers who had worked in many others, I found that independently owned clubs often operated with an open-ended definition of what was sexy that could encompass diverse demographics and performance styles while corporate clubs tended toward homogeneity in club management, customer relations, and choreography. Starting in the 1970s with the advent of the "gentlemen's club"—and especially since the development of international strip club chains like Spearmint Rhino in the 1990s—dancing sexy has become a global commodity, draped in demographically designated accoutrements and stripped of its potential to create spaces for the expression of women's erotic pleasure—and power.

The Basic Moves in Black and White

At my second lesson with Michelle I was introduced to her business partner, Wes, a former Alvin Ailey dancer who worked as a male stripper. Wes knew his way around a pole, and because we shared a background in modern dance he was able to instruct me with more nuanced exhortations than "no, sexy." Each teacher assumed responsibility for passing on a different set of skills. Michelle taught me hip-rolls, floor work, poses, and shimmies. Wes focused on using the pole, developing a routine, and poise. Like Michelle, Wes wanted me to "dance sexy," but he had a specific methodology in mind: he insisted that the way to be sexy was to discover one's own movement preferences and then indulge and exaggerate them onstage. He thought that girls who like to move in quick sharp bursts should hone their edges and those who felt most sensual in sinuous, sustained movements should emphasize their fluidity—and that all dancers should explore the movement qualities that were opposite to their own in order to provide contrast and dynamic variation. According to Wes, different men liked different types of women and different types of movement qualities: the key to dancing sexy was to commit fully to a particular set of qualities, a specific persona.

As a dancer and Laban Movement analyst, I was intrigued by this individualized, movement-oriented approach to sexuality. However, once I began working as a stripper, I realized that the opportunity and appreciation for individual expression varied greatly depending on the venue. Like most dance idioms, exotic dance encompasses a specific set of technical and qualitative characteristics. These characteristics are in the process of being more broadly codified—and commodified—by the fitness industry under monikers like "strippercize," "cardiostrip," and "pole dancing for fun and fitness," and some teachers within the International Pole Dance Fitness Association (unsuccessfully) circulated a petition to include pole dancing in the 2012 London Olympics. However, despite current trends in a variety of industries—striptease itself, fitness, and mainstream entertainment—toward standardization, individual and cultural differences remain.

As I have noted, discussions of choreography are somewhat rare in striptease scholarship, and even very good analyses sometimes ignore differences in movement vocabularies that may be tied to race and/or class. Both Hanna and Liepe-Levinson provide lucid descriptions of dance moves that they observed during wide-ranging studies of primarily white, heterosexual clubs in the United States in the 1990s. Hanna approaches her subject as an anthropologist and movement analyst and categorizes movements in terms of locomotion, gesture, place, levels, costuming, and so on. She writes: "In exotic dance, the performer uses body movements often simulating culturally constituted rhythms of lovemaking, for example flirting, foreplay, and intercourse ... The semantics of exotic dance draw heavily upon metaphor and metonym expressed through a dance-vocabulary of movements highlighting secondary sex characteristics, such as breasts, buttocks, and hips, in addition to the genitals."[6] Hanna brings attention to the aesthetic values of exotic dancing and to the fact that those values are "culturally constituted." She delineates specific movements such as crawling on the floor, hip rotations, breast shimmies and various kinds of self-touch, including intimate exposures that Hanna calls "going pink." Many of these movements are highly stylized, and can be only tangentially imagined as representing actual sexual activity. Rather, they participate in a particular cultural construction of sexuality: one that is largely white, heterosexual, middle class, and American.

Liepe-Levinson devotes two chapters of her book to choreography and brings a more critical perspective to her descriptions. She notes "basic moves" like the shimmy, the bump and grind, body stroking, and the strut, and provides a historical context for each. She describes early striptease[7] as "a whole-body choreography that defied conventional ideas about the naturally sedate, physically contained comportment of females, which included the old adage of the night—'Ladies do not move.'"[8] From this perspective, striptease dancers asserted their erotic subjectivity not only through their radical demonstrations that ladies do in fact move, but through the "whole-body"-ness of their choreography: rather than isolating body parts, these dancers moved as fully integrated, complete bodies. Performing solo, they confronted audiences with directness and humor, often commenting on their dancing as they danced.[9] Though they may have been performing for the titillation of a male audience, early striptease dancers also enacted new visions of female empowerment.

Liepe-Levinson's central argument is that striptease disrupts as much as reinforces stereotypical gender norms, and she perceives this paradox in some of the movements she describes. For example, of the bump and grind, she states:

> The image of an upright, glamorous Burlesque queen gyrating her way through a routine may indeed represent quintessential striptease through her portrayal of an ultra- or hyper-femininity. However, the actual movement of the bump and grind, especially when highlighted by the prone position of the stripper, are arguably more in keeping with the social expectations about the aggressive activity of males during sex (vis-à-vis various pelvic thrusting and grindings). Since prone-position bumping and grinding so clearly refers to masturbation and copulation, and since these moves suggest the "active" sex partner as well, such performances by female strippers are doubly transgressive.[10]

Liepe-Levinson writes that her focus on white, heterosexual clubs was informed by her broader interest in investigating "the strangeness of [her] own political and personal spheres."[11] In my own experience and observations, however, prone-position bumping and grinding was a move that was considered "low class" by many girls and performed more often in working-class clubs and by nonwhite dancers.[12]

Backstage and in online communities like stripperweb.com, dancers designate some moves as trashy, or classy, or slutty, or "trying too hard." In most clubs, dancers make use of the floor in their performances, crawling sinuously and demonstrating flexibility with exaggerated stretches. However, many older dancers, especially those who have worked in shadier venues, view the floor with the disgust of a germophobe, and perceive dancing on the floor as degrading. Similarly, violating the smooth surface of the body by "going pink"—spreading the labia and allowing audiences to peer inside—is often construed as vulgar by dancers aiming for "class."

Some dancers perform dazzling gymnastic routines on the pole, while others maintain that the introduction of the pole destroyed the art of striptease

Figure 7.1. Dancer at New York City Club. Photograph by Elyssa Goodman.

dancing by reducing a subtle idiom to base tricks. While much of the movement vocabulary of striptease is utilized across class, race, and venue-specific lines, certain movements are classified as markers of particular matrices of identity. Strip club conglomerates like Rick's Cabaret reify these differences by designing different clubs for different demographics—"high-end" clubs that cater to "white collar businessmen," rougher clubs for "working men," and venues like Club Onyx for "black and Hispanic professionals and athletes," each under its own brand name.[13]

Even within the confines of a single club, there are often differences between what kinds of movement dancers and customers perceive as sexy. Exotic dancers describe their performances as largely improvisational; as in contact improvisation, there are technical skills and combinations, but they are employed in an ad hoc, flexible framework. On stripperweb.com, a "newbie" forum offers advice from experienced dancers. In response to a query about "the basic moves," Mia M. wrote: "The three basic stripper moves: 1) Move slowly;

2) Make eye contact; 3) Smile. Anything else you do is just icing on the nekkid cake." Other dancers wrote: "Just go up there and do what feels natural. Don't make a routine because it will look scripted and boring . . . As long as you are having fun, that's all that matters." And: "Just relax. People are usually busy looking at your body before they get all hung up on your choreography. I would advise trying to be 'smooth' and sexy in your movements . . . the first week I danced I was advised about this."[14]

For customers, on the other hand, the main objective of striptease dance may be the advantageous display of key body parts. A male patron, Phil-W., added, "Excellent advice . . . The average dancer will try to put on a sexy/sensual show by moving in the most seductive way. The average customer, driven by your standard basic male instinct, will be trying to get the best view of the finer points of your anatomy . . . Sorry to sound cynical about this, but having good moves is probably secondary to making sure your customer has the best possible look at you."[15] The dancerly directions to "move slowly" and "be smooth" seem in line with the customer's desire to "get the best view": it is certainly easier to visually apprehend the parts of the whole if that whole isn't swiftly slipping into new configurations. However, presenting "the finer points of your anatomy" is antithetical to the whole-body choreography of early striptease—a fixation with specific parts diminishes the ability to appreciate the whole.

Backstage Bill's

After three lessons, Michelle declared me ready to go on stage. I auditioned for Bill, the proprietor of Backstage Bill's and its semi-attached sister club Backdoor Bill's, a "juice bar" that featured full nudity.[16] I performed for the first time that night, as "Jessie," in a pseudo-cowgirl costume pieced together from items from the Salvation Army, and then began dancing several shifts a week. I had performed as a "straight" dancer for years and had my training with Michelle and Wes to buoy my confidence, but I was in no way prepared for the rigors of my new gig.

Exotic dancers are usually considered independent contractors, rather than employees. Dancers do not get paid by the club, but rather pay the club "house fees" (anything from forty to one hundred dollars or more per shift) for the privilege of working there.[17] In most cases, if a dancer doesn't earn enough money to make the house fee on a given night she is still required to pay it, and thus ends up losing money after a long, depressing night's work. If she's late to her shift, or drunk, or bothers the bouncer, she gets fined between fifty and one hundred dollars; if she fails to show up for a shift she gets fired. Dancers make some money from tips for stage dances, but most of their income comes from private or lap dances, which usually take place in a separate area of the club and pay twenty dollars per song. Stage dances thus serve not only to entice the audience to give tips, but also to advertise for lap dances. This means that the dance has to embody a specific kind of sexual expression that entertains in the moment but also promises that more and better might be available in the future, in private, for a price. And the performance doesn't end when the dancer leaves the stage—she stays in character as she mingles with the customers trying to garner lap dances.

Christina, the Rubenesque thirty-five-year-old I had observed at my first lesson, was just one of many dancers at Backstage Bill's who did not conform to a stereotypical bourgeois image of lithe sexual availability. Christina had recently had a Caesarian section, and worried that the audience might see her scar; another older dancer, Heather, always wore thigh-high boots so that she could conceal her knee braces.[18] There were many African American dancers, often attractive younger women who might have been working at more upscale clubs had they been white. There were dancers from Colombia, the Dominican Republic, and Venezuela, dancers from Russia and other parts of the former USSR, dancers from down the street, dancers over forty, dancers who were tiny, dancers who were tall, and dancers who were quite robust, even chubby. Summer had a degree in psychology from UCLA and had previously run her own S&M dungeon in Beverly Hills; Heather was home-schooling her daughter using her own mixture of Montessori and Rudolf Steiner methods; some dancers had never attended high school; many lived from night to night, staying in motels because they couldn't save enough money for a deposit and first-month's rent.[19] Although the milieu of the strip club is not commonly considered by organizations promoting diversity, it often seemed to me that the population of dancers at Backstage Bill's could have been put on a poster for multiculturalism.

This diversity and eccentricity was reflected in the choreography and the performance qualities that unfolded on stage. Though they might not have been as articulate as Wes in describing what they were doing, many dancers seemed to subscribe to his philosophy of highly individualized expression. Foxy, a statuesque African American woman who favored 1970s cat-suits and a glorious beehive wig, employed a lot of disco moves in her dances, swinging her head around in a circle in the vertical plane and adapting John Travolta's strutting moves from *Saturday Night Fever*. Like many other performances at the club, Foxy's routines were idiosyncratic, not easily categorized or labeled: she borrowed from a range of pop-culture references and dance styles that crossed stereotypical borders of gender and race. Quite the opposite of Foxy's fierceness, two Venezuelan sisters gently rocked their hips while they gazed ecstatically into space: their dance style seemed to be aimed at keeping basically still so that customers' attention could linger on their otherworldly beauty (one version of "the best possible look"). Marissa, a willowy young dancer from Ukraine, levitated upside-down around the pole with ease. Angelique performed urgently quick hip-shimmies and prone-position bump and grinds, always laying a protective towel on the floor beforehand. A large bouncy blonde from Las Vegas, Summer employed humor in her performance, making eye contact and conversation with customers and castigating them if they didn't tip her well enough. In Hanna's terms, some of the dancing at Backstage Bill's was more metonymic than metaphoric: for some dancers dancing sexy meant an embellished pantomime of sexual intercourse. For others, however, performing "sexy" meant flirting; for still others, laughter or even a display of the dancer's own erotic pleasure.

Certain elements of striptease movement vocabulary meshed well with the dancing I already knew. I enjoyed the feeling of freedom from gravity that the pole allowed, and developed a few relatively simple phrases that I could use on stage. Striptease dance, like a number of contemporary dance techniques, emphasizes a multiunit use of the torso (an articulation of the hips separate from movements of the ribcage and shoulders), successive flow of motion through the joints (wavelike, "smooth" movements of the upper body), and an implicit and explicit acknowledgment of the pelvis as the center. Letting movement flow with fully realized shifts of weight from one leg to the other and allowing for a rhythm of suspension and release felt both instinctive and sensual to me, and I enjoyed the feeling that I could choreograph for the sake of how the movement felt, rather than just how it looked—that my subjective experience of the movement was connected to the objective experience of the viewer.

Diamonds

Diamonds is just outside of Hartford, Connecticut, about an hour north of Backstage Bill's. Situated on a service road of I-91, the club boasts a well-lit, video-monitored parking lot and a covered walkway between its topless and fully nude sections, through which the scantily clad dancers scurry back and forth during the New England winter. Dark plush carpet covers the floors, and the circular bar is more prominent than the small stage. I called ahead to ask about auditioning and had been told to come on a Tuesday evening. I was directed to a surprisingly formal-looking office in the back and after filling out some paperwork (something Backstage Bill's would never have tolerated), my "audition" consisted of removing the costume that I had carefully chosen for the occasion—I didn't have to dance at all.

Somehow I was hired, despite being ten years older and twenty pounds heavier than the vast majority of the other dancers. And there were a lot of other dancers: while Backstage Bill's might have fifteen dancers working at one time, Diamonds often had sixty or more, all of whom looked very much alike. With few exceptions, the dancers at Diamonds were eighteen to twenty-four years old, white, very thin and fit, with straight shoulder-length blond or light brown hair. None of the dancers could be described as "Rubenesque" (though certainly some of the customers might), and none were as athletically muscular as some of the dancers at Backstage Bill's; the dancers' bodies looked as though they had been meticulously groomed for being seen rather than trained for *doing* anything. Their costumes were almost always skimpy dresses, most of which would have been almost acceptable at any dance club—there were no disco cat-suits or cowgirls. There were also no scars, wrinkles, bulges, and certainly no pubic hair. These were Bakhtinian "classical" bodies, defined by a "closed, smooth, impenetrable surface."[20] They stood in opposition to the "grotesque" body, "composed of fertile depths and procreative convexities,"[21] and instead corresponded with "aspirations of bourgeois individualism."[22] The dancers took on this image in their performances on stage. They all moved in sustained, curvilinear phrases, gently stroking their bodies, never making quick or sharp movements. Walking around the perimeter of the small stage, dancers scanned the audience for likely private customers.

Most of the dancing at Diamonds exhibited variations of what Laban Movement Analysis calls Remote State: a combination of the Efforts Space and Flow. The Space Effort is associated with vision and focus, with seeing as opposed to feeling. Diamonds dancers moved with a heightened awareness of their presentation of the "best possible look"; however, their own focus was often vaguely centered on a spot just a few inches away from themselves, part of a version of Remote State termed "Inner Remote." Inner Remote is what one might observe in someone playing a video game, watching television, or hanging out at a boring party—someone going with the flow, paying some sort of attention to something, but not engaged in a meaningful, embodied way with anything. It is an Effort State befitting the smooth, placid classical body: A direct look, a return of the gaze, would implicate the dancer in the complex and necessarily grotesque realm of sexuality and desire.

What was strikingly missing from performances at Diamonds was Weight Effort. Weight is about the mover sensing herself, and perceiving Weight is how we sense her presence; without it, it is nearly impossible to make a connection to another person. Weight Effort is also necessary for any sort of "dancing sexy" that mimics or refers to actual sex. At Diamonds, there were no pelvic thrusts, no shimmies, and no bumping and grinding. No one could be said to be transgressively imitating the "active" role in sexual intercourse. The dancing at Diamonds was all about metaphor, but not metaphors for sex; rather, sex was deployed as a metaphor for consumption. Unlike the raw sexuality of much of the movement at Backstage Bill's, the dancing at Diamonds catered to an American fantasy of delightfully clean, uniform women who could be purchased and consumed.

Because there were so many dancers working at the same time, several dancers would go onstage at once. The overflow of dancers also meant that I worked mostly with strangers on every shift. The prevailing attitude among the dancers was one of competition rather than camaraderie: I got to know many of the dancers at Backstage Bill's, but hardly went beyond a stage-name basis with anyone at Diamonds. Dancers were alienated not just from one another, but also from our customers. Customers were for the most part quite guarded, bracing themselves for the hard hustle necessitated by the dancer-to-customer ratio, and I never developed relationships with regulars as I did at Backstage Bill's. Although an overabundance of dancers might seem to be a boon to customers, for whose attention dancers then have to compete, it compromises the possibilities for intimacy that may have drawn them to a strip club in the first place. For the same reason, I also had my worst-paid night at Diamonds, despite its opulent surroundings and rich clientele, bringing home just eleven dollars (after my eighty-dollar payout) for a seven-hour shift.

Figure 7.2. Dancer at New York City Club. Photograph by Elyssa Goodman.

The diversity of both dancers and customers at Backstage Bill's made the process and meanings of class distinction complicated and dynamic while power relations were more fluid. Conversely, Diamonds created a relentless message of rigid class difference: the physical layout of the club positioned most tables far from the tiny stage; dressing rooms were cramped and dilapidated; work regulations were formal and strictly enforced; the décor was richly appointed; drinks were expensive with no discount for dancers; and the number of dancers in competition with each other was excessive. Although outside the club the dynamics might shift, within the club dancers were workers, at the economic mercy of the clientele as well as the management. On weekend shifts, the DJ played Mötley Crüe's "Girls, Girls, Girls!"[23] five times a night, each play signaling to dancers that no matter where we were or what we were doing, when we heard the song we were to drop everything and rush to the dressing room.

There we were given copies of the club's current calendar, which we were meant to hawk to the audience. We were lined up and paraded swiftly across the stage as if in a beauty pageant and then forced to swarm into the audience trying to sell a package deal of a calendar and a lap dance for twenty-five dollars. If one were lucky enough to convince someone to take this deal (which for me was rare), one had to turn fifteen dollars over to the manager for the calendar, thus being paid half the usual rate for the dance. For me, this ritual highlighted everything that is wrong with the conflation of corporate and corporeal culture: as dancers, we were packaged, standardized, and managed in the same way as the shrink-wrapped calendars we were pushing on our customers.

Dancing in the Brandscape

The crucial difference between Backstage Bill's and Diamonds—what explains the differences in the populations of dancers and customers, in the décor, in the working conditions, in the dancing—is that Backstage Bill's is a strip club, but Diamonds is a brand. In her widely influential book *No Logo*,[24] Naomi Klein offers a working definition of "brand": "Think of the brand as the core meaning of the modern corporation, and of the advertisement as one vehicle used to convey that meaning to the world."[25] In her introduction to the tenth anniversary edition of *No Logo*, reflecting on the decade since its publication, Klein writes that in the 1990s, "corporate epiphanies were striking CEOs like lightning bolts from the heavens: Nike isn't a running shoe company, it's *about the idea of transcendence through sports*."[26] Whether the brand is the meaning of the corporation or the corporation merely one extension of the brand is an open question; unlike goods and services, brands take on a life of their own. A brand doesn't reside within the bounds of its corporate logo, its products, or its managers; rather it is continually constituted through interrelationships among consumers, companies, and cultures. Brands are so inextricably interwoven into "culture, politics, and ideology," according to Jonathan Schroeder and Miriam Salzer-Moring that "we live in a branded world: brands infuse culture with meaning, and brand management exerts a profound influence on contemporary society."[27] While Klein (along with a growing anticorporate political movement) bemoans the ever-increasing power of brands in every facet of cultural life, brand managers work ceaselessly to convince consumers to participate in a joint effort to not merely buy but "live the brand."[28]

While discussions about corporate influences on cultural production often involve questions of commodification, for this discussion branding is a more cogent concern. In *Global Culture Industry: The Mediation of Things*, Scott Lash and Celia Lury draw valuable distinctions between commodities and brands: "The commodity is produced. The brand is the source of production. The commodity is a single, discrete, fixed product. The brand instantiates itself in a range of products, is generated across a range of products. The commodity has no history; the brand does. The commodity has no relationships; the brand is constituted in and as relations. . . . The commodity is dead; the brand is alive. . . . The brand [is a] quality of *experience*. This experience is situated at the interface—or surface—of communication of the consumer and the brand. It is part of events; it is eventive."[29] This language strikes me as somewhat hyperbolic, but the breathless energy in Lash and Lury's and Klein's writing reflects the overwhelming power that brands assert in our cultural, social, political, and, as I experienced firsthand, erotic lives. Diamonds isn't merely its two Connecticut outposts, it is also calendars, merchandise, and a reputation as "the Scores[30] of Hartford": as one online reviewer writes, "Diamonds is not a place to go for a beer and some laughs. Rather, it is a night out and an experience to be remembered."[31]

Both experience and the memories experience generates reinforce the consumer's relationship with the brand, and thus contribute to the ongoing process of the brand's development. More and more since the 1990s, corporations have created physical spaces in which this relationship can be further elaborated and embodied. These spaces—such as Niketown or Apple stores—serve as "brandscapes," places in which interior design, customer service, sound, costume, and the movements and activities of both employees and consumers are coordinated and controlled to generate allegiance to the brand.[32] Diamonds is confined to New England, but other corporate clubs, like Rick's Cabaret and Spearmint Rhino, are global brands that extend into Europe, Asia, the former Soviet Union, and South America. Moreover, they exert a hegemonic influence: the power of global brands is such that they "shape consumer lifestyles and identities by functioning as cultural models that consumers act, think, and feel through."[33] In the 1990s Spearmint Rhino,[34] for instance, established a mode of being and doing in strip clubs that became a model for other "gentlemen's clubs": its plush furniture, animal-printed wallpaper, noncharacter costumes, flat screen televisions showing sporting events, and scripted conversations between dancers and customers are reiterated in clubs from Las Vegas to London to Moscow. Cultural model brands create modes of behavior, for both dancers and customers are shaped and standardized through surveillance, interior design, and indirect and direct regulation. For example, the Spearmint Rhino dancer contract, in use throughout its empire, specifies choreographic, costume, and customer interactions in immense detail and includes proscriptions against inviting spouses to the club or allowing customers to dance; it also contains a proviso that "The dancer warrants to the Client [Spearmint

Rhino] that she will continue to keep herself fit and ensure that she has all the necessary skills to perform dancer services."[35] It is hard to imagine an aspect of the activities and experiences of dancers or customers that is not regulated: the basic dancer contract is approximately forty-five pages, and some location-specific versions are eighty pages long.

This kind of standardization and regulation is part of what George Ritzer calls "McDonaldization": the increasing branding and franchising of all kinds of service industries through efficiency, calculability, predictability, and corporate control of employees and consumers. Sociologists Barbara Brent and Katherine Hausbeck apply Ritzer's theory to sex work in their 2002 essay "McDonaldization of the Sex Industries? The Business of Sex," focusing largely on Nevada's legal brothels. They note a number of strategies through which interactions that most people would characterize as deeply personal and idiosyncratic are regulated and controlled: the introduction of "club money" (often referred to as "funny money" in clubs), "Taylorization" of sex acts,[36] centralization of management, and enforced predictability in the comportment and language of workers. The "sublime irony of McDonaldized sex," they write, is that "It is the bureaucratically ordered structure that makes certain kinds of consumer pleasures possible and that creates a larger range of consumers for the growing adult industry, even as this process leads to greater dehumanization, less diversity of desires, and more stratification."[37] The corporate chain structure creates more and more easily accessible spaces in which consumers can enjoy striptease and legitimizes that enjoyment through branding. However, that structure also inevitably alters the very enjoyment it claims to proliferate, necessarily encoding, classifying, and containing intimate and unruly desires.

Brent and Hausbeck's description of McDonaldized brothels matches my feelings about dancing at Diamonds and my observations at other corporate clubs. However, as a model for examining the process of corporatization in striptease, McDonaldization doesn't adequately address the ways that branding agendas have permeated—or as Klein would argue, colonized—the *experiences* of both dancers and customers. And, in fact, Hausbeck and Brent revised their thinking a few years later, in "Marketing Sex: US Legal Brothels and Late Capitalist Consumption," arguing: "This 'McDonaldization' of services relies on rationalized work processes, centralized workspaces, controlled environments, interactive scripts, standardized employment contracts and highly predictable production/consumption rituals to increase efficiency and profit and standardize emotional services. However, as the service industry has become more touristic, these rationalized outcome-oriented approaches have given way to decentralized, do-it-yourself workers compelled to sell uniqueness, variety, and individuality."[38] Despite the actual standardization of service work, consumers often want to feel that their experiences are personal and unique, especially within the "intimate" realm of sex work. Experience is the key bearer of the brand, as Lash and Lury (and numerous other marketing scholars) note, and in the 1990s became a new frontier for brand managers. While the 1980s were characterized by the conspicuous consumption of physical objects—Nike sneakers, Guess jeans, Sony Walkmen—the 1990s saw a shift toward a desire for consumable experiences—"a night out and an experience to be remembered."

By the mid-1990s, however, these sorts of experiential "economic outputs"[39] were no longer sufficient to satisfy consumers' growing need for a feeling of connection or purpose: as David Norton notes in "Towards Meaningful Brand Experiences," in a cultural moment sodden with irony and skepticism, consumers "looked to experiential offerings as a way of getting more enjoyment out of their time, and, importantly, as a means of feeling connected, important, and understood."[40] I can think of no better description of the type of experience that is bought and sold at a strip club. Strip clubs offer consumers multiple layers of meaning and fulfillment: a connection to other customers through the shared experience of spectatorship; a sense of importance derived from both the customer's ability to purchase intimate moments with dancers and from his presence in a taboo space; and, essentially, a feeling of being understood by individual dancers.

This marketing of meaning and emotion calls to mind an alternative model to McDonaldization: what Alan Bryman calls "Disneyization," the "process by which *the principles* of the Disney theme parks are coming to dominate more and more sectors of American society as well as the rest of the world," through theming, hybrid consumption, merchandising, and performative labor.[41] Addressing inevitable comparisons with Ritzer's McDonaldization, Bryman writes that Disneyization operates in "a consumerist world in which McDonaldization has wrought homogeneity and in its place projects an ambience of choice, difference, and frequently the spectacular."[42] Certainly the promotion of emotional labor—the demand that Disney theme park workers act out enthusiasm and charm despite debilitating working conditions for example[43]— and of consumable fantasy—as in the parks' motto "Where dreams come true"—are strategies of upscale and corporate strip clubs as well. Dancers must

Figure 7.3. Dancer at New York City Club. Photograph by Elyssa Goodman.

perform not just the choreography of striptease, but its spoken and gestural scores of ease, sexiness, and empathy, regardless of the bodily and/or emotional injuries they may be experiencing on any given night. As in other Disneyized environments, customers at corporate strip clubs are encouraged to choose among individual members of a usually quite uniform field of dancers, and to revel in the spectacle of fleshy display. I also imagine that the percentage of dreams coming true at most strip clubs is about the same as that at Disney World, and the irrational persistence of those dreams equally robust.

However, Disneyization overlooks the interplay of standardization and emotional labor that operates in a number of servicescapes, including strip clubs. Corporate strip clubs depend on a cunning combination of standardization and regulatory authority and a calculated deployment of emotional labor and fantasy. With my tongue only partly planted in my cheek, I would like to propose yet another iconic-American-brand-based "-ization" that might better serve an analysis of corporate striptease: Starbucksization. Starbucks combines the assembly line methods of McDonald's with the experiential and emotional engagement of Disney World. As Naomi Klein notes, "Starbucks isn't a coffee shop chain, it's about *the idea of community*."[44] In a 2006 interview, Starbucks CEO Howard Shultz stated, "We're in the business of human connection and humanity, creating communities in a third place between home and work."[45] Although corporate chains might seem anathema to the very notion of a third place, Starbucks's "staggering success is due in large part to its skill in creating, standardizing, and implementing an upscale third-place ambiance on a global scale."[46] The ambiance of Starbucks alludes to a nostalgically imagined, European(ish) café, but not to the extent that the a/illusion comes into conflict with the actual, often suburban, and very much American servicescape. The emergence of Starbucks-produced CDs and films,[47] played at and sold through its cafes, extends the brand and reinforces the notion that Starbucks is a lifestyle far more than it is a place to get a cup of coffee.

Expressed through décor, food and beverage offerings, displays of logoed merchandise, and sound design, the Starbucks lifestyle conjures an upscale but not uptight sensibility, inviting patrons to imagine themselves into a privileged-class identity as they enter into the brandscape. Though the products and services are different, the invitation—or, depending on one's perspective, imperative—Starbucks offers consumers is similar to that extended by Diamonds and other corporate strip club chains. Strip clubs, like coffee shops or pubs, act as a third place, and Starbucks's strategic staging and standardization of emotional experiences can serve as a way of understanding similar processes undertaken in clubs. Starbucks, unlike McDonald's or Disney, embeds indicators of class identification in its brandscapes, and serves up daydreams of upward mobility with every Venti Skinny Vanilla Latte. As at Starbucks, what is being bought and sold in strip club chains is not simply a commodity, but a branded, theatricalized experience that engages the customer's emotional, embodied imagination. But while Starbucks inculcates warm and fuzzy feelings about expensive coffee and coffeelike drinks, lite jazz, and Fair Trade, the experiential offerings of corporate strip clubs are designed to link intimacy to class aspiration and connect intimations of erotic pleasure to the pleasures of consumption.

Play to Pay

All experiential brands depend to some extent on fantasy: we dream of becoming star athletes in Nike sneakers, of being hip and tech savvy with our iPods and iPads, of being upper-middle class—but not stuffily so—in Starbucks cafes.[48] Our capacity to imagine and embody potential fulfillment is part of the process through which corporations bind us to brands. At strip clubs, however, fantasy is both process and product in a heightened way, because the fantasies in play are (at least superficially) explicitly sexual, intimate, and taboo.

The room created for sexual expression, the sense of excess and transgression, and the uncertain but often invoked borders that separate life in the club from life outside point toward an understanding of the strip club as not only a third place, but in some sense as a third *space*—a space beyond the spheres of social norms and hierarchies, a liminal (or "liminoid"[49]) space in which power relationships and social identities are contested. How strip clubs function as such spaces has been extensively discussed elsewhere;[50] what I hope to bring attention to here are the ways in which corporate marketing agendas have overtaken a potentially subversive place/space that might at first seem resistant to such occupation.

Of course strip clubs, like many other "liminal" spaces, are also—and always have been—sites of commerce and consumption.[51] However, there is still a difference between dancing wildly in a thrift store getup at Backstage Bill's and swaying gently in a low-cut evening gown at Diamonds—there is a difference between dancing a commodity and dancing a brand. Strip clubs, like the live music events described by Naomi Klein in *No Logo*, have been colonized by brands;[52] but while Klein decries a branded world in which "art v commerce is no longer a battle but rather a *coup d'état*,"[53] the branding that takes place in strip clubs is enacted not only through corporate sponsorship and logos, but through the bodies of dancers. The processes by which this branding occurs involve dictates from management (mandating minimum six-inch heels, for example); directions and limitations imposed by space and interior design (a small stage, or the presence or absence of a pole); and the ineffable, intractable club culture continually generated by management, customers, and dancers (appreciation of certain movement vocabularies and the denigration of others, contact expectations of lap dances, and so on).

In *Performing Consumers: Global Capital and Its Theatrical Seductions*, Maurya Wickstrom explores the ways that corporations employ the emotional labor of consumers in order to generate fealty to their brands. In strip clubs, both customers and dancers function as producers and consumers—both create and consume the fantasies and experiences that are the "products" of striptease—and both perform a specific kind of emotional labor. Wickstrom terms this type of labor "corporate performance" and argues that it is linked to our capacity for imitation and make-believe, writing that, "Through the sheer force of our embodied identifications, our mimetic aptitude, we can create a made up real which calls into question the veracity of any determining original. We can play in a strange doubleness, creating something that is not real but feels as if it were. Mimetic theatricality moves us onto the spectrum of the really made up. . . . this mimetic content of the theatrical [has] little to do with truthful imitation, and everything to do with the productive capacities of embodiment and the protean self."[54] When we move through the line at Starbucks, speaking lines in "really made up" Italian and consuming highly sweetened, "really made up" coffee drinks, we act out the brand with our voices and bodies as well as our imaginations. At Diamonds and other corporate strip clubs, dancers and customers perform a demographically designated brand that shapes erotic desire in much the same way that Starbucks inculcated a global taste for frothy lattes. Every time I donned a hot pink dress I had bought at the mall or eschewed floor work for yet another strut around the pole, I lived and moved its upper middle-class, middle brow, white, "lite" brand of sexuality, one which seemed all too appropriate to its location on the outskirts of a city that had once been touted as the insurance capital of the world.

Conclusions and Transgressions

In the world of performance and dance studies, we like to look to the ways that the body rebels against authority; as Terry Eagleton notes, "there is something in the body which can revolt against power which inscribes it."[55] However, this optimistic focus fails to take into account how we capitulate to power through modes of embodiment and play that are almost exclusively described in terms of subversion or transgression. The fluid, multiple, labile subjectivity that mimetic play encourages—our ability to imagine and act out other selves and other worlds—is precisely what makes us vulnerable to corporate power. Through the playful performance of our embodied imaginations, we can become whatever the brand tells us we want to be, and then become something else, and something else again, as demanded by the different "brand worlds"[56] through which we wander.

It would serve my argument if I could write that I stopped stripping because I felt so oppressed by the homogeneity and weightlessness of the culture at Diamonds, but that is not the entire story. At the root of my decision was a simple truth, one that is not present for many dancers: I had a choice to stop because I had other options. I wasn't living night-to-night at the local Days Inn and, although at one point during my stripping year my bank account dropped to forty-three dollars, I knew I had family and friends and a supportive partner who would help me make my rent. However, my experiences at Diamonds did spur me to quit stripping, and quitting was in some sense as personally momentous as starting. Stripping had allowed me to move in new ways, to embody new and sometimes uncomfortable ideas about myself as both a desiring subject and an object of desire. Performing this kind of dance, and having my performances appreciated by customers, changed the way I felt about my body: always considered "voluptuous" (a frequently deployed euphemism in the dance world for "fat") in the realm of concert dance, the excesses of my body were valued in striptease, and I grew to value them, too. I developed a deeper embodied understanding of Weight Effort and the power of moving to fulfill my own kinesthetic and erotic sensibilities rather than solely attempting to imitate the movements of a choreographer or please an audience.

But there was something almost uncannily familiar from other service jobs in stripping at Diamonds: subject to management guidelines, costumes became uniforms; improvisations became routines; conversations became scripts. The mandate to "play" made playing impossible. I began to resent the club and the customers, and to commit small acts of resistance: I wore four-inch heels rather than the regulation six, and once danced without shoes at all; I showed up late with long, fake excuses, delivered with "real" tears, just to see if I could act well enough to avoid the fine; I dressed in bizarre, bondage-ish costumes that I knew no one at the club would like. Finally, I did something that I knew would mean I could never return to the club: I pocketed the fifteen dollars I earned on a calendar sale and lied to the house manager, telling him, straight-faced, that of course I had given him the calendar back as usual. With sixty girls working the shift, I knew there was a chance he wouldn't catch me, but I also knew that he thought that strippers were lying thieves in any case—and that now I had become one. It was time to go.

In decrying strip clubs, anti–sex industry feminists often argue that dancers aren't merely objectified, but (insert horrified gasp here) commodified, that their bodies are being bought and sold very nearly as they might be in prostitution. However, as in other forms of service and sex work, what is for sale at a strip club isn't a physical commodity—even one as fantastic as a woman's body—but an experience, a "means of feeling connected, important, and understood"[57] that reinforces the consumer's sense of "uniqueness, variety, and individuality."[58] In corporately owned clubs, power over that experience has been largely taken from dancers and customers by brand managers who have sought to control its every element, from costume to choreography to speech, in order to create and refine brand identity and increase profits. I do not wish to fall into the trap of a limiting and inaccurate binary in which independent strip clubs are viewed as "empowering" and corporate clubs as "degrading"; certainly both sorts of clubs can either create or destroy the potential for agency for dancers and customers in different contexts. And I want to resist the temptation to indulge in reductive anticorporate discourse that ignores what corporations may have to offer striptease. Dancing in a corporate strip club may be less fun than doing so at an independent club, but it is often safer. Customers may feel more secure as well, knowing that there is corporate accountability among employees. The familiarity of chain clubs is comforting and reassuring, coaxing consumers into a sense of striptease as mainstream and themselves as good, middle- or upper-middle-class guys out for a bit of naughty fun.

However, I do want to ask if safety and comfort are what we want from experiences of desire and intimacy—if the secure boundaries created by visuality and the self-congratulation encouraged by branding don't quash the very possibilities for connection and change that desire creates. If we restrict desire to the anodyne pleasures of familiarity and safety, we lose the pleasures of difference, of friction and frisson and movement. Dancing sexy means dancing difference, moving across and between opposing positions: subject and object, sensing and seeing, agency and abjection. Striptease can both reify *and* resist dominant notions of female subjectivity, suppress *and* express subversive desires—erotic or otherwise. But as exotic dance moves into the marketing mainstream, its transgressive potential is being erased by the imperatives of the brandscape. The corporate takeover of striptease, as American as Frappuccino, is rapidly repackaging the most mysterious human emotions into easily branded experiences no more personal or powerful than those to be found in any coffee megachain.

Notes

1. Notable exceptions to this criticism include Judith Lynn Hanna's extensive work applying semiotic analyses to exotic dance vocabularies (see www.judithhanna.com for a complete list) and Katherine Liepe-Levinson's historicized descriptions of striptease choreography in *Strip Show: Performances of Gender and Desire* (London: Routledge, 2002).

2. Catherine Roach, *Stripping, Sex, and Popular Culture* (Oxford: Berg Publications, 2007), 11.

3. Bernadette Barton, *Stripped: Inside the Lives of Exotic Dancers* (New York: New York University Press, 2006), ix–x.

4. This is an argument that has been offered especially in relation to dance with nonprofessional populations, or community dance; see Ann Cooper Albright, *Choreographing Difference: The Body and Identity in Contemporary Dance* (Middletown, CT: Wesleyan University Press, 1997); Petra Kuppers, *Community Performance: An Introduction* (London: Routledge, 2007); Jan Cohen-Cruz, *Local Acts: Community Performance in the United States* (New Brunswick, NJ: Rutgers University Press, 2005).

5. Judith Lynne Hanna, "Undressing the First Amendment and Corseting the Striptease Dancer," *Drama Review (TDR)* 42, no. 2 (Summer 1998): 38–69, 38.

6. Ibid., 45.

7. "Early" refers to the period approximately from the inception of striptease as a form of vaudeville in the mid-nineteenth century until the mid-1960s and the arrival of topless go-go dancing.

8. Liepe-Levinson, *Strip Show*, 111.

9. See Rachel Schteir, *Striptease: The Untold History of the Girlie Show* (New York: Oxford, 2004); and Ben Urish, "Narrative Striptease in the Nightclub Era," *Journal of American Culture* 27, no. 2 (June 2004): 157–65.

10. Liepe-Levisnon, *Strip Show*, 113.

11. Ibid., 4.

12. Like others writing about sex workers and striptease dancers, I use "girls" not to "imply youth or immaturity" as Kirsten Pullen notes (see *Actresses and Whores: On Stage and In Society* [Cambridge: Cambridge University Press, 2005], 191), but because that is the word by which most female dancers refer to themselves.

13. Tony Hoffman, "Rick's Cabaret Bares Its Hidden Growth Strategy," *Equities* (Fall/Winter 2005): 3.

14. Stripper Web, "'THE' basic stripper moves," last accessed October 3, 2016, http://www.stripperweb.com/forum/showthread.php?65134-quot-THE-quot-basic-stripper-moves&highlight.http.

15. Ibid.

16. Laws regulating strip clubs vary widely from state to state and county to county and often link alcohol licensing to some level of clothed-ness. Many clubs on the East Coast get around the proscription on selling alcohol in the presence of completely naked girls by joining a topless bar that serves alcohol with a "juice bar" that doesn't; patrons can leave their drinks at the bar and wander between the sections.

17. These figures, as the others in this section, seemed consistent among clubs that I visited on the East Coast and in California, and among clubs discussed by other dancers with whom I spoke and on online forums.

18. "Older" is of course a relative term. In most strip clubs, anyone over twenty-six belongs to this category.

19. This is a way of life common among many low- and hourly wage workers, not just exotic dancers and sex workers; see Barbara Ehrenreich, *Nickel and Dimed: On (Not) Getting by in America* (New York: Metropolitan Books/Henry Holt and Co., 2001).

20. Mikhail Bakhtin, *Rabelais and His World* (Bloomington: University of Indiana Press, 1984), 317.

21. Ibid., 39.

22. Mary Russo, "Female Grotesques: Carnival and Theory," in *Feminist Studies/Critical Studies,* ed. Teresea de Lauretis (Bloomington: University of Indiana Press, 1986), 219.

23. There was some unintentional irony in this song choice, in which the band sings the praises of the strippers they've bedded while on tour, and includes a lyric about Thee Dollhouse in Fort Lauderdale, the first "Gentlemen's club" in Michael J. Peter's empire and the place where the lap dance began.

24. Some marketing scholars take issue with Klein's journalistic methodology and question her descriptions of the mechanisms of brand domination; however, even her critics tend to concede to her major arguments. See Alan Bradshaw, Pierre McDonagh, and David Marshall, "No Space: New Blood and the Production of Brand Culture Colonies," *Journal of Marketing Management* 22 (2006): 579–99.

25. Naomi Klein, *No Logo: Money, Marketing, and the Growing Anti-Corporate Movement* (New York: Picador USA, 1999), 5.

26. Ibid., xvii.

27. Jonathon Schroeder and Miriam Salzer-Moring, eds., *Brand Culture* (London: Routledge, 2005), 1.

28. See Nicholas Ind, *Living the Brand: How to Transform Every Member of Your Organization into a Brand Champion* (London: Kogan Page, 2007).

29. Scott Lash and Celia Lury, *Global Culture Industry: The Mediation of Things* (Cambridge: Polity Press, 2007), 6–7. Lash and Lury's *Global Culture Industry* responds to Theodor Adorno's mid-twentieth-century notion that culture itself was becoming a commodity. In the twenty-first century, they argue, culture has already been commoditized and is now becoming merely a facet of the creation of worldwide brands.

30. Scores was an iconic upscale club in New York in the 1990s and early 2000s, often touted by frequent patron Howard Stern.

31. "The Ultimate Strip Club List." last accessed October 3, 2016, https://www.tuscl.net/city.php?ID=741.

32. I am borrowing Maurya Wickstrom's use of this term, which she in turn borrows from Otto Reiwoldt, who writes of retail environments intended to "get the customer to identify with the world of the brand, creating a brand awareness and providing it with a deep set emotional anchor" (Otto Reiwoldt, *Brandscaping: Worlds of Experience in Retail Design* [London: Momenta, 2002]; cited in Maurya Wickstrom, *Performing Consumers: Global Capital and Its Theatrical Seductions* [New York: Routledge, 2006], 14). This is somewhat different from other uses in consumer research literature, in which "brandscape" "generally refers to consumers' active constructions of personal meanings and lifestyle orientations from the symbolic resources provided by an array of brands" (Craig J. Thompson and Zeynep Arsel, "The Starbucks Brandscape and

Consumers' [Anticorporate] Experiences of Glocalization," *Journal of Consumer Research* 31 [Dec 2004]: 632).

33. Thompson and Arsel, "The Starbucks Brandscape," 632.

34. Spearmint Rhino is one of world's largest strip club chains, with outposts in the United States, Canada, United Kingdom, Central Europe, Russia, and Australia.

35. Spearmint Rhino Dancer Contract, p.13, 5.1.

36. Barbara Brent and Katherine Hausbeck, "McDonaldization of the Sex Industries? The Business of Sex," in *McDonaldization: The Reader*, ed. George Ritzer (Thousand Oaks, CA: Pine Forge Press, 2002), 104.

37. Ibid., 117.

38. Barbara Brent and Katherine Hausbeck, "Marketing Sex: US Legal Brothels and Late Capitalist Consumption," *Sexualities* 10, no. 4 (Oct 2007): 428.

39. Joseph B. Pine and James Gilmore, *The Experience Economy: Work Is Theatre and Every Business a Stage* (Cambridge, MA: Harvard Business School Press, 1999), ix.

40. David W. Norton, "Towards Meaningful Brand Experiences," *Design Management Journal* 14, no. 1 (Winter 2003): 22.

41. Alan Bryman, *The Disneyization of Society* (Los Angeles: Sage Publications, 2004), 1–2.

42. Ibid., 13.

43. See The Project on Disney, *Inside the Mouse: Work and Play at Disney World* (Durham, NC: Duke University Press, 1995).

44. Klein, *No Logo*, xvii.

45. CBS news. "Howard Schultz: The Star of Starbucks," last accessed October 3, 2016, http://www.cbsnews.com/stories/2006/04/21/60minutes/main1532246.shtml. The term "third place," coined by Ray Oldenberg in his book *The Great Good Place* (New York: Paragon House, 1989), describes public spaces that are neither in the domestic sphere (the "first place") nor the work sphere (the "second place"), but instead operate in a separate category, facilitating casual conversation, friendship, and a sense of place and community.

46. Thompson and Arsel, "The Starbucks Brandscape," 633.

47. For example, the film *Akeela and the Bee* (2006) was produced by Starbucks Entertainment, and the Starbucks Hear Music label has put out albums by Paul McCartney and Luciano Pavarotti, among others. In 2006, Starbucks announced a collaboration with Apple, and there is a Starbucks Entertainment section of Apple's iTunes store.

48. Herbie Hancock, the jazz pianist whose album "Possibilities" was sold at Starbucks, believes that "Going to Starbucks, you feel kind of hip. I feel kind of hip when I go to Starbucks; that's how I know!" (Susan Dominus, "The Starbucks Aesthetic," *New York Times*, October 22, 2006).

49. Victor Turner's concept of "liminality" in relation to performance and ritual describes events that exist at the threshold (limen) between one world and another, in which everyday mores and social structures are suspended for a time; Turner distin-

guished between performances in pre- (liminal) and post-industrial (liminoid) societies. See Victor Turner, "Play, Flow, and Ritual: An Essay in Comparative Symbology," in *From Ritual to Theatre: The Human Seriousness of Play* (New York: Performing Arts Journal, 1982).

50. Liepe-Levinson *Strip Show*; Katherine Frank, *G-Strings and Sympathy: Strip Club Regulars and Male Desire* (Durham, NC: Duke University Press, 2002); R. Danielle Egan, *Dancing for Dollars and Paying for Love: The Relationships Between Exotic Dancers and Their Regulars* (Basingstoke: Palgrave Macmillan, 2006).

51. For example, new age spiritual retreats, drum circles, body-mind therapeutic centers and practices, music festivals, experimental theatre, etc., all involve commercial as well as more esoteric concerns.

52. Also see Bradshaw, McDonagh, and Marshall, "No Space."

53. Ibid., 580.

54. Wickstrom, *Performing Consumers*, 6.

55. Terry Eagleton, *The Ideology of the Aesthetic* (Oxford: Oxford University Press, 1990), 28.

56. Bradshaw, McDonagh, and Marshall, "No Space," 581.

57. Norton, "Towards Meaningful Brand Experiences," 22.

58. Brent and Hausbeck, "McDonaldization of the Sex Industries? The Business of Sex," 428.

8

Bgirls as Drag Kings

ANSLEY JOYE JONES

"The idea that a b-boy or b-girl should be judged on their skills rather than their gender (or any other factor, for that matter) is central to the ideology of the dance," states hip hop writer Joseph Schloss.[1] But what happens when sexism is central to the culture's perception of skill? Traditionally hip hop has been a patriarchal culture. "Hard" attitudes molded hypermasculine dancing and gestures and fueled the breaking battles. In these battles, gestures are either scatological or sexualized, which in many cases provokes sexual assault and gender-based violence. Misogyny is so deeply embedded in every aspect of breaking culture that it leaves very little room for any other physical representations—and for bgirls, this creates performative problems unknown to the bboy.[2] The culture is obsessed with annihilating "weakness." This is evident in the training process and the bgirl acculturation into what is termed "foundation."[3] Because patriarchy positions the woman as "weak," all things feminine must be extracted from the bgirl's psyche: Any gesture, behavior or movement performed in a "weak" (slow or nonexplosive) fashion is replaced with male-oriented gestures, behaviors, movements, and dynamics. The bgirl is pressured to carry on the tradition of hypermasculinity through her breaking and discouraged from doing "feminine" gestures—unless it is to ridicule the opponent's weaknesses. Although history proves she has other options, in order to be accepted, bgirls must follow the dominant bboy model. This culturally hypermasculine genderizing is required of bgirls, but it promotes the language of the bboy/bboying *only*, focusing on making bboys out of girls and women.[4] Joseph Schloss writes about the term bboying, "While this may appear to be begging the question, I would argue that the ambiguity of the term reflects a kind of social ambiguity: to what degree, and in what senses, is a b-girl a kind of b-boy?" However, I argue that trying to be something they are not (bgirls must become bboys) is *not* the way. In fact, this opposes the culture's assertion of being true to one's self. "The most important thing that foundation teaches," Schloss states, is "how to develop your own individual identity in the context of the group, which necessarily entails understanding your own strengths, weaknesses, and personal history. Foundation allows you to bring your own past experiences into your present identity in a way that is specifically designed to work towards your advantage."[5] This idealization functions well if you are male.[6] However as a practicing bgirl, this toxic experiential struggle to resist a forced masculinity helped me recognize I was fighting for respect the culture had not reserved for me, or any woman, or any idea of femininity. The sexist philosophy or collective consciousness that underlies breaking requires the bgirl to undergo a kind of psychological abuse.

As a bgirl acculturated into breaking during the new millennium, competing and dancing in the Southeastern United States from 2005 to 2010, I began to consider the bgirl's paradoxical position from a theoretical point of view—in order to better analyze the feelings and conflicts that I, and other female breakers, confront. The physiology of the woman is shamed, either in terms of how she looks or how she dances. Ephrat "Bounce" Asherie remembers being told, with scorn, "Why don't you dance like a boy?"[7] Many bgirls delight in being mistaken for bboys, hiding breasts and hips in gigantic pants and tops, deploying what I have termed "male sexual-reproductive power language" (miming rape)[8] when dancing. For instance, the crotch-grab is used specifically when bboys want to uphold their dominance as males; it also appears at the end of a series of movements, giving the dancer extra "validity." However when a bgirl crotch-grabs it has more complex meanings: She may be grabbing female genitals but she does it to replicate a masculine gesture of sexual dominance, mimetically "becoming" male to overcome her rival. This communicates her affirmation of male sexual dominance and promotes self-inflicted gender-based violence: When she mimes rape against another bgirl she concurrently displaces "rapist" onto her own body.[9]

These are powerful psychological genderfuck forces that the bgirl must manage. In the first years of the millennium bgirls were caught in a bind between an extreme example of a dominating hypermasculinity, and an alternative androgynous identity created by bgirls from the 1970s to the '90s. In researching the bgirls' roots and position in hip hop (and hoping to discover more about women's contributions), I found useful insights and an analytic frame in the writings of theorist Kathryn Rosenfeld. Rosenfeld's work[10] was particularly helpful in teasing apart the various components of bgirls' problematic performance, which trained them to use specific gestures that disempower and oppress women. If bgirls are to find a feminine voice and performance mode—which has begun to emerge in the last five years—an analysis of the traditional physical vocabulary and its meanings will help pave the way.

Bgirls as drag kings may appear to be an outrageous theory. But it is through the embodiment of black hypermasculinity and "genderfuck" presented in the styles of movement, clothing, and battling that bgirls resemble drag kings.[11] In Kathryn Rosenfeld's "Drag King Magic: Performing/Becoming the Other" she states, "by performing/becoming the other, drag kings engage in a practice of magic which transforms both the margin and center."[12] The magic Rosenfeld recognizes in drag performance is the magic bgirls experience when battling. Part of this magic incorporates androgyny, which encompasses all genders in a single entity. Through liminal androgyny, they not only transcend the adolescent bboy's sexist ideology that "girls can't do this," they concurrently challenge the larger patriarchal society's gender norms by gaining power through battling and empowering themselves.

According to Rosenfeld, some drag kings represent specific types of maleness while others emphasize a fluidity of gender, so Rosenfeld separates drag kings into two categories: "mimetic" and "liminal." I am borrowing these two categories of drag kings to describe how bgirls transform both the margin and the center of traditional gender norms, especially concerning female sexuality and reproductive power through battling. In breaking, female sexual reproductive power would be transformed into gestures, like miming the pregnant belly. When drag kings appear macho, they are "more layered and nuanced than macho in the mainstream."[13] Rosenfeld argues, "By drag kings performing maleness—by performatively/mimetically "becoming" men—drag kings simultaneously alter the nature of power-over [sic] as it operates in the general culture, and claim power for themselves."[14] On the positive side of mimetic empowerment, bgirls performing masculinity (whether queer or straight) can create new possibilities for a number of different masculinities and femininities within breaking. Through mimesis, many bgirls, especially those who openly identify with queer culture, recognize this and claim power for themselves. Paradoxically however, mimesis is just as disempowering as it is empowering. As Rosenfeld states, "It is important to add race as treated by drag kings to the discussion, not only because it makes for a more complete picture, but because

Figure 8.1. Bgirl Ephrat "Bounce" Asherie in a "back-break." El Barrio Freshest, Harlem, New York, April 2014. Photograph by Brandon Giddens-Morris (aka "Boystatic"). Photograph courtesy of Ephrat "Bounce" Asherie.

it further exemplifies drag kings' 'power play.'"[15] Mimesis is limiting in its empowerment for bgirls because many of the ideas mimicked are misogynistic, and therefore oppress womanhood. This means (according to Rosenfeld) that white drag kings have both no power and some power when they mimetically embody masculinity. Race, however, problematizes things in the matter of degree; the *black* drag king is caught in a potent doublebind. First, the black drag king's mimesis of male whiteness (which also subsumes the "privilege of whiteness") is disempowering because of its impossibility: biologically black cannot be biologically white. Second, the black drag king's (or black bgirl) mimesis has more power because of its intracultural mirroring—they are black females mimicking black males. Third, and this applies to both black and white drag kings, disempowerment resides in biology. A biologic female is still a biologic female, even with a dildo.

The practice of breaking has unique parameters of power-privileges. It is a domain of black masculinity that all bgirls enter, which includes certain behaviors all bgirls must attempt to embody. If the bgirls buy into the full masculinity of breaking, they de facto become mimetic drag kings, taking part in their own suppression.

Rosenfeld explains that drag is a performance of gender, but it also extends into race, at least stylistically and through performative characteristics.[16] In hip hop, specifically, the stylistic and performative characteristics are stereotypically black and male, and the glorification of black masculinity and the supression of black femininity is racially coded. Mimetic bgirls dress like men, walk like confident black males, disguising parts of the body to pass as male, such as dressing in oversized all-male clothing, de-emphasizing (flattening) their breasts, locking or braiding their hair in male African/black styles (certain styles are considered more "boyish" than others), wearing typical bboy hats or tying back their hair in a bandana. Rosenfeld discusses that "passing"—historically in reference to the black community—has double meaning. As Bryant Keith Alexander argues in his book *Performing Black Masculinity: Race, Culture, and Queer Identity*, "passing is a performance of suppression that is associated with the origin of denial."[17] Bgirls perform their own suppression through "throwing the cock,"[18] which denies the female body power, and the phallic link of "becoming/performing male" represses the option of what I call "womb-power" within battling.

For example, certain clothes have become iconic symbols of hip hop and black masculinity. Some black men describe any "tight" pants (considered uncomfortable) as "nut huggers."[19] This idea references the stereotyped sexually aggressive black male who supposedly possesses an "enormous penis and testicles" (they even need room to swing). Many emcees even rap about walking with a limp, as if their penises are so huge that they are incapable of walking correctly, accepting the historical stereotype of black male hypersexuality. In the song, "Beamer, Benz and Bentley" (Beamer is a BMW car; Benz is a Mercedes Benz, and Bentley is a Bentley) rapper Chris "Ludacris" Bridges states "call me a jerk but I ain't going through that tight phase/clothes still baggy enough to let my nuts hang."[20] So in mimesis, bgirls also wear baggy pants that signify this "heavy penis," enhanced by grabbing the crotch and thrusting mimicking the male. Does the bgirl unconsciously do this only because she feels the need to disguise her body? Or, is there another reason, such as adapting the "gangsta" rapper look?[21] As Alexander states, "We can recognize the 'gangsta' concept as a culturally indigenous example of black masculine fashioning."[22] Because of this image, many bgirls feel that walking in a certain way, even throwing up hand signs that symbolize where they are from (much like gangs) becomes a part of their identity. For example the peace sign (fingers form the "V") was/is thrown in a certain way by African Americans called "deuces" (the "V" made to the side like scissors means "see you later" as opposed to the upright peace sign). Many bgirls have adopted specific "signs" of representing their cities or crews. Nicole "Severe" Rateau says one of her favorite gestures is the "A town-down" (the index finger and the middle finger form an upside down peace sign with the thumb between the two) because she "is from Atlanta" and it was made popular by Usher "Usher" Raymond, Christopher "Ludacris" Bridges, and Lil'John in their song titled "Yeah."[23] There is also a general stereotype of black men as sexually lustful, "the black rapist." Bgirls enact this "angry" sexualized masculinity when they dance, and perform other stereotypes of black masculinity.

As Rosenfeld states, "The centrality to drag of costuming and style leads back to questions of mimesis and desire."[24] Mimetic bgirls do not experiment with or reference femininity in their styles, or in the gestures they use in battling. Gestures within battles are monitored by the panoptic bboy in the consciousness of the mimetic bgirl. When mimetic bgirls deploy male battle gestures, they become the objects rather than the subjects of the male gaze/the dominant male, or the phallic-gesturing male.[25] Gestures by bgirls that elicit the male gaze are flirtatious or incorporate themes of seduction. The index finger is used as a seductive tool ("co' mon, baby"), which bgirls claim they use in order to "catch the attention of" or "throw the bboys off of their game." Bgirls gave examples of other female gesturing. Blowing kisses was a very popular gesture that at least six bgirls labeled as a "feminine gesture."

Bgirls Tammy "Kadence" Tso and Dawnette "Patience" Joseph explain that there are more creative ways to use the "cock" for women. Kadence states that turning the guys around on themselves is a way of getting back at the bboys. Patience gives a more detailed account of what is done. "If there are two guys battling each other you can go up to one guy and chop his off and then use that to cock[26] the other dude."[27] Although this is "alternative," when the bgirl acts as if she has a cock or uses that "cock" as Kadence describes she is still using male anatomy as an instrument of power and referencing the domination and power of rape. In an interview with bgirl Ellz, she explains her viewpoint about the use of phallic gestures. "I try not to use anything [pause] too crazy. I try to avoid stuff like that. It's just—I don't have to do that in order to let someone know I'm gonna wipe the floor with 'em. I can just look at 'em in the face and do that."[28] Even though Bgirl Ellz does not use the phallic gestures per se, she nevertheless practices patriarchy. "Like, if I'm battling against a guy I will definitely use... flirtation in the dancing to try and throw them off," bgirl Ellz says, "because they get distracted easily or stuff like that. But if I am battling a girl, it's just... kinda making sure that they feel over-powered and making sure they feel that I am the dominant one."[29] But bboys are not always thrown off by these sexual gestures because of the bgirl's masculinized appearance. Refocusing of the bboy's attentions away from the bgirl's skill and talent to her body as sexual object contradicts the purpose of why bgirls cover up their femininity in the first place. When bgirl Ellz discusses battling women, she strives to be "dominant" while her female opponent is "dominated." This replicates patriarchy; someone has to be the "man" and someone has to be the "woman." Hence, bgirls actually employ a kind of panopticism (Michel Foucault's theory of self-censorship) over the womb-power within themselves, reverting to the idea of the male gaze and the view that men are dominant-superior and women are submissive-inferior.

Mimetic bgirls find power in being able to use phallic gesturing against bboys. In one scenario, the mimetic bgirl dances up to her male opponent and humps his face. This gesture is symbolic of male-sexual dominance. Bgirls have a power they previously did not own (through throwing the cock), but devastatingly, phallic gestures used *against* bgirls *by* bgirls are one of the ultimate suppressions of female sexual and reproductive power. When a bgirl mimes raping another bgirl with her imaginary penis the bgirl is suppressing through rape her own and her opponent's sexual and reproductive power as well as the power of all women. In referring back to the drag king's "power play" Rosenfeld discusses, the power struggle within a battle, at its most extreme, is between men and women's power of sexuality and reproduction. Bgirls are not only performing/becoming male, they are fighting against their own bodies' possibility of power. This becomes problematic not only because of the possibilities of queer-girl power but for all types of feminine power manifested in battling.

Rosenfeld ultimately states that the power of drag kings lies in mimesis because they invoke change by taking back power and empowering themselves. Because they are not biologically trying to change into men, be men, they embody that power and use it for themselves. However, because mimetic bgirls strive to be accepted/pass as men by disguising female anatomy[30] and repressing any female authority by employing phallic gestures when battling with the

Figure 8.2. Bgirl Ansley "Jukeboxx" Jones in a "Z" freeze. Tallahassee, Florida, 2016. Photograph by Becki Rutta. By permission of Rutta Studios.

male gaze/phallic gestures that reinforce the patriarchal position. This raises the question: "How is mimesis empowering for bgirls?"

My theorization is the opposite of Rosenfeld's mimetic power: I believe that the power exists with the "liminal" bgirl who becomes androgynous—and the liminal is the genderfuck that occurs here. Rosenfeld believes genderfuck to be a way to successfully *masculinize* and therefore concludes that mimesis is empowering. However, I believe liminality is a way to successfully merge femininity and masculinity into the unrecognizable, which expands both femininity and masculinity and creates more options for the bgirl and ultimately the "b-world."[31]

Because "elements of masculinity are clearly evident, yet concealed in extremely feminine packaging," androgyny allows the liminal bgirl to battle against traditional patriarchal gender roles with feminine power.[32] Bgirls who float between the gendered states and play with the ideas of femininity and masculinity through dance are categorized as liminal. As Dara Milovanovic states, "Male clothes liberate women. Their sex is not concealed, rather it is emphasized."[33] It is important to note that it is not male clothing itself but the appropriation of it that allows for this freedom. For instance, Milovanovic in her reading of Bob Fosse's clothing choice for his female dancers explains, "male attire is appropriated by women with their repeated use of bowler hats, highly stylized jackets, or pinstriped bikini-briefs" and that "Hats are male: they conceal the face and introduce an air of austerity or playfulness."[34] In addition, liminal bgirls tend to play with the masculine and feminine consciously through their gestures in battling, thus expanding definitions of both. Liminal bgirls utilize traditional feminine qualities mediated through liminal, comedic means by dancing out the power of the generative mother in female reproductive-power gestures.

For liminal bgirls, appropriated black male attire may be a mashup of pink trucker hats and baggy pants that display panties instead of boxers, and jerseys that show the midsection. For example, a liminal bgirl might pair men's pants with a bikini top or wear all men's clothing (with a "girly" color of course) while wearing large earrings and heavy makeup. For example Moanne81[35] states "when I see a b-girl who perfectly manages the tightrope walk between tight and baggy, sporty and feminine, I admire that."[36] Liminal bgirls do not use phallic gestures. Instead, they use gestures that comment on the power of femininity and the female body. Milovanovic states, "An androgynous looking woman becomes associated with masculine elements of mind and reason, rather than the feminine elements of nature, feelings and emotions, which are often connected to instability and weakness."[37] Likewise, Monica "TahXic" Kelly states, "I completely embrace the fact that I am a woman and I use it to my advantage. I think my masculine qualities are manifested in my mind and personality, while my feminine qualities are manifested more physically."[38]

For this reason, liminal bgirls use mind and reason through strategies within the battle, and they are able to recognize the advantages of using feminine gestures against men. The fact that women can play multiple sexual identities and switch from one second to the next, they can—and do—use the feminine burns (i.e., a gesture or move so potent that it incinerates the opponent). Liminal bgirls do not merely use traditional gestures of femininity; they utilize gestures that women can use—but men will not. Men tend to resort to feminine gestures in order to emasculate their opponent. For example many men are afraid to shake their shoulders for fear of being seen as gay. Instead they will shimmy their shoulders briefly then point at the opponent to say "you're a fag."[39] Severe explains a gesture that she uses for men. "Um, if I'm battling a guy and he's doing a lot of derogatory gestures because I'm a female I'll do [mime] something like he has a small dick." TahXic also creates gestures related to this idea. "I came up with some good burns when I did battle. With one I would get down on my knees in front of the guy I was battling, and pretend to pull out a telescope from behind me, extend it al-ll-ll-ll [her emphasis] the way close to their 'you know what' and kinda scratch my head like 'Huh? What am I looking at? And where is it?'"

Feminine sensibility has tweaked the gestures with comical liminality. Liminal bgirls are not subject to the male gaze but gain agency by manipulating it and placing themselves in liminal roles of power. Severe states: "Sometimes you can play up being 'girly' in a smart and comical way by like, looking at your nails or checkin' your hair just to be kinda like 'There's no sweat.'" In a battle I engaged in against Timothy "K.T. (Killer Tim)" Langston, I also won by being bored and "painting my nails" as he vigorously danced full out. Even though technically he was better, the fact that I was able to make the crowd laugh made me the real winner. This underscores how Severe could win with intelligence, humor, and a quick wit, elements that have been eliminated in today's big-time formal competitions.[40]

The liminal androgynous bgirl is not yet "pretty"; she is using the transitional state *before* she is "pretty" as a comical battle strategy. The gesture is potent, amusing, and belittling because it is "in-between." Liminal bgirls desexualize the situation, thereby transferring any power of the male gaze to themselves. The double-punch of woman/mother is exploited as well. In woman power–oriented gestures bgirls may grab their breasts to symbolize the power in the female anatomy (much like that of the bboy crotch-grabbing) transforming bboys into their children. For example, breasts "feed" the bboy, from which he gains all of his power (this is used by bgirl Rokafella). In another example of a power-mother gesture, I used a liminal gesture to beat an actual phallic gesturing young bboy in a crew called "Shit Bricks Crew," the kids from HBO Crew[41] at a battle called "Tribal Floor Wars" in Florida. The bboy began the battle. As he toprocked, he mimed masturbating and ejaculating on me. When I approached him I wiped the ejaculatory fluids off, signaled him to my belly like I was pregnant with him and executed a reverse suicide (landing flat on my stomach). The crowd and judges yelled "ooohhhh!" and this angered the young bboy. He was so mad that he slid up to my leg and humped my leg repeatedly, actually making physical contact. I yelled to the judges to disqualify, since he was attached to my leg and was sexually harassing me. The judges stopped the battle, saying nothing about the bboy's behavior toward me other than "no touching." The bboy ended up winning. Afterward he shook my *male* crew-members' hands. But not mine. This illustrates not only the power of the liminal gesture but unequivocally shows the existence of, and legacy of, misogyny.[42] Examples of liminal bgirls battling, such as this one, show the formidable magic that can exist in these burns.

Marilyn Francus, author of "The Monstrous Mother: Reproductive Anxiety in Swift and Pope," discusses the negative image of the "fecund female" in the West. Traditionally negative ideas about the female body are reversed and made powerful when the liminal bgirl transforms into generative mother to battle bboys. Bboys have a peculiar and dissonant relationship with their sexual-reproductive gestures and claiming power as "men."

When bboys originally created what has become known as "Foundational" bboy movements, they were adolescents or pre-adolescents. Whether consciously or not, there were strong attachments (and resistances) to the mother who has power over the boy, which get represented in the movements and enacted in the basics of breaking. Bboys work on the floor, like the crawling baby. Then they change instantly from the baby to the man, perfectly physicalizing in a nanosecond what it is to be in the pre-adolescent, then adolescent, state. So bboys also "play" in a liminal state between the child and the man. As a "child" he is subject to the entire range of power that the generative mother possesses. Bboys, in fact, represent the in-between sexual and physical state of baby and man. Another macho-yet-childlike example of the bboy is the pride they take in enduring bruises, cuts, and scrapes. In the documentary *The Freshest Kids: The History of the Bboy*, the Nigga Twins state: "We didn't dance on linoleum, we didn't dance on cardboard. We danced on the cement!" Hard or rough surfaces become a challenge to "face down" in order to become a man, or, what signified a *real* bboy. It is glorified as a state of manhood, especially for boys. By enduring bruises and scrapes, he is trying to separate from his dependence and need for comfort from the nurturing mother. Marilyn Francus explains that this makes the female dangerous. By satisfying his needs, she reinforces his stasis and his dependence on her.[43]

By performing the liminal, not-yet-but-mother-to-be, women hold varying powers over bboys. For example, a bgirl is battling a bboy who throws the cock at her. She may take his body, signal putting him in her womb while miming a pregnant belly. But she decides to eliminate him by taking abortion pills. Or she may make a "mistake" by slipping and falling, aborting/miscarrying the bboy/baby as well. Another example of what the generative mother could do while pregnant with her bboy, is to blithely smoke a cigarette and drink alcohol. She then mimes giving birth to the bboy she is battling within seconds of her bad actions; but he is not developed enough to battle her. Women have the power to choose to mother a child or not: a paradoxical interplay of male negativity, concepts defined by misogynistic sexism about the female body, pro-choice, and child neglect are the stuff of female reproductive burns. Francus explains: "The refusal to mother is the only active monstrosity available to the domesticated mother, for unlike the self-empowered fertile female who has many options, the domesticated mother has all too few."[44] Although this may have been true in a society governed by normative gender stereotypes, in breaking, the liminal bgirl can choose and refuse. Both hold significant power.

In female reproductive power gestures, the vagina is always the ultimate reference of power. The stereotypical "mystery" of the vagina is used against the bboy. Her vagina may become a "black hole," be deadly as quicksand, or resemble the *vagina dentata* that Freud postulated as the fearful tool of castration. For example a bgirl is "cocked" by a bboy. She then runs two fingers up her vagina lips and her fingers turn into a pair of threatening scissors.[45] Excretions associated with the vagina as well are imagined as toxic, like acid rain, much like the bboy uses his semen against his opponent. Bgirls may mime using menstrual blood as acid thrown in the eyes of the bboy. Bgirls may also use the lack of fluids to signify that she is sexually uninterested; if the bboy uses the penis against her and her vagina may be mimed as if it was sandpaper, or, ratcheted up one more level, it becomes an old-style winding pencil sharpener that sharpens and files down the penis. She finishes by blowing off the excess dust of the now pencil-thin penis.[46]

Though we may not have as many liminal bgirls as we do mimetic, we certainly have more bgirls accepting feminine qualities. For example Bgirl Roxy dances with such powerful femininity it is hard not to recognize her as a liminal bgirl. In between her sets she frequently places her hands behind her head while she leans on one hip with the opposite foot resting on its toes. Unsure if she intends to play with her hair or not, it comes off as a comedic gesture. Her clothing is pink and blue—but her style uses hard power moves. With this mixture, Roxy epitomizes the liminal bgirl.

Today, some liminal bgirls are returning to a "feminine" style, like that described by bgirl "Baby Love" who danced in the 1980s during the time when hip-hop party dances were popular.[47] There are also bgirls who choose to be

Figure 8.3. Bgirl Ansley "Jukeboxx" Jones in a one-armed "Y" freeze. Tallahassee, Florida, 2016. Photograph by Becki Rutta. By permission of Rutta Studios.

completely "masculine." What makes this exciting is that it reflects the new trend toward bgirls making new choices rather than clinging to the older masculinities. This redefines how they choose to present themselves and how they will be received.

From the late 1990s to 2005, bgirls were largely mimetic although a few were emerging into liminality. The majority of the women dressed like bboys and strived mimetically to "act" like men. However, around 2010 a shift began to take place. Bgirls are no longer *only* mimetic. The bgirl collective consciousness is moving closer to the liminal state. Bgirl and house dancer Vanicia Flores Messick in conversation at the 2014 Southeast Bboy Championships stated, "I don't really care what others think of me," verbalizing her confidence in her liminal mindstate that dismisses negative interpretation by others, leaving room for multiple movement possibilities.

Solidarity among bgirls, however, is the optimal liminal power gesture. Solidarity will recognize a thirty-five-year lineage of women's contributions in hip hop dance, and thereby be able to maximize a wider gender expressivity. Bgirls have the potential to create new versions of power moves that employ liminality. For example, the classic windmills could be repositioned into "queenmills": the bgirl could cross her legs "like a proper young lady" as she madly spins on head and shoulders. My prediction is that once a healthy number of bgirls are using and inventing female gestures, those bgirls who have been, and are, turned off by the power moves and hypermasculinities, will begin to infuse the scene with new energy. When dancing in toprock, there is ample time and opportunity for new expressivity. For example, in the battle between Roxy and Ayumi,[48] Ayumi can be viewed as a mimetic bgirl and Roxy as liminal. When watching the battle, Roxy uses only liminal gestures while Ayumi uses much more masculine gestures. The masculine gestures are so normalized that Roxy's gestures stand out and actually elicit applause from the audience when she does them, something that does not happen when other dancers battle, whether they are bboys or girls.[49]

Expanding the language in this way not only restores some of the playful female spirit of the bgirls of the 1970s and 1980s in the gestures, it simultaneously reinstates the humor and wit that had gotten devalued by "pure movement" and brute power moves. Liminal bgirls' fluid mix of both genders can transform the culture, expanding the vocabulary for all. Liminal gestures serve as an entry point to actualize the best purposes. Joseph Schloss writes: "Hip-hop culture gives its participants the power to redefine themselves and their history, not by submission or selective emphasis, but by embracing *all* of their previous experience as material for self-expression in the present moment." He then quotes Trac 2 saying, "'That's why the dance form is so phenomenal.'"[50] Women are slowly but certainly moving forward as a collective, expressing in motion and gesture the reality of their female potential, claiming their rightful space in the larger hip hop culture. Being a "real" and powerful breaker will no longer be an act of female suppression, or selective emphasis on hypermasculinity. Instead it will be an act of female celebration that widens the expressive scope of the form for everyone.

Notes

1. Joseph G. Schloss, *Foundation: B-boys, B-girls and Hip-Hop Culture in New York* (New York: Oxford University Press, 2009), 66. This quote from this important work is both correct and incorrect. Ideally it should be true. However, what Schloss does not acknowledge is the discrimination bboy pioneers practice when discussing aspects deemed as "feminine," which includes displaying the physical form of the female and any feminine qualities that are considered "weak." This affects cisgender and transgender bgirls and members of the LGBTQ community that express any level of femininity or femaleness.

2. Ibid., 65–66. Bgirl Emiko is interviewed on the differences between bboy and bgirl events. She explains her annoyance with the "girl tendencies" some of the other women had—for example, being more "sociable" (demonstrating how effective the systematic oppression and annihilation of the "feminine" identity has been). Schloss explains: "In Emiko's eyes, the other girls were violating battle protocol by attempting to be sociable before the competition. By making these overtures on the basis of gender, they were not only forcing Emiko to choose between two aspects of her identity (woman versus bgirl), but also doing it in a way that was specifically detrimental to her ability to compete in the battle. If she tried to support her fellow b-girls, she would not only lose a part of her character she was trying to project in the battle, but would also have to carry around the knowledge that she had done so *because she was female* (emphasis mine)." Emiko is participating in her own oppression and the oppression of other women and, if she does not, she is "guilt-tripped."

3. Ibid., 67. "Foundation" is understood as the basic techniques of breaking. It is the continuation of the movements, attitudes, and ideas of the original bboy pioneers who established Foundation when they were twelve- to sixteen-year-old adolescents and indoctrinated in society's idea of patriarchy. Joe Schloss exposes and validates this tradition with exemplary instances of misogyny in his chapter "'Getting Your Foundation': Pedagogy." He interviews Richard Santiago who explains that he trains bgirls the same way he trains bboys. "There's no gender breakdown, this is what you got. You want to do it, you do it! (Santiago, interview)."

4. Ibid., 15. Explaining his choice of "options" in how to refer to breakers, Schloss concludes: "The final option is to simply use the term *b-boy*, with the explanation that this is widely viewed in the community as a generic term that includes women." This particular functioning of the term is sexist.

5. Ibid., 67.

6. This b-boy "naming" option infects attitudes and threatens the potential for real self-growth for any sex or gender orientation.

7. Bgirl Ephrat "Bounce" Asherie, as quoted in e-mail from Asherie to Sally Sommer, September 23, 2016.

8. March 6, 2014, I presented "Bgirls as Drag Kings" in Dr. Lisa Munson-Weinberg's "Sociology of Hip Hop" class at Florida State University. Dr. Weinberg used the class's reactions to show how patriarchy operated in the classroom. When discussing male anatomy and excretions, the class was silent. But when discussing the female anatomy and excretions the class reacted with shock, disgust even.

9. The crotch-grab is the predecessor to a gesture called "throwing the cock," explained in further detail in note 15.

10. Tss Crew, "32 Overlooked Rape Lyrics in Rap," http://uproxx.com/smokingsection/2013/04/50-absurd-rape-lyrics/#page/2. Although covering the lyrics of rap is not in the direct scope of this paper, it shows the pervasiveness of misogyny and rape culture in hip hop as a whole, both underground and mainstream. For example, rapper Hopsin states: "Rape wives and then laugh at husbands." DJ Paul from Three 6 Mafia also has misogynistic lyrics about rape and domination like others, *"I had to rape his b*tch cause the hoe was stacked, I fucked her from the back, with my gun to her back."*

11. Kathryn Rosenfeld, "Drag King Magic: Performing/Becoming the Other," *Journal of Homosexuality* 43:3–4 (2003): 208.

12. Ibid., 201.

13. Ibid., 206.

14. Ibid., 203.

15. Ibid., 210.

16. Ibid. All of these characteristics are stereotypes of black males.

17. Bryant Keith Alexander, *Performing Black Masculinity: Race, Culture, and Queer Identity* (Lanham, MD: AltaMira Press, 2006).

18. "Throwing the cock" or "cocking" is part of the gestural language in breaking battles. It is performed by miming an impossibly large penis with the hands extended (one hand at the base and the other at the end of the penis) and thrusting the hips simultaneously as if to say "take that." It is generally done after a dancer finishes a series of movements called a "set."

19. The only practical reason for bboys/bgirls wearing baggy pants is that they are more comfortable to dance in and they refer to the "gangsta" rappers' style. However the majority of bboys do not wear overly baggy pants. It is the bgirls who do this.

20. http://rapgenius.com/Lloyd-banks-beamer-benz-or-bentley-remix-2-lyrics, accessed December 2010.

21. Baggy pants do not echo gang life. There is a stylistic difference between baggy pants and pants hanging below the buttocks. One of the many stories surrounding the origin of the style of pants below the buttocks is that it "copies" prison clothes. Prison clothing (particularly in big cities), at least since the '70s, has been the one-piece jumpsuit.

22. Alexander, *Performing Black Masculinity*, 221.

23. Severe, telephone interview with the author, October 26, 2009.

24. Rosenfeld, "Drag King Magic," 204.

25. Refer to Laura Mulvey's theory of male gaze, although it is used only as a jumping-off point for discussion.

26. To "cock" means essentially to rape.

27. Patience, telephone interview with the author, October 6, 2009.

28. Bgirl Ellz, telephone interview with the author, March 2, 2009.

29. Ibid.

30. Many bgirls have stated that if a silhouette were filmed of them they would not want anyone to know they were female.

31. The breaking world.

32. Dara Milovanovic, "Androgyny, Glamour, Fetishism, and Urbanity: An Analysis of Bob Fosse's Choreography" (master's thesis, Florida State University, 2003).

33. Ibid., 7.

34. Ibid., 12. Hats are considered "male" by traditional societal definitions.

35. Unable to get family name.

36. Martha Cooper, Nika Kramer, and Rockafella. *We B*Girlz* (New York: PowerHouse Books, 2005).

37. Dara Milovanovic, "Androgyny, Glamour," 7. It is important to note that the ideas of masculine and feminine qualities are traditional/stereotypical.

38. TahXic, e-mail message to the author, January 1, 2010.

39. This is a common insult used by bboys to demean other bboys.

40. Battles such as Red Bull BC1 and Battle of the Year.

41. HBO used to mean "Home Boys Only," although they may have changed their name to indicate another meaning.

42. Another problem with patriarchy in breaking is that it deliberately, and more specifically, indoctrinates young girls and boys (specifically) into a culture of violent misogyny.

43. Marilyn Francus, "The Monstrous Mother: Reproductive Anxiety in Swift and Pope," ELH 61, no. 4 (Winter 1994): 829–51, http://www.jstor.org/stable/2873360, accessed October 2009.

44. Ibid., 845.

45. Sonette Ehlers, "RapeaXe," website about the invention of RapeaXe, http://www.antirape.co.za/. These gestures can open up possibilities in the larger culture con-

cerning rape, such as the invention of the antirape device "RapeaXe" developed by Dr. Sonette Ehlers from South Africa. While this is certainly not the answer to rape and sexual assault, it shows that women are trying to solve issues from their own standpoint, especially in breaking.

46. These are female-reproductive gestures that I used in battle.

47. Guevara, Nancy. "Women Writin' Rappin' Breakin,'" in *Droppin' Science: Critical Essays on Rap Music and Hip Hop Culture,* ed. William Eric Perkins (Philadelphia: Temple University Press, 1996), 49–62. Baby Love is quoted: "Girls got all kinds of styles. They got b-boy style then they mix it with b-girl style or with lock. B-girl style is more feminine. It's basically the same with different names." Baby Love goes on to explain the femininity as "jazzy." Guevera concludes that "slower and smoother breaking moves were considered more appropriate for females."

48. RONATOUNE, "AYUMI vs ROXY (URBAN CONNECTION 2011) WWW.BBOYWORLD.COM," https://www.youtube.com/watch?v=K-tNvR2aw-U.

49. Bboys can be liminal and use liminal gestures as well. I have yet to see bboys challenge the status quo other than a bboy from Atlanta, Zach (aka Veezy) who uses a lot of House dance femme gestures when he breaks.

50. Schloss, *Foundation*, 44.

III
Public Spaces, Political Statements

9

Receptions of *Descent* and Politics of *Agora*

9/11 Changed the Way They Saw It; Everybody Jumped into the Pool

SALLY R. SOMMER

One month before the 9/11 al-Qaeda attack on New York City's Twin Towers, Noémie Lafrance showed her site-specific work *Descent* as a twenty-five-minute work-in-progress. The dance's structure was elegant. From the top of twelve flights of marble stairs, eight beautiful women descended, dancing, murmuring, moving languidly, followed by about two dozen audience members. The perfectly proportioned 200-foot marble staircase spiraled downward in geometric precision, each loop reflecting the one above in a vertiginous optical illusion of a mirror-within-a-mirror. Moving in unison, the dancers leaned over the banisters, performing gestures of companionable domesticity—washing hair, resting on the railings with arms spread wide. The stairwell enveloped spectators and dancers, as if in a convivial tenement, a feeling underscored by the dancers' movements. Lafrance intended *Descent* to be a meditation on women as subjects and objects of desire within the domestic realm—and so it was received at those initial performances in August 2001.[1] By the official opening of *Descent* in November 2002, however, the reception was quite different. Following 9/11, a highly charged context metamorphosed *Descent* into an elegy.

In the 9/11 aftermath, New Yorkers were confronted daily with strict new policing and security checks in city buildings, and TV replays of burning buildings with people racing away or descending stairs. Homemade fliers begging for information about missing friends and family members were taped to walls, and downtown the acrid odor of electrical fires seeped into everything. The city was trapped in a culture of disaster, which affected how Lafrance's dance was received at its 2002 official opening. *Descent* was transmuted into a lament that illustrates how textual meanings shift under contextual pressures. New horizons of expectations altered the audiences' reception.[2]

General reception theories, personal memories of spectatorship, and recent practices of "psychogeography," offer new perspectives on Lafrance's modalities of dance-making and performance that were displayed in *Descent* and *Agora* (2005). "Psychogeography" is the practice of drifting (*dérive*) through urban spaces without a planned destination, mapping the cityscape according to structures of emotions, energy fields, and memories—whether real or imagined. In theory, these maps are subversive because they disrupt traditional cartographies and the hegemonic powers that made them.[3] Because psychogeographers' maps trace paths of desire, overlaying emotions, images of past and present, the detritus or materiality of buildings, streets, and places, these maps represent more accurately how individuals navigate the city. As personal experiences and city "readings," they lend themselves well to artistic practices.[4] Lafrance uses the architecture and cityscapes as both scenography and character in her works. Exceptionally tuned to the fugitive ambiences, the physicality of the site itself is the force that propels her. She discovers her site and then envisions the dance that will occur there—as she did with *Descent* and *Agora*. Psychogeography evolved from a lineage of thought about reception theory, which, as it progressed during the twentieth century, shifted from literary discipline (from Hans-Robert Jauss, Stuart Hall, Guy Debord) into the social sciences and performance camps. Throughout the transition, spectatorship gained prominence.[5] A pivotal change occurred with the Parisian Situationists; Guy Debord was a crucial thinker in developing this theory, progressing from being first a Letterist (1950s), then a Situationist (1960s), then a Psychogeographer (1970s), which made him instrumental in theorizing the move from the literary and image-ist mediums into performative actions.[6] In the performative realm, autonomous interpretations made by the audiences were recognized as more important than the producers' intentions (Dennis Kennedy, Richard Schechner, Steve Pile, new historicists). The old binary schema of the hegemonic-power producer and passive-subaltern receiver subsided; it was accepted that the makers' meanings and the audience's meaning-making could be, and usually are, quite different. When actively mixed together in performance concepts of "spectator" and "maker" become slippery, acknowledging the fact that performance and meaning happen in the temporal space between the thing being observed and the observer. Potentially, everyone can be an agent and object of observation, and those fluctuations vary from second to second. Then, there are unexpected political events whose repercussive pressures add yet another element of meaning-making that can radically alter perceptions. In *Descent*, outside politics would shape perceptions of Lafrance's work; in *Agora*, the politics of the work would shape the political perceptions about the site.

Post 9/11, a profoundly changed semiotics of naked bodies and stairs was operant. In 2002, Bruce Springsteen's popular song "The Rising" became the city's requiem, giving expression to a city's mourning.[7] An homage to the more than 343 Fire Department of New York (FDNY) firefighters who died the day the towers fell, "The Rising" ascribed new meanings to otherwise quotidian urban architecture: stairs were heroic, sacrificial. They were graves. They ascended. Stairs were also the material and metaphoric center of *Descent*.

By *Descent*'s premiere in November 2002, Lafrance had substantially enlarged her work. Now sixty minutes long, the dance had a cast of twelve *corps* dancers, two featured soloists, an audience guide, an enhanced musical score of ambient sounds, and new costumes. The choreography was further developed, with additional activities and brief domestic vignettes performed on various stair landings. As *Descent* began, spectators stood on the top floor with the guide, staring down the vertiginous stairwell, irresistibly drawn toward its dim void. Then out of the darkness one woman's spectral, white-powdered nude torso draped itself over the railings several stories below, her auburn hair cascading down as she slowly moved up the stairs, rolling her torso over and over on the banister. It was disconcerting, disorienting. At the next landing, tilting her body far out and over the banister, she flung her arms up as if calling out, and was joined by the other dancers reaching out in unison, one on each of the twelve landings. The image spilled down in diminishing perspective.

They were beautiful. Involved in everyday actions, like washing arms and hair, whispering, laughing, stringing ropes between banisters to hang out clothes to dry, letting feathers from a ripped pillow drift down the stairwell, they were softly erotic—and eerie. "They look intensely up at us, insisting that we become part of the spooky spatially distorted environment."[8] As the dance descended, the audience followed, scrutinizing the strange surroundings—filigreed iron banisters, dirty windows, cracked walls, and worn marble—in a kind of *dérive* reading of the history of this particular historic building. Lafrance purposely suffused her dance with a sense of periodicity that was never precisely defined; it could have been the past, the future, or another world, constructed as an episodic series of resonant scenes. Layers of time peeled

Figure 9.1. *Descent*, dancers on banisters of Clock Tower, New York, NY. Nov 2002. Photographer, Claire Le Pichon. Courtesy of SensProduction.

away. "[B]edroom groupings on the landings recall the Victorian era when this McCoy, Meade & White building was constructed," noted critic Mindy Aloff. "Tenement groupings, where women lean precipitously over banisters giving onto a 200 foot stairwell, suggest the 20th century when the city of New York acquired the building, which now houses the domestic violence court and services for juvenile offenders."[9] About midway through the descent, some of the dancers slipped upstairs above the audience. Suddenly, in a turnaround, the dancers above were looking down at us (were we the performers?) and we stared up at them gazing down at us. In her mission statement Lafrance explains her methodologies in making a site-specific piece: "The process [interestingly she does not use the first person] pursues the intrinsic meaning of the place for its historical, symbolic and energetic values and explores how places are marked by the 'life' of people and objects and vice versa. The final product is imbued with the atmosphere of the space . . . the performance unfolds as an intimate and unpredictable voyage for traveling view."[10]

This striking overlap in language reveals how Lafrance's creative process resonates with the processes of psychogeography—a name she had heard of although she was not familiar with its complex theories.[11] Guy Debord formulated the practice of *dérive* in order to discover the "form[s] of emotional work that comprise the urban experience."[12] Steve Pile, a current psychogeographer, stated it more clearly in 2014: "What is real, then, about cities is as much emotional as physical, as much visible as invisible, as much slow moving as ever speeding up, as much coincidence as connection."[13] In the ideal, psychogeography was conceived of as a way to break up hegemonic powers and incite political change. Steve Pile takes the next logical step and pushes the Situationists' psychogeographic explorations into elusive psychic and motional fields to reveal another kind of ephemera. "Nor do I necessarily think that cultural forms of expression necessarily reveal in some direct and obvious ways their feelings. Instead, these structures should be thought to be fabricated, devious, contradictory, mobile, changing and changeable. To evoke the more febrile, secretive and ambivalent aspects of emotional life, I prefer the term 'phantasmagoria.' The term phantasmagoria implies many things. In some ways, it describes an experience of movement, of a procession of things before the eyes. In other ways, it invokes the importance not only of what can be seen, of the experience of the immediate, but also of life beyond the immediately visible or tangible."[14]

There are two kinds of "processions" here: one is the action of drifting through the city; the other would be the still observer before whom a cinema of possibilities passes. In both cases there is a sensibility of temporal slippage that fuses past, present, and future. Lafrance, too, creates multilayered processions and seeks scenographies in provocative architectures.[15] Instead of wandering through a planned city, in *Descent*, the audience entered a historic place, went upstairs, and then walked downstairs as the performance unfolded below and above them. New meanings accumulated on Lafrance's original intentions about women as subjects and objects of sexual desire in the domestic realm.

For the audience, the situation was fraught from the moment they entered the building. New security checks required for all city buildings post-9/11 meant each person had to pass through a metal detector and have bags checked by unsmiling New York City police officers looking for weapons and bombs. If anyone had forgotten 9/11, this checkpoint brought home that we were under siege.

New Yorkers were still reeling from the attack, the three thousand dead, the barrage of TV images seared into the mind's eye: the towers being hit by one plane, then another. Bodies and desks tumbling down in a snowstorm of paper, followed by the slow-motion implosions of the collapsing skyscrapers with enormous clouds of grey ash seeming to pursue the people fleeing before them. But time was not as compressed as TV presented it. From the moment of first impact on the north tower to the collapse of the south tower, one-hour-and-forty-two minutes passed. During that time, hundreds of FDNY firemen entered the towers and climbed the darkened stairs to rescue trapped victims and battle fires as terrified office workers filed down.[16] Again and again photographs and videos were shown of doomed firemen gathering together in preparation. It was hard slogging. Wearing heavy helmets, black boots with four-inch soles, yellow-and-black coats, carrying tanks and gear, they were going to ascend the stairs. Once they entered the buildings—stepping out of what was surely one of the most beautiful days of the year—they entered total darkness.[17]

Haunted by these images, Bruce Springsteen wrote "The Rising" in January and released it in July. Composed as a panegyric to the FDNY heroes, the song became the megahit of that year, earning three Grammys.[18] The evocative lyrics and driving pulse of the chorus revivified tragic images. Springsteen gave a first-person voice and emotional narrative to events by telling the thoughts of a single fireman (he represents the FDNY 343) as he climbs the stairs. The music industry's power to disseminate product, and the ability of popular song to emotionalize events, transformed Springsteen's song into a messianic keening, overshadowing newspaper or television reports. Pop culture, if successful, distills—perhaps clichés—sentiments and memories with mythologies that give meaning to suffering. Song embeds meaning through rhythm, an infinitely more powerful and fundamental communicative system than words. Among many post-9/11 songs Springsteen's was neither the first nor the last. But it was the most effective. To be effective (here I purposely conflate "popularity" and "effective") the musician/poet does not merely replicate feelings, he lures the listener inside the song, inside the rhythmic pulse to carry them—however fleetingly—into the center of significance. "Music, like identity, is both performance and story, describes the social in the individual, and the individual in the social."[19] Music exists in/as the action. "[I]n talking about identity we are talking about a particular kind of experience . . . Identity is not a thing, but a process—an experiential process which is most vividly grasped as music."[20] The singer only has a few minutes to persuade the listener that what he is saying matters. If successful, he and the song become the rhetoric. Springsteen excels at this. He looks and sounds like the working-class men he exalts, and in "The Rising," he glorifies everyday work that gives and takes lives.

> "The Rising"
> Can't see nothin' in front of me
> Can't see nothin' coming up behind
> I make my way through this darkness
> I can't feel nothing but this chain that binds me
> Lost track of how far I've gone, how high I've climbed
> On my back's a sixty pound stone
> On my shoulder a half mile of line[21]
> *Chorus*:
> Come on up for the rising
> Come on up, lay your hands in mine
> Come on up for the rising,
> Come on up for the rising tonight.[22]

When the dancers and spectators physically bunched together on the stairs for *Descent*, it coalesced accumulations of stories and images (idiosyncratic to each person). Roles of performer and watcher switched during the performance. Like the escaping office workers, the audience became performer(s) reenacting the descent of stairs to the safety of the ground. Initially the dancers were below, and the audience looked down the stairwell's dim recess through the twelve levels of spiraling steps. However, when some of the dancers appeared above, and we were looking up at them looking down at us: Were they the women left behind, or, the spirits of the men who died? Time swirled forward and backward. Spectators were caught in between, physically stranded between upstairs and downstairs, between past and future. Descending into the murkiness, the audience inverted the upward ascent by the FDNY but, simultaneously, also presaged the next hours when the FDNY again entered the darkness, this time going down to search for buried survivors inside "the pile," the dangerous and collapsing hill of grey ash and enormous pieces of building debris.[23] "Among the homages to New York created since the attack of September 11 nothing has yet surpassed a dance-installation called *Descent*," wrote dance critic Mindy Aloff; "one sees the figures receding through the deep space like so many doomed moths in a darkly mirrored room.... One is also led to think about the levels of human interaction that have taken place in or near here over the past century, as very gently, the piece leads us downwards."[24] Although this was not the intent of the choreographer, in that piece, in the way the audience and performers were situated on the stairs, at that particular moment in history of traumatic archived memories—*Descent* skirted the edges of a ritualized commemorative performance.

Diana Taylor, writing about formalized, ancient Mexican religious ritual performance celebrations of *la virgen de Guadeloupe*, labeled these constructed events "scenarios" in order to distinguish them as more than narrative, more than an all-encompassing scenography. *Descent*, of course, is neither socially nor religiously inculcated in the same way as Taylor's religious rituals. "A scenario is not necessarily, or even primarily, mimetic. While the paradigm allows for a continuity of cultural myths and assumptions, it usually works through *reactivation* rather than duplication [emphasis mine]."[25] An odd and powerful commemorative ritual that arose tangentially from the FDNY tragedy is the worldwide "9/11 Memorial Climb" (listings come from as far away as Vietnam and New Zealand).[26] Firemen from across the nation and world, along with relatives, colleagues, and friends of first responders of all kinds annually make a 110-story climb in memory of the 343 fallen FDNY heroes. In fact, none of the FDNY could have gone above the 88th floor at the World Towers, but they were prepared to ascend to the top.[27] In the 9/11 Memorial Climb, participants wear weighty firemen's gear, the strongest also humping 110 pounds of equipment. This muscular and mental memorial reenactment is a ritualized transmission of traumatic memory, embodying both history and a mythology. Close identification occurs between the reactivator and the idealized "fallen hero." Each climber carries the photograph of one of the fallen—although at times it is unclear if the fallen are always from the original FDNY 343 or from members of a local firehouse. Repeating a physical action instills a muscular immediacy that fuses the present and past. This event is trained for, rehearsed, and consists of learned sets of movements to properly reenact the climb.[28] Very often lines of climbers snake up and down stadium steps, and depending on the weather and geographic locales, it can be a blistering hot endeavor. Hundreds of videos, photographs, and mission statements mark the importance of this ritual of transmission (Googling "9/11 stair climb" earned 87,600 hits). Taylor's scenario theories are particularly useful in looking at the 9/11 Memorial Climb in relationship to similar areas of social functionality inherent in *Descent*. This provokes questions about proximity—the physical closeness of performer/watcher (who plays which role when?); the timing (the performance was close in time to the event); the proximity of 346 Broadway "Clock Tower" to Ground Zero where demolition was still in progress. "Rather than a copy, the scenario constitutes a once-againness. . . . Scenarios, like other forms of transmission, allow commentators to historicize specific practices. . . . The scenario places spectators within its frame, implicating us in its ethics and politics."[29]

Yet for *Descent*—and here is an arresting fact—the significant and peripheral juxtapositions of events outside the performance, the images, movements, texts, song, and interplay of memories were powerful unintended consequences. Lafrance did nothing *consciously* to deviate from her original intentions about women viewed as sexual objects and subjects in the domestic sphere when she enlarged the dance between the August 2001 work-in-progress showing and the November 2002 opening. She did not even know Springsteen's song—listening to it for the first time in 2015.[30] After the first performance of her work-in-progress she had, however, been looking for other sites with resplendent staircases. Her idea was to place *Descent* in various locations around the city, "change it up a little in that way," but she let that idea go when she realized she would not find another staircase as perfect as the one she had.[31]

She did not change *Descent* to respond to 9/11 and recalled "to my surprise and delight, I heard them [the audience] talking about it [9/11]. But it is not something I tried to do." Lafrance liked hearing the audience make those connections because "it signified the importance and ownership of the audience of the piece." Audience inclusion is crucial in Lafrance's ideals about her work. "Thinking back what is kind of amazing, is the amount of me *not* being concerned with that event [9/11] in my reconstruction. . . . But who knows what goes on in any unconscious? I think that's the beauty of it. . . . What I think is going on in the soul and mind of the artist is you are working on a personal expression and a collective expression at the same time. I was probably [in] my collective expression, discussing this experience. I mean it *was in my body* [the 9/11 trauma]. . . . [R]eflecting on the work. . . . I think a lot of my work had a very political approach, but I wasn't particularly conscious of how to position it in the context of a political conversation."[32]

When a work was/is good, it improves under shifting contexts; allusions unnoticed before come to the forefront; images gain more profound resonances; the piece becomes more relevant. This occurred with *Descent*. Expanding on the 9/11 responses, Marco Abel, writing about Don DeLillo, states: "[the] most significant intervention in the post-9/11 discourse is that present-day attempts to imagine a (traumatic) event's sense cannot operate exclusively on the level of the event's content (the representational what) without attending to the rhetorical mode of presentation, the ethical how."[33]

In post-9/11 context, the rice-powdered dancer that began the piece looked like the ash-covered runners racing before the clouds of smoke—or a Butoh figure of death. A solo dancer wearing a bright red dress (was she dressed to go out?) ran downstairs but disappeared, seeming to melt into the cement wall.[34] This is, of course, exactly what occurred with the Twin Towers. In the raging fires and wreckage, everything—and everyone—turned to ash. Of the more than 3,000 dead, only 291 intact bodies were recovered. One of the FDNY first responders remembered: "I didn't see victims. They were dust. And I was inhaling them. So . . . you're literally taking these people in. And there's no one for us to help. When the wind blew, you couldn't grab them. They were gone."[35]

As we arrived at the bottom two floors, the feathers were drifting down the stairwell and the dancers, who were lying on the stairs and had been slowly sliding down the last flight—stopped. At the dance's finish, a pile of bodies is stretched on the stairs and we are left with the question: Were they climbing up, or, were they climbing down?

Figure 9.2. *Descent*, dancers lying on stairs. Clock Tower, New York, NY. Nov. 2002. Photographer, Claire Le Pichon. Courtesy of SensProduction.

Three years later, however, Lafrance would become an artist-citizen with a political agenda when she made *Agora* (2005). "*Agora* was inspired and created in celebration of the historic McCarren Park pool site, a 50,000 square foot abandoned pool in Williamsburg. The site-specific dance performance invited the community to re-experience a moment in movement in the monumental public space."[36] Her first task was to bring activity to the dead space (the pool) at the edge of Greenpoint in Brooklyn. Certainly, the publicity surrounding *Agora* before the performance, plus the thousands of people who came to see it, were important interventions on behalf of the community. Politicians were invited to come to a rehearsal—they took notice. The timing was right. The energizing force of Lafrance's indefatigable discussions with the city was pivotal. Slow-moving talks between the community and city about the pool finally turned into a productive dialogue. Clear Channel Entertainment donated more than $200,000 to help stabilize existing pool structure.[37] Lafrance's dance transformed the site into a viable performance venue and neighborhood site for other events: there were concert events (sponsored by Clear Channel Entertainment), several local Brooklyn film festivals, community craft fairs, and flea markets. Finally, after real renovation, McCarren was fully restored in 2012 as a city pool, claimed as one of the city's best places to swim on hot summer days.[38]

Still, when Lafrance began her initial "imaginary" of the piece it was "not in the spirit of activism but because I was interested in the aesthetics of the site."[39] Personal aesthetics are first for Lafrance, and it is from that prime position that the political and ethical unfold. "As an artist, you *do* things—then it has all these meanings."[40] She always works from the preeminence of physical action and place. This aligns her with new psychogeographers, walking and creating their cartographies of ambiences; and it also aligns her with the utopic Marxist Situationists of the 1960s, who wanted their refigured space to affect sociopolitico changes. Lafrance discovered the McCarren Pool in 1996 when her own *dérive* led her a couple of blocks from her Brooklyn loft. Originally built in 1936 by the Works Progress Administration (WPA), the 50,000-square-foot pool accommodated up to 6,800 people. Then in 1983 the city closed the pool, surrounded it with a chain-link fence, and let it fall into wretched disrepair. The large Moorish-style bathhouse and all the pool's walls were covered in graffiti; the basin was filled with broken couches, syringes, dog feces, shattered glass, weeds, and trash. "I thought it was superb," Lafrance remembers;

"Grand on such a large scale, like New York City buildings." Pool lights set in the walls for nighttime swimming were like gigantic portholes in a wrecked ocean liner. "I knew I wanted to do a piece there."[41] Her instantaneous emotional imaginings of that place parallels the kind of encounters promoted by geographer/theorist Doreen Massey. "She [Massey] gives particular importance to the potential surprise of space and to the encounter with the unforeseen, . . . an approach that emphasizes dynamic simultaneity, where space is in process and incomplete, where it eludes final determination and representation."[42] Lafrance was also immediately struck with the paucity of ideas about what to do with McCarren. "My vision for the space has a longer thread than just [my] project," she said. "We want this space for community use, for other performances and for it to be used as an experimental space where people can develop site-specific ideas."[43] Most important, she brought muscle and activity to the rubbish-filled pool when she and a cadre of friends slipped through the broken chain-link fence with shovels and brooms and actually started to clean up some areas to begin rehearsing. By starting with action, she brought attention from the neighborhood and local government to what she was doing—then she could tell them what she wanted. She had the visions. The politicians had the money. After dogged discussion with the office of Brooklyn Parks Commissioner (BPC) Julius Spiegel for almost one year, Lafrance became politicized because of the endless negotiations. Finally she got permission to do her piece using thirty dancers.[44]

Agora opened September 13, 2005. "[With] simultaneous events covering the vast expanse of the pool basin, *Agora* produced the illusion of travel through the different layers of visceral urban experiences."[45] All kinds of dance and activities from the silly to the sublime intersected inside the pool like a double-exposed movie progressing with strange temporal elongations and laminations of simultaneous actions.

"A couple of kids gather at one end [of the pool] and smash bottles, dancers with skateboards strapped to their backs do tricks and elaborate partner work, a roving band of dancers follows a boombox in a grocery cart."[46] A troupe of sweet young girls dressed in white tunics, like little Isadorables, swept across the pool running and leaping. Elizabeth Streb's dancers rebounded in and out of a small wading-pool. A gang of men dressed in suits and fedoras suddenly appeared, passed by a dancer who seemed to be doing slow elegant laps back and forth across the pool. "But beyond these interspersions of dancey dance, the

Figure 9.3. *Agora*, dancers in McCarren Park Pool. Brooklyn, NY. September 2005. Photographer Richard Termine. Courtesy of SensProduction.

space percolated with activity. . . . All time converged in the pool as if someone had shaken out a very big sack of brightly-colored balls and let them bounce and roll where they will."[47] At the end of the piece, everybody was invited to jump into the empty pool and party. Seven years later, in 2012, with the grand opening of the restored McCarren Pool, that did become the reality.[48]

Lafrance's aesthetic is about *how* a series of images plays out rather than "the *what*" of content—which implies there is a correct perception, a viewpoint to be defended and continued. Interpretations are ceded to the spectators "response-ability" as Marco Abel calls it. In his essay about "image processes," Abel emphasizes that any work about 9/11 must "stylistically configure" a multiplicity of truths so "response-ability as [is] always and necessarily a question of how rather than what; (e)valuation rather than representation; the power of the false rather than the regime of truth."[49] The same could be said of *Agora*.

Descent and *Agora* have accrued extraordinary vitality in their afterlife. They retain resonances of social and civic meanings within circles of scenarios—ritualized reactivations defined by Diane Taylor as "Rather than a copy, the scenario constitutes a once-again-ness. . . . Scenarios, like other forms of transmission, allow commentators to historicize specific practices. . . . The scenario places spectators within its frame, implicating us in its ethics and politics."[50] Using this as an analytic frame, *Descent* was an unintentional scenario of 9/11. Clustered on stairs, the spectators were as much a part of the scenography as the walls and railings. They were active observers, and ambient "characters" in the performance event. Activism as awareness is inherent in the ways that Lafrance designs and structures her work. In *Descent*—caught in the melancholic political atmosphere of post-911 in a building near Ground Zero—there were heightened emotional, spiritual, and ethical overtones to progressing downstairs with the dancers. In a surprising coincidence thousands of national and international participants in the 9/11 Memorial Stair Climbs inadvertently created an international scenario on a grand scale that re-lives the sacrificial ascent of New York City's firefighters.

The performance of *Agora* ended with the rallying call, "Everybody jump into the pool!" In many ways, *Agora* was a small and significant catalytic scenario that set the stage for the larger social scenario to be realized seven years later when swimmers actually jumped into the water at the official (re)opening of the McCarren Park Pool in 2012. *Agora*, which means "assembly" or "gathering place" in Greek, primed the pool with life. Lafrance, who always works from the primacy of action, says that you take a space and put activity in it—then it has meaning. Now when people swim in McCarren's 50,000-square-foot pool they are unwitting reenactors in a grand and joyful civic scenario.

The politics surrounding 9/11 changed the way audiences saw *Descent*, whereas *Agora* changed the way the politicians and neighborhood saw the McCarren pool. Structured within both works' dynamics are interactions that stimulate mobilizations and encourage making connections. In both cases, Lafrance's work initiated a kind of ongoing-ness of sociopolitical reverberations. The open nature of her work (with no linear narratives or specific meanings) compels the viewers to make meaning and access scenarios of their own imaginings. These could be seen as mental *dérives* that wander through many-layered realities in the landscapes of their minds, gathering details along personal paths that find emotional architectures and ambient terrains.

The ways Lafrance chooses sites and constructs serial images of suggestion (rather than representations) echoes psychogeographic ideologies. Her art offerings are configured for enacting audiences who enjoy a broad spectrum of participation and responses. This also dovetails with Abel's tenets (influenced by André Bazin) that the ethical responsibility of anyone who "engages images" is to open possibilities: "*Seeing*, in other words, is less a matter of (in) correct perception than a question of how subjects can respond to events."[51] Lafrance formalizes and merges her art and ethical belief that there is no single answer, no single narrative but "an experience of place, of being somewhere, feeling what it is like to be in such a place, an experience of seeing things in a different way and seeing the beauty of things as they are."[52]

Notes

1. Noémie Lafrance, Sens Productions, "Descent," accessed November 1, 2016, http://sensproduction.org/descent; Noémie Lafrance, interview by author, January 14, 2015, New York, NY.

2. For the purposes of this essay, more recent performative theories of reception will be used. However, reception theory embraces multiple positions on a spectrum between two polemic propositions: one cedes power to the author-producer (hegemonic power); the other places power with the receiver-reader-audience (subaltern-passive). The term "horizons of expectations" was first used by an early reception-theorist, Hans-Robert Jauss, in a 1967 essay, "The Change in the Paradigm of Literary Scholarship." Readers experienced changeable "horizons of expectations" at different time periods and/or according to what information they acquired; this caused a consequent shifting of "aesthetic distance," i.e., the distance between the author and reader agreeing versus a growing separation between author's intentions and readers' reception. A lucid synopsis of early reception theory is Michael Eckert, "Reception Theory: A Critical Introduction by Robert C. Holub," *Criticism* 27:3 (Summer 1985): 310–12.

3. David Pinder, "Arts of Urban Exploration," *Cultural Geographies* 12 (2005): 395.

4. Ibid. Pinder reports a witty performance of psychogeography which, for me, represents how we all use psychogeography in our navigations: Karen O'Rourke's project "New York body'n' soul map" in 2003, take[s] on new meaning through becoming the focus of story-telling and through the accumulation and mapping of details. Her project called out to local residents: "Send us your tiresome commutes, your everyday errands, your shopping sprees and secret shortcuts, your wrong turns, bike rides and bus routes. Write your paths through the city and we'll map them for you."

5. Brennon Wood, "Stuart Hall's Cultural Studies and the Problem of Hegemony," *British Journal of Sociology* 49:3 (September 1998): 399–414. Stuart Hall in 1981 "Notes on Deconstructing 'The Popular'" ceded audiences more power. He parsed reception theory (in broad terms) to "encoding" (power) and "decoding" (receivers) and orients audiences in three more nuanced positions of decoding meanings: dominant-hegemonic (agreement); negotiated position; oppositional position.

6. Duncan Hay, "Transforming Psychogeography: From Paris to London" (paper presented at the 2008 Literary London Conference, London, Brunel University, July 2–4, 2008, *Walled City*, posted October 18, 2012, walled-city.net/transforming-psychogeography-from-paris-to-london/.

7. Christine Lee Gengaro, "Requiems for a City: Popular Music's Response to 9/11," *Popular Music and Society* 32:1 (2009): 26.

8. Lisa Jo Sagolla, "Descent," *Backstage,* November 20, 2002, 41.

9. Mindy Aloff, "Noemie LaFrance, Crouching on the Steps [Descent, in New York]," *BalletTanz*: On Stage, January 2003, 38.

10. Noémie Lafrance, Sens Productions, "About," accessed November 1, 2016, http://sensproduction.org/about.

11. Noémie Lafrance, interview by author, New York, NY, January 14, 2015.

12. Guy Debord's catalytic idea posits that image representation has taken the place of "real" experience which, in turn, inspired him and the Situationists toward more active citizen-producer, whose drifting walks enacted performative theories of "psychogeography."

13. Steve Pile, *Real Cities: Modernity, Space, and the Phantasmagorias of City Life* (London: Sage, 2005), 3.

14. Ibid.

15. Aloff, *BalletTanz*, 38.

16. Towers being hit: North Tower at 8:46 a.m., South Tower at 9:03 a.m.; collapses of North Tower at 9:59 a.m.; South Tower at 10:28 a.m. "Collapse of the World Trade Center," last modified February 9, 2015, http://en.wikipedia.org/wiki/Collapse_of_the_World_Trade_Center#Aircraft_impact.org/wiki/Collapse_of_the_World_Trade_Center#Aircraft_impact.

17. WTC911demolition, "First Response—Ground Zero America," *YouTube* video, 43:58, July 3, 2011, https://www.youtube.com/watch?v=nq7rdhZfyJc#!; "September 11 Attacks," last modified February 14, 2015, http://en.wikipedia.org/wiki/September_11_attacks#Events.

18. "Bruce Springsteen: Grammy Awards," last modified February 14, 2015, http://en.wikipedia.org/wiki/Bruce_Springsteen#Grammy_Awards.

19. Simon Frith, "Music and Identity," in *Questions of Cultural Identity*, ed. Stuart Hall and Paul Du Gay (London: Sage, 1996), 109.

20. Ibid., 110.

21. "On my shoulder half a mile of line" refers to the coiled 2½" wide hoses, plus nozzles and clamps, that the FDNY carry on their shoulders. Backpacks weighed between 50 and 75 pounds (as noted on official NYFD site) plus many FDNY carried 30-pound tanks. *New York City Fire Department*, "Candidate Physical Ability Test (CPAT)," 2014, http://www.candidatephysicalabilitytest.com/the-cpat-success-guide/.

22. "The Rising (Bruce Springsteen Song)," last modified December 12, 2014, http://en.wikipedia.org/wiki/The_Rising_%28Bruce_Springsteen_song%29; stereomusicvideo, "Bruce Springsteen—The Rising (official video)," 4:28, February 6, 2011, https://www.youtube.com/watch?v=6i-fiRgbpr4; "The Rising—Bruce Springsteen," Google Play Music, https://play.google.com/music/preview/Tfijq5ognts6ocxpwiqn5kbknya?lyrics=1&utm_source=google&utm_medium=search&utm_campaign=lyrics&pcampaignid=kp-lyrics.

23. "9/11 by the Numbers," *New York Magazine*, January 2011, nymag.com/news//articles/wtc/1year/numbers.htm; Chris Smith, "Braving The Heat," *New York Magazine*, January 2011, nymag.com/nymetro/news/sept11/features/5199/; WTC911demolition, "First Response—Ground Zero America."

24. Aloff, *BallettTanz*, 38.

25. Diana Taylor, "Acts of Transfer," In *The Archive and the Repertoire: Performing Cultural Memory in the Americas* (Durham, NC: Duke University Press, 2003), 32.

26. Ibid. Taylor writes, "Many contemporary performances carry on these representational traditions as they continue to form a living chain of memory and contestation," like the National Fallen Firefighters Foundation's "9-11 Stair Climbs," http://www.firehero.org/events/9-11-stair-climbs/9-11-stair-climbs: "History of the 9-11 Memorial Stair Climb." The first stair climb held to support the mission of the National Fallen Firefighters Foundation was held on September 11, 2005, when five Colorado firefighters convened at a high-rise building in downtown Denver to climb 110 flights of stairs in memory of their FDNY brothers who were killed in the terrorist attacks of 9-11. The following year, twelve firefighters participated, representing four fire departments from the metro Denver area. Each subsequent year, attendance grew, until it was capped at 343 participants in 2008. Since its beginning, the Denver 9-11 Memorial Stair Climb has evolved into a much anticipated annual event, and generated interest from individuals across the country who hoped to adapt the format and host an event in their cities. In 2010, the original Denver team partnered with the National Fallen Firefighters Foundation to create a template that would enable coordinators to successfully replicate a 9-11 Memorial Stair Climb anywhere in the United States.

27. WTC911demolition, "First Response—Ground Zero America."

28. National Fallen Firefighters Foundation, "Training Resources," http://www.firehero.org/events/9-11-stair-climbs/training-resources/.

29. Taylor, "Acts of Transfer," 32.

30. Ibid.

31. Noémie Lafrance, interview by author, New York, NY, January 14, 2015.

32. Ibid.

33. Marco Abel, "Don DeLillo's 'In the Ruins of the Future': Literature, Images, and the Rhetoric of Seeing 9/11," *PMLA* 118:5 (2003): http://www.jstor.org/stable/1261462.

34. Sally Sommer (audience member), November 2002. There was an almost invisible space between the stair and the wall where she slid down.

35. Fireman Walsh, as quoted in Chris Smith, "Braving The Heat," *New York Magazine*, January 2011.

36. Noémie Lafrance, "Agora," http://sensproduction.org/agora.

37. Pia Catton, "The Unsung Heroine Of the McCarren Park Pool," *Wall Street Journal*, August 26, 2012, http://www.wsj.com/articles/SB10000872396390444506004577613583253184216; Kristen Iverson, "The Rebirth of McCarren Park Pool Started with One Woman: Noemie Lafrance," *Brooklyn Magazine*, August 27, 2012, http://sensproduction.org/sites/default/files/wysiwyg/images/BMMPPDRAFT1.jpg.

38. Ibid.

39. Noémie Lafrance, telephone interview with author, February 4, 2015, New York, NY.

40. Ibid.

41. Sally Sommer, "Everybody into the Pool (and Dance)," *New York Times*, Arts & Leisure, September 4, 2005.

42. Doreen Massey, as quoted in Pinder, "Arts of Urban Exploration," *Cultural Geographies*, 391.

43. Sommer, "Everybody into the Pool (and Dance)."

44. Catton, "The Unsung Heroine of the McCarren Park Pool." In late 2004, "she approached the office of the Brooklyn Parks Commissioner, who at the time was Julius Spiegel." Lafrance asked permission to use the dry pool and was told the site was in such bad condition "the public could not be allowed in before a long list of repairs was accomplished. They thought I was going to say, 'OK. Thank you. Bye,'" she recalled. "But I said, 'No, give me the list. What are we talking about? Holes in the ground? There's glass? Please be more specific.'" According to Ms. Lafrance, "around March 2005 the office gave her a to-do list. Meanwhile, the huge concert promoter Live Nation, hoping to present concerts at the pool, put $200,000 toward the clean-up. (Live Nation had no comment. City Parks Foundation, which facilitated the effort, also had no comment.)"

45. Noémie Lafrance, "Agora."

46. Andy Horwitz, "Agoraphilia," culturebot arts + culture + ideas. September 14, 2005, www.culturebot.org/?agoraphilia.

47. Eva Yaa Asantaewaa, "Dancing with Eva Yaa Asantewaa: Exclusive Reviews," September 15, 2005, http://sensproduction.org/sites/default/files/wysiwyg/images/Dancing%20with%20Eva%20Yaa%20Asantewaa.jpg.

48. Catton, "The Unsung Heroine Of the McCarren Park Pool."

49. Abel, "Don DeLillo's 'In the Ruins of the Future,'" 1236.

50. Taylor, "Acts of Transfer," 32.

51. Abel, "Don DeLillo's 'In the Ruins of the Future,'" 1238.

52. Noémie Lafrance, quoted in Krista Wilson, "Noemie Lafrance," *Atomica* 3:3 (Spring 2006), accessed November 1, 2016, http://sensproduction.org/sites/default/files/wysiwyg/images/ATOMICA.2006.jpg.

10

The Land of Dance Crimes

Social Dancing and the New York City Cabaret Laws

INA SOTIROVA

On a Sunday afternoon in August 2000, hundreds of people of all ages and races dance through the Lower East Side. "Dance is not a crime!" Their chant echoes through the streets. "Dance is not a crime!" Signs bop above their heads: *Legalize dancing! Dancing is fun; Dancing keeps you physically fit.* The Million Mambo March is in full swing. For the finale, they congregate at Tompkins Square Park. "New York City used to be called 'Fun City,'" Robert Prichard proclaims over a megaphone, "Now it's the land of nightlife taskforces and dance crimes."[1] The crowd roars in disapproval.

Led by the Dance Liberation Front (DLF), the march and ensuing party in the park are part of a series of dance actions protesting Prohibition-era legislation that strictly regulates dancing in the city. Prichard is one of the three DLF cofounders. Along with his friends and fellow Lower East Side residents, Jen Miller and Francis Hall, "we were forced to commit ourselves to the cause after bars in our neighborhood were padlocked because their patrons decided to get a groove on," DLF's manifesto explains.[2] Under the notorious Cabaret Law, originally passed in 1926 and still in effect well into the twenty-first century, dancing is forbidden wherever food and drink is served—unless the venue has a special, so-called Cabaret license. "The restriction is doubly complicated," New York University law professor and civil rights attorney Paul Chevigny explains, "because you not only need a license, but you have to be in a zone of the city that is zoned for dancing."[3] Over the course of his career, Chevigny was involved in not one, but two major court cases attacking the controversial legislation, which he wrote about in his book *Gigs: Jazz and the Cabaret Laws in NYC* (2004). A third lawsuit, filed in September 2014 by Brooklyn attorney and bar owner Andrew Muchmore, is challenging the Cabaret Law "in federal court on grounds that it violates freedom of expression and due process guaranteed by the First and 14th Amendments, respectively."[4] Three years later, he is still awaiting a decision.[5] "Obtaining a license is 'just unbelievably complicated and cumbersome,'" Muchmore told the *Wall Street Journal*. The same article states that "the cost of a license ranges from $150 to more than $1,000, depending on the venue's size and the duration of the license, which can be for up to two years." The Journal also reports that no Cabaret Law violations were issued in 2013 and only one in 2012, but just six years earlier, the bill for dancing citations added up to $43,342.64, with individual fines ranging between $100 and $500.[6] And according to a 2002 *National Post of Canada* article, between 1997 and 2000, New York City shut down sixty-nine venues for illegal dancing.[7] One of them was Baby Jupiter, a small East Village bar and performance space, where DLF's founders enjoyed hanging out and, occasionally, dancing. Francis Hall remembers that when the venue was fined and then padlocked because people were dancing, he and his friends thought this was "absolutely insane" and felt they had to do something.[8] They formed the Dance Liberation Front and started holding massive dance actions, like the Times Square Twistathon, a 600-person conga line up Avenue A, a giant Hokey-Pokey circle surrounding City Hall, and the Million Mambo March.

Fighting absurdity with a good dose of humor is a DLF trademark. At the Times Square Twistathon, for example, Hall wore "military fatigues to represent the revolutionary side and . . . a big pink tutu to represent the dance side." These protests, he explains, are "silly in nature but serious in our desire to eradicate this law." Although Hall admits to not having "much of a sense of rhythm" and hardly ever dancing, he's upset by "the idea that I don't have a right to, if I want to. It also disturbs me that it's not protected as free speech."[9] On the loudspeakers at Tompkins Square Park, he's adamant: "We are here to protest an unjust law based in racist ideology and we will *not* stop this fight until we have regained our right to boogie!"[10]

Back in 1926, when the Cabaret Law was originally introduced, Mayor Jimmy Walker had just come into office and the Harlem Renaissance was swinging. Jazz roared, booze only came bootlegged, and the increasingly popular African American dances like the Shimmy, the Charleston, and the Lindy Hop—seen as wild, provocative, and completely out of control—scandalized the moral norms of white America. In recommending the enactment of the Cabaret Law, the Committee on Local Laws wrote: "These nightclubs are

Figure 10.1. Francis Hall at a DLF dance action in downtown New York, NY, dressed in a costume inspired by Kraftwerk's hit song, "We Are the Robots." June 11, 2011. Photo by Ina Sotirova.

simply dance halls, where food and drink is served at exorbitant prices to the tune of jazz and tabloid entertainments ... Well, there has been altogether too much running 'wild' in some of these night clubs and, in the judgment of your Committee, the 'wild' strangers and the foolish native should have the checkrein applied a little bit."[11]

Avram Turkel has carefully studied what he calls "the long and sordid history of the Cabaret Laws and racial relations in New York City."[12] Between 2003 and 2005, in his role as legislative director to former New York City Councilman Alan Gerson (District 1), he worked on diverse legislation proposals, including an unsuccessful attempt to reform the city's dancing regulations. "There came a point [in the 1920s]," he explains, "where lots of white folk were going uptown to listen to jazz and to dance, and that was deemed a bad thing by our city elders and they wanted to shut down a lot of these venues uptown, and when I say uptown, I do mean black-owned venues, black-run venues, places with black music."[13]

Originally, the law encompassed not just dancing, but live music as well. It "required cabaret licenses for horns, drums, dancing, and music combos with more than three musicians," DLF research found, "in addition, the performers themselves were required to obtain licenses."[14] Instruments popular in white society and ballrooms, however—like pianos, organs, accordions and string instruments—were exempt from the licensing restriction.[15] As the Dance Liberation Front puts it, the City of New York had "decided to invoke onerous regulations designed to outlaw the perceived dangers of wild rhythmic improvisational music and interracial dancing."[16] Because of Prohibition, liquor licenses were not a viable means of exerting control over nightlife, so authorities came up with another tool. By requiring licenses for live music and dancing, Turkel contends, they could—and did—effectively punish those clubs and club owners that allowed interracial dancing to take place on their premises at a time (1926) when "mixing of the races was deemed unseemly and ill-advised."[17] It is impossible to know exactly how many Harlem clubs were shut down or refused a license, but there is no doubt that the Cabaret Law was widely used by city authorities in their attempt to discipline and moralize society. It is also unclear how long this went on, but as time passed and circumstances changed, the city's priorities also shifted.

"Enforcement of these kinds of regulations was very, very low in the 70s," civil rights attorney Chevigny explains, mainly because "the city was close to broke. They didn't have any extra money to do anything, so all kinds of activities like live music and dancing were done all over the place."[18] But this began to change after Mayor Ed Koch came into office in 1978. His administration zealously implemented neoliberal policies favoring big capital and real estate development over the vibrant cultural and artistic life that had been flourishing throughout Manhattan thanks to low rents and relatively little hassle from the police.[19] Gradually over the next decade, Chevigny points out, "the city's land values began to rise and the tax base rose so there was more money for enforcement" of all types of regulations, including the obscure Cabaret Law.[20] A long-time resident of Manhattan's Upper West Side and a lover of jazz, during the 1980s Chevigny was a regular at the Burgundy Café. The intimate, low-key jazz bar on Amsterdam Avenue and West 82nd Street was just around the corner from his home and provided exquisite live music. Due to the size of the location, there were never more than three musicians playing at a time, but saxophones and basses were common and very much appreciated by the clientele. In the prelude to his book, *Gigs: Jazz and the Cabaret Laws in NYC*, Chevigny recalls noticing that by the mid-1980s "horn players were increasingly rare" at the Burgundy. When he asked the owner about it, her response was "would you believe it's illegal to have a saxophone in here?" Baffled, he started researching the law and getting in touch with affected musicians. Not surprisingly, considering the legislation's goal to keep Harlem's nightlife in check, what he found was that the live-music clause disproportionately discriminated against instruments and musical combinations typical of jazz.[21]

Outraged, Chevigny became one of the principal attorneys in a case attacking the licensing requirement for live music, and his book came as a result of the long but successful legal battle of *Warren Chiasson et al. v. New York City Department of Consumer Affairs* (1988),[22] in which, Chevigny affirms, the New York Supreme Court ruled in favor of "a First Amendment interest in live music."[23] In January 1988, six decades after the Cabaret Law's introduction, the restrictions on live music were knocked down, but those on social dancing remained untouched. What Chevigny, his colleagues, and his clients could not have foreseen as they fought for their own narrowly defined rights of artistic expression, is that the liberation of live music would soon backfire on dancing New Yorkers. Now, Chevigny recognizes that shortly after the control of live music was removed, the city "tightened up on dancing."[24]

Club dancers like Archie Burnett and Byron Cox will be the first to testify to the noticeable revival of the Cabaret Law. Despite their generational difference—Burnett is in his late fifties and Cox barely in his forties—they both knew New York City as an eclectic and energizing place for ordinary dancers and their art. "Part of that fertile environment," Cox says, "was that you could dance, you could express yourself, and the Cabaret Laws make that very, very difficult." He remembers a time when "there used to be 10 or 15 options a night to dance . . . [to] hear different music [and] see different expression. People traveled from other countries to be here" to experience and partake in New York's vibrant dance culture.[25] For social dancers like him and Burnett, dance is a means of connection and communication, as Cox puts it, "on a very, very human level and void of many of the limitations, like language, age and all these other things that many times keep us apart as people."[26] Dancing in a social environment, such as the dance floor of your favorite club, fosters a sense of familiarity and extended family, melting individual differences into one collective experience and reducing feelings of social isolation. In these spaces of uninhibited self-expression, the body becomes a physical instrument and medium for expressing and releasing emotions much more effectively than spoken language, while the act of dancing together to a common beat becomes both a marker and a creator of community.

Cox knows firsthand how incredibly therapeutic social dancing can be. Prior to September 11, 2001, he was a corporate man, working as a communication technology specialist at a hedge fund. On the morning of the World Trade Center attacks, he had a job interview at one of the towers. He was running late, however, and, stuck in traffic, he did not reach the fatal destination. But his friend's father, whom he was supposed to meet, perished under the rubble. Dealing with the tragedy was a challenge for Cox, who found solace at underground dance parties. There, he discovered a utopian community, bounded by the language of music and dance where, he says, "you get to celebrate life and you get to share that with people despite your economic status or social standing."[27] When we shed these masks, he adds, "then we're forced to face oneself."[28] In an interview with British author Tim Lawrence, Burnett has described it as participation "in a musical-kinetic form of individual dissolution and collective bliss,"[29] while Lawrence talks about underground dance "as an open, participatory, experimental, non-competitive community that is organized around progressive pleasure."[30] Experiencing this and being a part of it not only helped Cox deal with the tragedy, it turned his life around. Today, he is a renowned house dancer and founder of the House Dance Project, a platform for sharing "the rich cultural experience associated with Underground Dance," as its Facebook profile reveals.[31] Aside from competing worldwide, he also teaches House Dance—a collection of dance styles and freestyle movements that emerged out of the nightclubs and underground dance parties of 1970s New York and Chicago.

The sense of community, shared joy, and unconstrained self-expression that helped Cox deal with the traumatic events of September 11 are the essence of this underground dance culture and a legacy of the contentious socioeconomic context of the 1970s and '80s. Archie Burnett, who has been a club dancer since the early 1980s, grew up in Brooklyn's Crown Heights during the '70s. An African American of Caribbean descent and strict religious upbringing, he remembers growing up in a rough neighborhood where street violence was a regular occurrence. Although not officially segregated, New York City was still clearly divided along racial lines. Firmly rooted in 1970s New York, underground dance culture "was born out of strife," Burnett asserts; "[it] was

Figure 10.2. Archie Burnett dances at a private Loft-style dance party. Brooklyn, NY. April 16, 2011. Photo by Ina Sotirova.

born out of wanting to belong to a society that had nothing to do with you, did not want you around *at all*."[32]

Lawrence is an academic expert on dance music whose 2003 book, *Love Saves the Day: A History of American Dance Music Culture, 1970–1979*, chronicles the birth, rise, and philosophy of New York's unique underground dance culture. In my documentary *freedom2dance* (2012), Lawrence argues that discotheque culture already existed in the 1960s, "but it had been very formalized, it had been very straight, there'd been all these social regulations about how you could or couldn't go on the dance floor."[33] In many ways, this reflected broader society where the rules of white patriarchal America prevailed. Despite the various civil rights movements, women, people of color, and other minorities, like gay and transsexual men and women, were largely marginalized and excluded from society well into the 1970s, '80s, and beyond. Gay men in particular were so repressed that they could be arrested for merely dancing together—there was an actual law against it. "So all of these groups were looking for an outlet to express themselves and to also find a way to have pleasure in a society where they lived fairly repressed lives."[34] The underground dance culture that emerged in the very beginning of the 1970s at places like the Loft and the Sanctuary gave these groups not only a venue for expression, but also a sense of belonging and community. These parties "gave them their freedom. They said 'you can come on the dance floor as you are, be as you are and express yourself.'"[35]

Freed from the social norms of the outside world, dancing became empowering. The underground dance clubs of the 1970s and 1980s, many of which were predominantly gay, helped to further build and strengthen a well-defined LGBTQ identity and community. It is no coincidence that the first symbol of the gay liberation movement is the Stonewall Inn, the iconic gay bar on Greenwich Avenue, where in 1969 a New York City Police Department (NYPD) raid—an otherwise common occurrence—turned into a violent riot.

"Whereas the dance floor was once the place for Man to meet Woman," Lawrence asserts, "the Loft and the Sanctuary recast it as a multicultural, polymorphous, free-flowing space where individuals could let go of their everyday selves and dissolve into the mutating desire of the crowd."[36] The dance experience at this type of underground venue was "ultimately focused on tribal transcendence, . . . grounded in a collective rather than individualistic notion of pleasure,"[37] liberating to both body and mind. These new kinds of underground dance parties provided a space free of discrimination and judgment where the diversity of human identity and expression was not merely respected, but celebrated. Although they operated largely as private members' clubs, they bred inclusive, diverse, and egalitarian communities based on the universal language of music, freedom, and movement. This, according to Lawrence, marks the dance culture that did not exist prior to 1970. It was precisely this environment that would also help Cox heal after 9/11. "There's no sexism, there's no racism, there's equal treatment [of] both gay and straight, there's no ageism," Cox affirms. "They seem to have solved many of the problems that still plague society."[38] Dancing in that sense became a means toward social progress, just as Loft founder David Mancuso had envisioned.[39] But, Cox points out, "if you wanna dance, like we do, you need space, you need folks to be able to come out and play, you need a venue that respects that, you need good music."[40] Referring to the renewed enforcement of the Cabaret Law, he concludes: "you stop having venues, and art is suppressed."[41]

Archie Burnett clearly remembers when, in the early 1990s, city authorities began using the obscure law to "shut down a lot of real tasty places where people could communicate" through dance. Many of the venues he frequented, if not shut down, were converted to regular bars with couches brought in to turn dance floors into lounge areas. But, he fervently argues, "socializing bar-sense is not socializing dance-sense."[42] Today, Lawrence affirms, dance culture in New York "is a pale shadow of what it was. If you compare the number of places where you can go out dancing today to the 1980s and even more, the 1970s, there's just no comparison."[43] Past data are hard to find, but the *National Post of Canada* claims that in the 1960s "there were 12,000 places for New Yorkers to get their groove on." In 2002, when the article was published, they were "barely 300,"[44] and the numbers keep shrinking. Department of Consumer Affairs records from 2008 show that the number of venues licensed for dancing dropped almost by half, to 179; by 2011, there were a mere 134 places in all five boroughs of New York City where people could legally dance.[45] In 2017, there are fewer than 100.[46]

Dance suffered "under this huge pressure of real estate."[47] New York City's Mayor Ed Koch in his 1978 inaugural address said gentrification was key to New York's revival and incentives were put in place for developers. Soon, and over time, many of the city's iconic dance venues were repurposed into expensive housing and luxury boutiques. "Landlords who rented their properties to party promoters across the 1970s and very early 1980s," Lawrence explains, went on "to strike significantly more handsome deals" with real estate and commercial entrepreneurs.[48] In an article for the *Journal of Popular Music*, Lawrence writes: "Concurrent property price inflation rocketed by 125 percent between 1980 and 1988" pricing party hosts, club owners, and artists "out of large swaths of Manhattan."[49]

With rising property values and the gentrification of entire neighborhoods throughout Manhattan and Brooklyn, the face and feel of the city drastically changed. By the mid-1980s, New York's SoHo neighborhood had shifted "from a zone that encouraged artistic and social experimentation to one . . . embedded in boutique consumerism and [luxury] real estate mania."[50] When the legendary Paradise Garage opened in the late 1970s, "there was no one living near the club," resident DJ David DePino told Lawrence. "On the corner was a parking lot. Eight years later the lot was gone and in its place was a very big and expensive apartment building. The developer and the local neighborhood association wanted the club gone so they persuaded the landlord not to renew the lease . . . Neighborhood associations are powerful. It's not something a landlord wants to have problems with."[51]

The revamping of previously industrial or commercial districts into fancy residential areas also fueled the tightening and enforcement of zoning regulations. Combined with the "Cabaret licensing laws, which are very repressive," this had an acutely adverse effect on New York City's dancers, their communities, and freedom of expression.[52] Paul Chevigny attests that "under [Mayor Rudolph] Giuliani's administration, there was a general inclination to enforce every kind of regulation that was on the books. Giuliani is a law enforcement sort of guy, so they had groups of city raiders who went out to clubs to check out whether they were complying with the rules."[53] One of those rules, of course, was unlicensed dancing. "The dance police," Avram Turkel sneers, "are essentially the task force that would go around ticketing venues for illegal dancing."[54] Overseen by NYPD and officially known as the Multi-Agency Response to Community Hotspots (MARCH), it was created under Giuliani and strengthened by the Bloomberg administration as "a group of different agencies all together coming to a venue to give you as many tickets as possible."[55]

In his role as legislative director at City Hall in the early 2000s, Turkel spent considerable time analyzing the city's controversial dancing regulations and working on a proposal for adequate reform. To begin with, he clarifies, the term "Cabaret Law is sort of a misnomer." What it really refers to is "an amalgam" of city laws and codes governing everything from building, safety, and noise regulations to zoning and finally, licensing.[56] The conclusion he came to is that even if the original 1920s law requiring a Cabaret license for dancing were to be removed from the Administrative Code of New York City, "you'd still be saddled with the underlying zoning" regulations. Put in place by Giuliani in an effort to raise quality of life for residents and businesses, these codes effectively classify most of the city's neighborhoods as strict "no dancing zones." Changing the zoning, however, involves a long and tedious process, which requires not only the approval of a string of city government agencies but the agreement of local community boards as well.[57] An informal but powerful regulatory body, the community boards are neighborhood groups actively involved in local decision making. But to most local community boards, Chevigny points out, "a discotheque is a fearful word."[58] The demise of the Paradise Garage proves this unequivocally.

A major issue with the current zoning regulation is that it lumps "establishments of any capacity with dancing" together with "eating or drinking establishments with entertainment and a capacity of over 200 persons."[59] These two, vastly different types of spaces—massive entertainment centers and dance venues "of any capacity" (including local bars and small dance clubs)—are collectively known as "use group 12" and are not sanctioned to exist and operate in residential and mixed-use districts. Dancing, even on a small scale, city officials and community boards decided, is only appropriate—and thus allowed—in industrial and commercial zones. "And the crux of it is," Turkel asserts, "that most of New York City is simply not zoned use group 12."[60] One of the very few areas within Manhattan appropriately zoned for dancing is the Meatpacking District, and club owners there hold an effective monopoly on legal dancing.[61] But clubs in that neighborhood tend to be overly expensive, offer a commercial sound, and cater to a particular type of crowd. In addition, they enforce strict, subjective, and discriminatory door policies. A *New York Post* article investigating club selectivity quotes one bouncer saying: "If you're not on the guest list, I would need to set you up for a bar minimum, a $100 a person... good for a couple of cocktails."[62] This is standard procedure in the Meatpacking District. Most venues also have rigid dress codes that require high heels for women and possibly equally uncomfortable dress shoes for men. People are often refused entry on the basis of their looks, gender, and perceived socioeconomic status, a practice that stands in stark contrast to the very ethos of New York's original clubbing subculture. At the entrances of these clubs, it is not uncommon to see groups of young men trying to bargain their way in, often unsuccessfully. Some only gain access at the price of "bottle service," which inevitably costs multiple thousands of dollars a pop. That becomes an extravagantly expensive cover charge. "The Meatpacking District has these big dance clubs and it has some expensive restaurants," Turkel argues, but when people go out to eat in the West Village or the Lower East Side, and they feel like dancing after dinner, "they should be able to do so in those neighborhoods, without going to the fast and furious Meatpacking District. Not everyone wants to be there with the glitterati."[63]

Plant Bar, in contrast, was a quaint local spot on Avenue C that existed between 1999 and 2003. "It wasn't a club, it was a bar so there was no cover charge," says Dominique Keegan, one of the owners. "It was just about having a cool bar for us and for all our friends [and for other] people like us." It was not envisioned as a dance bar, he says, because, being in a residential neighborhood, the venue was zoned out of the possibility of even applying for a Cabaret license. So Plant Bar opened up with a jukebox. However, both owners were

Figure 10.3. No dancing sign hanging on the wall at Von Bar on Bleecker St., New York, NY, August 27, 2011. Photo by Ina Sotirova.

DJs, and they eventually "couldn't help" bringing in turntables, installing a good sound system and playing dance music. "We had really good sound so it was a really, really nice place to go and dance and enjoy yourself," Keegan proudly admits. But it did not last long.[64]

"About a year and a half in [c. 2000], we had our first cabaret violation, which was a ticket for dancing." On a night he was DJing at the bar, Keegan recounts, "a guy came in undercover, witnessed five people dancing" and wrote up a ticket. In court, the owners were warned that "if we were caught dancing again, we would potentially be padlocked." Like many bars at the time, they put up a sign: *No Dancing Please*. Others have opted for *No Dancing Permitted: by order of N.Y.C. Dept. of Consumer Affairs*, or the rather ludicrous: *Refrain from Dancing*. "We tried to curb dancing in the bar and make it a little bit more mellow but business really suffered because people really liked to come there and dance," Keegan recalls. "When we would approach [them] and ask them to stop dancing, they would just be confused and not really understand why."[65]

Plant Bar, like countless other venues, came up with strategies for eschewing the restrictions. Keegan divulges that after the first ticket they installed a switch by the front door that was connected to a blue bulb in the DJ booth. If the doorman suspected anyone of being an undercover police officer, he would flip the switch, turning on the blue light that told the DJ "to basically turn that record off to just stop the dance floor dead in its tracks."[66] "It's actually totally legal" as a means of communication between staff, Keegan adds, and worked quite well.[67]

Renowned civil rights attorney and former head of the New York Civil Liberties Union, Norman Siegel has represented various clubs with dancing violations—and Plant Bar was one of them. Keegan recalls that, after communicating with the Department of Consumer Affairs, Siegel was given the impression that the city was not going to "persecute bars under this law anymore" and would "basically start ignoring it." Following the World Trade Center attacks on September 11, the city's administration had much bigger problems to deal with so it cooled off on the enforcement of the Cabaret Law. Plant Bar was given the green light and, "as people started dancing, business came up again and the bar kind of returned to its former glory."[68] Unfortunately, the liberalization of dance in New York City was short lived. "When Michael Bloomberg succeeded Giuliani in 2002," Jesse Jarnow wrote in the *Village Voice*, "MARCH activities rose immediately by 35 percent and kept growing."[69] Then a deadly fire demolished a heavy metal club 175 miles away, and it triggered a renewed crackdown.

In February 2002, just a month and a half after Bloomberg took office, "a night of rock 'n' roll turned into a deadly, raging inferno," announced newscaster Tom Brokaw on *NBC Nightly News*. Heavy-metal band Great White was just warming up the crowd at a venue called The Station in West Warwick, Rhode Island. Fireworks accompanied their stage appearance, but the show quickly turned lethal when the walls and ceiling caught on fire, engulfing the small building in a matter of minutes. "Almost 100 people were killed when they were caught in the stampede to escape the smoke and rapidly spreading flames," NBC's Brokaw reported. Another 180 were hospitalized with severe burns and smoke inhalation.[70] The following weekend, Keegan clearly remembers, the New York City Department of Consumer Affairs sent out the task force. Plant Bar was again fined for dancing, and another week later, after a third Cabaret Law violation, it was padlocked. It reopened as a local bar with a jukebox and a redesigned space with no dance floor, but closed down the following year, unable to get the business running again.[71]

This was not the first time New York City responded to club fires by tightening up on dancing. In 1999, Department of Consumer Affairs Commissioner

Jules Polonetsky defended the enforcement of the Cabaret Law by claiming they were important safety measures. "Imagine a fire in a big, dark, noisy, smoky nightclub," he said in an interview for *NPR News*. "The law clearly recognizes that the potential for harm is significantly greater, so the goal is to make sure that, frankly, these areas are safe for people."[72] Polonetsky was referring to another fatal incident—the fire at Happy Land Social Club in the Bronx, New York, which killed eighty-seven people in 1990. City officials at the time reacted to the tragedy by establishing the Social Club Task Force, which evolved into MARCH under Giuliani.[73]

Other laws, however, already govern bar-goers' safety, Turkel states, and if they were properly legislated and enforced, safety wouldn't be an issue.[74] According to news reports, The Station was not licensed to operate pyrotechnics. Furthermore, because of its limited capacity, the venue was not required by law to have fire sprinklers, so it did not. Witnesses reported no fire extinguishers in sight either.[75] Happy Land also had serious safety issues. According to reports by the *Washington Post* and *NBC Nightly News*, the club was operating illegally, having already been ordered shut down sixteen months earlier for fire code violations.[76] On the night of the fire, "it had no business being open," Turkel asserts; it was also "overcrowded and ill-used."[77] By some accounts, the emergency fire exit was chained shut to impede people from sneaking into the club.[78] Tragically, this also prevented their escape from the lethal flames and smoke. The *Washington Post* reported that, save for the few survivors, "everyone else was trapped inside the narrow, windowless, two-story brick row house," where "the only staircase led down to the inferno" and "the only exits were two small front doors."[79]

The fire code, with its mandatory sprinklers, fire extinguishers, adequate fire exits, and signs, is "extremely important," Turkel insists, "that's what keeps you... safe." Building Code is also crucial, he explains, for it regulates capacity. Permit of occupancy rules already require greater square footage per person if a venue plans to feature dancing, so dance spaces receive lower capacity limits. Ironically, under the current Cabaret licensing system and zoning, safety is actually compromised because the occupancy permits of local bars, like Plant Bar, do not correspond to their actual usage. This is another reason why Turkel is unyielding in his criticism: "[D]ancing on its own is not a trigger for any particular license or zoning regulation. It shouldn't be."[80] Plant Bar's attorney, Norman Siegel, also maintains that instead of targeting dancing, the city ought to deal with the real issues, like safety, noise, and overcrowding.[81] Case in point: when Plant Bar received its second ticket for dancing, Keegan admits the place was packed over capacity. "You'd figure they'd be busting people on that, not on dancing."[82]

Noise is the second-biggest issue cited in favor of the Cabaret Law, particularly when it comes to residential neighborhoods. Although, Turkel says, "noise regulation makes a lot of sense," the Department of Consumer Affairs already regulates noise independently of dancing.[83] Meanwhile, the jazz-loving civil rights attorney Paul Chevigny debunks the argument's very assumptions: "There isn't any way, as far as I know, to prove that it is a dance place as such that produces noise. The music may make noise," he reasons, but if you have "maybe 25 people dancing" at a local bar, "there's no noise effect at all and in fact, they may actually be quieter because they're busy dancing with one another, they're not getting drunk and shouting and starting fights."[84] He believes "the underlying problem is that people fear dancing. They say they fear it on the basis that it's crowds of kids and they're going to take drugs and they're going to be out in the streets raising the devil and making noise."[85] But the issue goes much deeper than that, he says: "there is this vein of social reprobation of dancing." Popular dances, often originating among minorities, lower classes, or foreigners, have historically been shunned by moral society. The waltz, he notes, "was considered a naughty dance" in the early nineteenth century, seen as "*risqué*, because a man held a woman in his arms and they danced around the floor and they might get dizzy, and this was . . . on the edge as far as morality of relations between men and women goes." In the 1920s "jazz dances were thought of as being animalistic and immoral." This, he concludes, is "the history of society's reaction to social dance" and underneath it all lies "the old, ancient fear of the emotional release that comes from dancing."[86]

Author Barbara Ehrenreich's work supports this argument. In her book, *Dancing in the Streets: A History of Collective Joy* (2007), she chronicles and analyzes the long history of repression against popular social dance. "Disputes over who can dance, how and where, are at least as old as civilization," she writes in an Op-Ed for the *New York Times*, "and arise from the longstanding conflict between the forces of order and hierarchy, and the deep human craving for free-spirited joy." She gives the example of European colonizers who "made it a priority to crush the danced rituals of indigenous people," because they were seen as "savagery, devil worship and prelude to rebellion." It was the archbishop of Constantinople who originally planted this idea, declaring at the end of the fourth century: "for where there is dance, there is also the Devil."[87] Yet "the need for public, celebratory dance seems to be hardwired into us" and has important social functions. "While language also serves to forge community," Ehrenreich writes, "it doesn't come close to possessing the emotional urgency of dance." Dancing, she concludes, "is not only mood-lifting and community-building; it's also a unique human capability."[88] As house dancer Byron Cox puts it, "[a] lot about the human condition... is expressed in dance." In a world where we are so estranged from one another, dancing allows people to reconnect not only with each other, but also with themselves.[89] "If you really want to know what it feels like to really be human and to live passionately, to see the color or feel the color in your life, try moving to a song that does that for you mentally," he advises.[90]

In 2005, determined to change the status quo, Cox and four other social dancers took the Department of Consumer Affairs to court. Almost two decades after successfully repealing the Cabaret Law's restrictions on live music, Chevigny attempted to do the same for dancing, this time along with Siegel and another law firm. "We brought the case on behalf of the dancers, rather than the clubs, to show there wasn't a commercial issue," he explains. Instead, the plaintiffs claimed that dancing is an important form of expression that should be protected under state law.[91] "The city, however, disagrees," *NPR News* reported. "Officials point to a 1989 Supreme Court case, *City of Dallas v. Stanglin*, in which the Court held recreational dancing is not protected by the First Amendment."[92] Subsequently, Chevigny clarifies, "they distinguished performance dancing," which is legally acknowledged as expressive art with constitutional protection, "but they don't think that social dance is one of the arts." In spite of the legal precedents at the federal level, Chevigny and his colleagues "tried to get the New York courts to say that under New York State law there is a free expression protection for social dancing."[93] But despite testimonies from dance scholars, historians, and a whole gamut of social dancers, from swingers and goths to hip hoppers and house dancers, the judges still upheld the federal court's 1989 ruling. Many find the courts' decisions hard to believe, or even understand. "The only way I could explain it," Chevigny says, is that "older lawyers, for the most part, are all two left feet. They can't dance and they don't care about [dance]." Then he adds with a smile: "that's not true of all of them." Even into his late 70s, Chevigny is an amateur tap dancer who maintains that social dance is an important form of communal expression, the regulation of which is "anti-social" and "against the community."[94]

Testifying in the lawsuit, ethnomusicologist Kai Fikentscher wrote in his affidavit: "dancing is a cultural identifier that sets a group apart [and] communicates the values and sometimes the mythology associated with [the] group."[95] He continues: "As an important social identifier, dance is a language, similar to spoken language because it can be learned. It is different, of course, from spoken language, because it expresses the person through the entire body. It celebrates the expressivity of the body, and through its communication, integrates the body with the mind in a way that other forms of expression do not."[96]

Avram Turkel also finds it bizarre that according to New York State law "sexually suggestive dancing on stage for money is protected speech, but . . . social dancing is not."[97] Yet for him the debate over whether dance is expressive or not is secondary. "I know from the perspective of the dancers, this is a moral issue, this is a free speech issue, this is about our right to dance," he says. "From my perspective, this is a small business issue. This is about small businesses in the city of New York being able to function within the law in such a way that makes money for them, makes money in taxation for the city and that makes our city a better place. People come to this town to go out," he asserts, "it's one of our major industries."[98] An industry report commissioned by the New York Nightlife Association and published in January 2004 identified 949 bars and lounges, 66 music venues, and only 60 dance clubs[99] and estimated that nightlife generates almost $10 billion.[100] The study also found that nearly 80 percent of "out-of-town attendees identified visiting a nightlife bar or club as their primary reason for being in the City." According to its calculations, the industry's economic impact is far-reaching, creating (directly or indirectly) almost 100,000 jobs and paying over $700,000 in state and local taxes.[101]

In Turkel's view, "creating and enforcing regulations that are overly restrictive, that are impossible really to enforce and that lump disparate groups together is not in our best interest and it's bad for business." He admits: "I don't dance that much, but if I'm in a local bar and a song comes on and I want to dance to it, should the bar owner really be closed down because two or three people are up dancing?"[102] Francis Hall of the Dance Liberation Front also voices concern over the practical application of the Cabaret Law. "What is dancing?" he ponders. "How can you regulate something that's so difficult to define? I think that modern dance in particular may have thrown out a lot of preconceived notions about what dance is. Does it necessarily have to be rhythmic to be called dance?"[103] Maybe. Bar owners report that tickets for Cabaret Law violations usually cite a few people "moving rhythmically to music."[104]

But, Hall postulates: "What if I was in a bar, with three people, and we all stood perfectly still, and said 'This is a social dance piece, called *The Stillness*.' Am I breaking the law?"[105]

Postscript

On October 31, 2017, the New York City Council voted to repeal the 1926 Cabaret Law on a bill introduced by Council Member Rafael L. Espinal.

Notes

The short documentary film *freedom2dance* (written, produced, and directed by Ina Sotirova, 2012) and the research and interviews conducted in the process of making it provide the basis for this article. Unless otherwise stated, all quoted interviews were conducted by the author.

1. Robert Prichard, in *freedom2dance*.
2. Dance Liberation Front (DLF), "Manifesto," unpublished document presented to author by Francis Hall.
3. Paul Chevigny, in *freedom2dance*.
4. Adam Janos, "For Nightclubs, Life Is No Cabaret without a License," *Wall Street Journal*, September 29, 2014, http://online.wsj.com/articles/brooklyn-bar-owner-challenges-new-yorks-cabaret-law-1412023210.
5. Office personnel at Andrew Muchmore's office, telephone interview with author, October 6, 2016.
6. Adam Janos, "For Nightclubs, Life Is No Cabaret without a License," *Wall Street Journal*.
7. Giles Hewitt, "You Can Dance in Afghanistan but Not in New York: License Needed: Club Owners Angered by Cabaret Laws Dating Back to 1920s," *National Post of Canada*, December 31, 2002, A13.
8. Francis Hall, interview with author, New York, NY, June 17, 2011.
9. Ibid.
10. Francis Hall, in *freedom2dance*.
11. *John Festa et al. v. New York City Department of Consumer Affairs et al.*, Supreme Court of New York, New York County, April 3, 2006, 17–18, http://ny.findacase.com/research/wfrmDocViewer.aspx/xq/f ac.20060403_0003141.ny.htm/qx.
12. Avram Turkel, in *freedom2dance*.
13. Ibid.
14. Francis Hall, in *freedom2dance*.
15. Paul Chevigny, *Gigs: Jazz and the Cabaret Laws in NYC* (New York: Routledge, 2004), 15.

16. Francis Hall, in *freedom2dance*.
17. Avram Turkel, interview with author, New York, NY, June 24, 2011.
18. Paul Chevigny, interview with author, New York, NY, April 12, 2011.
19. Tim Lawrence, "Big Business, Real Estate Determinism, and Dance Culture in New York, 1980–88," *Journal of Popular Music Studies* 23, no. 3 (2011): 288–306.
20. Paul Chevigny, interview with author.
21. Paul Chevigny, *Gigs*, 15.
22. *Warren Chiasson et al. v. New York City Department of Consumer Affairs et al.*, Supreme Court of New York, New York County, January 28, 1988, http://ny.findacase.com/research/wfrmDocViewer.aspx/xq/fac.19880128_0040893.NY.htm/qx.
23. Paul Chevigny, interview with author.
24. Ibid.
25. Byron Cox, in *freedom2dance*.
26. Byron Cox, interview with author, New York, NY, March 11, 2011.
27. Ibid.
28. Ibid.
29. Tim Lawrence, "Beyond the Hustle: Seventies Social Dancing, Discotheque Culture and the Emergence of the Contemporary Club Dancer," in *Ballroom, Boogie, Shimmy Sham, Shake: A Social and Popular Dance Reader*, ed. Julie Malnig, (Urbana: University of Illinois Press, 2009), 199–214.
30. Tim Lawrence, "Disco: Liberation of the Body," in *Liberazione* newspaper, Italy, June 18, 2006, http://www.timlawrence.info/articles2/2013/7/16/disco-liberation-of-the-body-translated-by-francesco-warbear-macarone-palmieri-liberazione-italy-18-june-2006?rq=Disco%3A%20Liberation%20of%20the%20Body.
31. About: Company Overview, @TheHouseDanceProject *Facebook* page, https://www.facebook.com/TheHouseDanceProject/about/?entry_point=page_nav_about_item&ref=page_internal.
32. Archie Burnett, in *freedom2dance*.
33. Tim Lawrence, in *freedom2dance*.
34. Ibid.
35. Ibid.
36. Tim Lawrence, "Disco: Liberation of the Body," in *Liberazione*, Italy.
37. Tim Lawrence, "Beyond the Hustle."
38. Byron Cox, in *freedom2dance*.
39. Tim Lawrence, "New York Stories: David Mancuso," *Red Bull Music Academy Magazine*, May 27, 2013, http://daily.redbullmusicacademy.com/2016/11/david-mancuso-dj-historyinterview.
40. Byron Cox, interview with author.
41. Byron Cox, in *freedom2dance*.
42. Archie Burnett, interview with author, New York, NY, June 20, 2011.
43. Tim Lawrence, in *freedom2dance*.

44. Giles Hewitt, "You Can Dance in Afghanistan but Not in New York."

45. Department of Consumer Affairs data provided to author in 2011 following multiple requests.

46. A search for "cabaret" within the Legally Operating Businesses in the City of New York returned a list of 94 business locations, a number of which appear to be striptease bars. NYC Open Data, accessed on May 7, 2017, https://data.cityofnewyork.us/Business/Legally-Operating-Businesses/w7w3-xahh/data.

47. Tim Lawrence, in *freedom2dance*.

48. Tim Lawrence, public lecture recorded by author, New York University, New York, NY, April 15, 2011.

49. Tim Lawrence, "Big Business, Real Estate Determinism, and Dance Culture in New York, 1980–88."

50. Ibid.

51. Ibid.

52. Tim Lawrence, in *freedom2dance*.

53. Paul Chevigny, in *freedom2dance*.

54. Avram Turkel, in *freedom2dance*.

55. Avram Turkel, interview with author.

56. Ibid.

57. Ibid.

58. Paul Chevigny, interview with author.

59. Zoning Resolution of the City of New York, Article 3, Chapter 2, 32-21 Use Group 12, A. Amusements, p. 24, accessed Aug 27, 2017, http://www1.nyc.gov/assets/planning/download/pdf/zoning/zoning text/art03c02.pdf?v=0407.

60. Avram Turkel, in *freedom2dance*.

61. Ibid.

62. Susannah Cahalan, "How Selective are NY's Hottest Clubs? Geeks and Guidos Brave the Velvet Wall," *New York Post*, June 13, 2010, http://nypost.com/2010/06/13/how-selective-are-nys-hottest-clubs-guidos-and-geeks-brave-the-velvet-wall/.

63. Avram Turkel, in *freedom2dance*.

64. Dominique Keegan, interview with author, New York, NY, July 14, 2011.

65. Ibid.

66. Dominique Keegan, in *freedom2dance*.

67. Dominique Keegan, interview with author.

68. Ibid.

69. Jesse Jarnow, "New York's Crackdown on Brooklyn DIY Spaces," *Village Voice*, December 28, 2011, https://www.villagevoice.com/2011/12/28/new-yorks-crackdown-on-brooklyndiy-spaces/.

70. Tom Brokaw, *NBC Nightly News with Tom Brokaw*, February 21, 2003.

71. Dominique Keegan, interview with author.

72. Megan Williams, "Analysis: New York City Mayor Shuts Down Nightclubs

Who Do Not Have a Dance Permit but Still Allow Dancing," *All Things Considered,* Natl. Public Radio, WNYC, New York, 18 Sept. 1999.

73. Jesse Jarnow, "New York's Crackdown on Brooklyn DIY Spaces."

74. Avram Turkel, interview with author.

75. Tom Brokaw, *NBC Nightly News with Tom Brokaw.*

76. Howard Kutz, "87 Die in Fire at Illegal N.Y. Social Club," *Washington Post,* March 26, 1990.

77. Avram Turkel, in *freedom2dance.*

78. Author's notes from interviews and conversations with dancers who were not there on the night of the fire, but otherwise frequented Happy Land.

79. Howard Kutz, "87 Die in Fire at Illegal N.Y. Social Club."

80. Avram Turkel, interview with author.

81. Patrick Arden, "Busting a Move: Law Prohibiting Dancing in Unlicensed Bars Challenged," *Metro Weekend Edition,* June 24–26, 2005.

82. Dominique Keegan, interview with author.

83. Avram Turkel, interview with author.

84. Paul Chevigny, interview with author.

85. Paul Chevigny, in *freedom2dance.*

86. Paul Chevigny, interview with author.

87. Barbara Ehrenreich, editorial, "Dance, Dance, Revolution," *New York Times,* June 3, 2007, http://www.nytimes.com/2007/06/03/opinion/03ehrenreich.html.

88. Ibid.

89. Byron Cox, interview with author.

90. Byron Cox, in *freedom2dance.*

91. Paul Chevigny, in *freedom2dance.*

92. Luke Burbank, "Lawsuit Champions Right to Dance in New York," *All Things Considered,* Natl. Public Radio, WNYC, New York, 28 Nov. 2005..

93. Paul Chevigny, in *freedom2dance.*

94. Paul Chevigny, interview with author.

95. Kai Fikentscher, Court Affidavit. *John Festa et al. v. New York City Department of Consumer Affairs et al.,* Supreme Court of New York, New York County, June 1, 2005, 84–85.

96. Ibid.

97. Avram Turkel, interview with author.

98. Avram Turkel, in *freedom2dance.*

99. Based on the listings in *Time Out New York Bars & Clubs* guide and the *New York City Nightlife Zagat Survey.*

100. This number takes into consideration spending on nightlife-related activities, like transportation, shopping for clothes and accessories, dining out, and other pre-party activities. It would probably increase substantially if it were to include spending on illegal substances and afterparty activities.

101. Audience Research & Analysis, "The $9 Billion Economic Impact of Nightlife Industry on New York City: A Study of Spending by Bar/Lounges and Clubs/Music Venues and their Attendees," Prepared for the New York Nightlife Association, January 2004, http://www.nysra.org/associations/2487/files/EconomicStudy.pdf.

102. Avram Turkel, interview with author.

103. Francis Hall, in *freedom2dance*.

104. Megan Williams, "Analysis: New York City mayor shuts down nightclubs who do not have a dance permit but still allow dancing."

105. Francis Hall, in *freedom2dance*.

11

Dancing in the Dark

Defining and Defending the Elusive Hipster Dance Aesthetic

PATSY GAY

On this Saturday night in Williamsburg, those in the know follow the pounding dance grooves (and an 8½ by 11 sign taped to the back wall that reads: "party timeeee—>") through a cute coffee shop/bar to their back room "live art gallery" turned, for the evening, into an indie dance party. The small—but well air-conditioned—black box–style space is dominated by a large suspended illuminated kinetic sculpture that one partygoer aptly described as a "disco mop."[1] On the stage, the three DJs who spin this monthly set alternate between flipping through stacks of big black CD binders piled atop a pair of folding tables and bopping around to their tunes. Tonight, the dance floor is crowded with a sea of people sporting vintage summer dresses, short-sleeved plaid button-ups, and graphic tees all dancing their hearts out to the blasting grooves. Welcome to a quintessential Brooklyn hipster dance party.[2]

In this article, through working from scholarly and popular media sources and utilizing movement analysis garnered through participatory research in Williamsburg clubs, I uncover the core aesthetics of the Brooklyn hipster dance style. These core components—cultural appropriation, movement bricolage, antivirtuosic, anticool—combine with the inherent paradoxical flux of hipster identity to collectively establish, at the heart of hipster dancing, a unique form of social transcendence on the dance floor.

The first wave of hipsters were the cool, rebellious, artistically inclined mostly white youths who were visiting African American neighborhoods, clubs, and bars and taking part in the avant-garde artistic and social world of the 1940s jazz era. Like their 1940s counterparts, contemporary hipsters are mostly Caucasian, reasonably affluent, educated, and disenfranchised youths in their late teens to early thirties. Hipsters are essentially a group without identity (they are white, liberal arts–educated young adults coming from middle-class backgrounds) who are looking to form an identity through their rebellion against mainstream society and social expectations. Hipsters in the United States had the bad luck to come of age during a prolonged economic depression. Betrayed by the American dream, hipsters—often underemployed or unemployed—funnel their education and intellect into their social endeavors. Hipsters today value experimental music, avant-garde art, and alternative fashion and engage in subversive social practices such as shopping at thrift stores, couch surfing, eating local organic foods, riding fixed gear bicycles, and for anything they possibly can "doing it yourself" (DIY). In most prominent American college towns and larger cities the hipster movement (or antimovement) is now ubiquitous. Across the country—and to a more limited extent around the world—hipsters gather at concerts, bars, and clubs, with dancing as an important impetus for hipsters to assemble and interact. Though the subculture has become increasingly prominent over the past years, few scholars have addressed it in any serious capacity or analyzed its unique style of dance.

Growing up in this modern information age, hipsters developed with unlimited access to a wealth of information historical and contemporary, local and international, mainstream and underground. As NYC-based artist and author Jace Clayton describes, "the rise of the hipster is intrinsically linked to widespread internet use, and the dwindling time in which a fashion moves from an expression of individual style to something photographed, blogged, reported on, turned into a trend, marketed, and sold."[3] Hipsterdom in America springs from a whole generation of youths (or at least the affluent, well educated among them) with unprecedented access to the vast expanse of the Internet: endless blogs, countless websites, and an ever-developing array of social media. For no other generation was the whole world's cultural past and present so close, so vital, or so available. Hipsters cash in on their social, economic, and educational privilege, taking full advantage of this "culture of availability" to draw on in the creation of their patchwork identities.

Raiding the trunks of cultural history, modern hipster culture is an amalgam of elements from a variety of eras in history, ethnic groups, and preexisting mainstream and subcultural movements. Even the name is borrowed from a previous subculture: referring originally to bebop's hepcats. Contemporary hipsterdom in every way realizes theorist Fredrick Jameson's postmodern literary concept of "pastiche," which is "like parody, the imitation of a peculiar

Defining and Defending the Elusive Hipster Dance Aesthetic · 253

Figure 11.1. Instagram photos from Crown Heights, Brooklyn, house party, May 2014. Photograph by Patsy Gay.

or unique, idiosyncratic style. . . . But it is a neutral practice of such mimicry, without parody's ulterior motives."[4] Hipster culture, as a patchwork of quintessentially postmodern pastiches, uncritically pulls from many diverse sources for material, which is combined in strange and unexpected ways, often without regard for original context.

Hipster clothing is probably the most immediately recognizable manifestation of this fabricated stylistic bricolage. The visual aesthetic that hipsters project through their dress unites them and asserts the group's existence as a distinct cultural faction. In a 2005 *New York Magazine* article, cultural journalist Zev Borow described the fashion scene, scathingly, but quite aptly, as being "like some out-of-hand fusion-cuisine restaurant menu that you need to smoke pot to even contemplate ordering from. You go out and see the Icelandic Björk look mixed with grunge from the nineties, with weird hats . . . with flowy ruffle skirts underneath corduroy and lots of yarn. Yarn!"[5] Hipsters routinely rock such disparate fashion staples as punk rock skinny jeans, Buddy Holly glasses, plaid shirts, acid-washed denim, vintage dresses, cardigans, leggings, and a dazzling array of sneakers. Some of the wilder past hipster trends include keffiyehs, Hammer pants, fanny packs, Native American prints, and Kanye glasses, while cosmic patterns and cowboy boots have enjoyed a recent vogue. It is exactly this hodgepodge style that paradoxically unites and defines hipster fashion.

This essential bricolage style of hipster fashion mirrors the diverse and unexpected music parings within a hipster club. The hipster dance floor is very much a social forum replete with talking, laughing, drinking, flirting, and of course dancing, with the DJ creating the experiential landscape in which these actions occur. In one night, the crowd can be presented with such disparate tunes as Martha and the Vandellas' 1963 "(Love Is Like a) Heat Wave," The Smith's 1984 "William, It Was Really Nothing," and LCD Soundsystem's 2007 "North American Scum."[6] Such a diverse spectrum of music is typical of this scene that thrives on strange combinations and atypical juxtapositions, and it encourages diversity and variety in the dancing.

The hipster-championed indie dance music genre of mashups further shows how hipsters not only appreciate combining dissimilar elements but also actually take pleasure in fabricating something new out of preexisting and discrete pieces. Musical mashups are songs created on the computer by integrating elements from two or more prerecorded songs. "I like to keep it as diverse as possible," says Greg Gillis (aka Girl Talk), perhaps one of the most popular artists in the mashup genre, "so if there was maybe an '80s pop song before this piece, you know something like The Rolling Stones would be nice now cause it's you know something a bit older and something rock and roll."[7] Girl Talk's 2010 album "All Day," according to a list published on the website of his record label Illegal Arts, contained samples of 374 separate songs.[8] Though the content is all borrowed, the originality and artistry—not to mention the way of getting around copyright laws—comes from how an electronic musician curates, breaks down, and manipulates these prerecorded musical elements. Utilizing music editing programs to juxtapose, sample, chop up, loop, speed up, and slow down, mashup artists transform a jumble of disparate pieces into a cohesive patchwork that is more (or at least different) than the sum of its parts.

The hodgepodge nature of hipster fashion and music is carried through into the heterogeneous and, at times, anachronistic movement pairings that hipsters use on the dance floor. The core move of hipster club dancing is generally a nonspecific sort of bopping in place. On top of this basic shuffling two-step, any variety of movement is piled, such as rock and roll twisting, skank-style kicking or crescendos of pogoing and ponies to express kinetic excitement (often in parallel with swells in the music).

There tends to be little getting down in hipster dancing—more typical is erect, but loose upper bodies with much shoulder shimmying. Much of the visual impact comes from a limitless variety of arm movements, especially swinging and flailing punctuated by directed gestures such as claps, disco points, or fist pumps. This basic substructure welcomes any number of different variations and additions into its folds. Unproblematically combining all of the above movements and more, hipster dance is at its core a collective movement mash.

In the name of hipster stylistic appropriation, a dancer can do literally almost anything out on that dance floor, and bringing in new and different moves is always encouraged. But the heart of hipster dance lies in more than just haphazardly borrowing from all sorts of different decades and social, cultural, and ethnic groups. Rather, the artistry within the form comes from how a club-goer juxtaposes one movement against the next. Sometimes a hipster allows multiple disparate dance moves to inhabit his or her body for an extended period of time—playing each different piece off one another and infusing the whole with new meanings. This aesthetic of performative mashups is an aesthetic of freedom and limitless possibility, since anything and everything can be appropriated.

While anything goes in a hipster club, dancers tend to eschew the intense physicality and sexuality of many modern-day social dance forms, favoring the apart style of early rock and roll dances. Even on a packed dance floor, there is little deliberate contact between dancers. When partner dancing does occur at a hipster club, it is just as often hand-holding and twirling or middle school dance-style arms around necks than it is body-to-body grinding.[9] This lack of coupling in the clubs could be a symptom of the hipsters' internalization of their liberal-arts-education-garnered gender theory. Or perhaps dancing cheek-to-cheek just is not possible when both parties are flailing and bopping hipster-style, without stylistic or physical synchronicity.

Scenesters celebrate odd, strange, and awkward movements and movement pairings, reveling in the weirdness rather than attempting to normalize, equalize, or regulate their dancing. Though the entire subculture of hipsterdom in

Figure 11.2. The hipster flail. Illustration by Christopher O'Connell. By permission of Christopher O'Connell, Brooklyn, New York.

general enjoys reappropriating the socially unacceptable, hipster dancing is one of the clearest elements of the subculture wherein "bad" style is consistently reborn as good. Dance scholar Latika Young quantifies what exactly the qualities are that makes society deem a given dance "dorky" in a 2008 article by saying: "Movement reads as awkward when it is uncoordinated, jerky, arrhythmic..., off tempo (of both the music and any sense of internal rhythm), when the limbs move in contradictory directions, the dancer makes faces and/or the dance cannot be aligned with any known style of dancing."[10] Dorky dancing is, essentially, any movement that, intentionally or not, goes against the dominant aesthetics of a culture. Hipsters incorporate dorky dancing into their own live, performative aesthetic of the uncool. Blogger Lola Wakefield, on her popular web "blogumetary" Stuff Hipsters Don't Like, recounts watching "hipsters with alcohol-induced confidence flail like a whirling dervish throughout an empty dance floor."[11] While this nonscholarly movement description is decidedly disparaging and condemning, it does aptly point out key aspects of hipster movement style such as abnormal rhythms and uncoordinated limb actions. Such nonmainstream choices place their subcultural movement practices within Young's criteria for awkward dance.

The purposefully weird and unsexy movements of hipsters clearly show an intentional disregard for the standards of "good" or "attractive" dance as seen in pop culture, professing instead an ironic and radical reverence for the uncool. Similarly, since dancing well is devalued, virtuosity becomes entirely unimportant. This is diametrically opposed to most social dance forms, which value skill and excellence: there will never be a "Cat's Corner" on a hipster dance floor. Rather, looking at aesthetic values, hipster dance has more in common with the New York City–based postmodern dance group the Judson Dance Theater. In fact, Yvonne Rainer's tongue-in-cheek "No Manifesto" ("NO to spectacle no to virtuosity no to transformations and magic and make-believe no to the glamour and transcendence of the star image..."[12]) could practically be the rallying cry of the hipster dance scene. For hipster dance, this unusual approach of intentionally dancing badly has the added benefit of making hipster dance impossible to do wrong because it is already, according to mainstream aesthetics, totally "wrong."

Aesthetically, hipster dancing, unlike the majority of dance being done in mainstream clubs today, is moving away from the dominance of African American styles. Over the course of 100 plus years, African American social dances—from the Cakewalk, to the Lindy Hop, to boying, to jookin'—have repeatedly started as underground forms and risen to mainstream popularity by captivating the bodies and souls of (young, white) Americans. The original hipsters, through their celebration of black culture including jazz and bebop dancing, participated in this whitewashing phenomenon becoming, as Norman Mailer coined it, "the white negro." As a subcultural dance form, modern-day hipster club dancing, however, intentionally rebels against many of the qualities of mainstream club dancing. Scenesters do not fill up hipster dance floors with sexy-cool, booty-shaking get down like partygoers do at hopping mainstream clubs. Many of the qualities from mainstream social dancing, which I find lacking—or at least radically deemphasized—at hipster clubs were adopted from African American social dance. These include such important Africanist aesthetics as the "get down" and the "aesthetic of the cool." Through this denial of the mainstream, the hipsters' no-to-little contact, awkward, bouncy dancing diverges at right angles from the dominant trajectory of club dancing.

In addition to rejecting the mainstream and its current domination by commodified and commercialized African American style, hipsters are also fetishizing the culture (or more accurately cultures) of whiteness as seen in their trucker hats, lumberjack plaids, and nerd glasses. "Caucasian kitsch," as John Leland describes it: "packages whiteness as a fashion commodity that can be donned or doffed according to one's dating needs. Post-hip [read: 'hipsterdom'] treats whiteness the way fashion and entertainment have historically treated blackness. It swaths white identity not in race pride but in quotation marks."[13] Today's hipsters are appropriating contemporary white cultural elements in the same way that their jazz-era hipster forbearers were whitewashing 1940s African American culture. Most strange, the hipster's mining of white culture in some ways levels the cultural playing field. Perhaps hipsters have achieved a postracial sensibility: namely by treating white culture just like black culture, Asian culture, Hispanic culture, and any other culture—as a rich wealth of resources to be discovered (the more obscure the better), borrowed (without regard for original cultural context), and exploited.

There exists within the hipster movement as a whole a pathological paradox of self-denial. Douglas Haddow aptly described this phenomenon as "an odd dance of self-identity—adamantly denying your existence while wearing clearly defined symbols that proclaim it."[14] Hipsters, though they acknowledge the existence of the scene and follow all the appropriate trends, typically refuse to admit that they are, in fact, hipsters. It is as if the true test of hipsterdom were denying your hipsterness; in this equation of mutually dependent, yet inherently conflicting, conditions, one can be a hipster and not a hipster all at once. I encountered this phenomenon while talking with a trendy twenty-three-year-old Cornell graduate back in 2010. We were listening to the experimental folk-pop artist Sufjan Stevens's Christmas album over a glass of one of his latest home-brewed beers in his Brooklyn apartment; he was wearing a navy and sea foam sweater, boat shoes, and what could charitably be called a beard—in other words, his choices of both style and lifestyle were hipster through and through. But when I asked if he self-identified as a hipster he laughed and said (potentially with self-conscious irony) no, "because I don't have a fixed-gear [bicycle]."[15] While his reasoning was certainly a joke, his lack of self-identification with the hipster scene was clearly not.

"Hipster" these days tends to be a negative label people apply to others. It has come to stand for all the evils propagated by this youth generation such as gentrification, commercialization, and technology-induced dehumanization. In a June 2014 article in *The Observer*, Morwenna Ferrier proclaimed the death of the hipster, saying "what was once an umbrella term for a counter-culture tribe of young creative types . . . morphed into a pejorative term for people who looked, lived and acted a certain way. . . . In reality, the word is now tantamount to an insult."[16] Though people have been claiming the death of the hipster for years (all the way back in 2005 Zev Borow wrote an article for *New York Magazine* called "Will The Last Hipster Please Turn Out The Lights? New York Cool Dies Its Thousandth Death. A Satire"), Ferrier is correct about the extreme negative connotation of the term in today's slang culture. If the hipster scene sticks around another twelve years after this death proclamation, perhaps the label will follow in the footsteps of the term "hippie," which shed much of its pejorative connotation with the passage of time.

In addition to wanting to avoid the negative connotations of the term, hipsters do not self-identify as hipsters because they are suffering from a postmodern paradox of individuality. Sociologists Kenneth Allan and Jonathan H. Turner explain in a 2000 article on postmodern theory how "as grand narratives lose their ability to embrace large groups with a sense of a collective identity . . . and as communication and transportation technologies systematically break down the symbolic barriers between groups, individuals and their identities increase in importance."[17] Thus, the hipster overemphasis on individuality—to the extent that someone will deny being a hipster despite his or her obvious associations with the group—is a function of existing within a fragmented and deconstructed postmodern cultural context.

The constructed nature of hipster identities makes them simultaneously extremely precious and easily mutable. A recent study—perhaps the first scientific piece to focus, at least partially, on hipsterdom—discovered that for "students whose friends list tastes in the 'indie/alt' music cluster are significantly likely to discard these tastes in the future."[18] This study quantifies the tendency of hipsters to intentionally change their own tastes once something becomes too popular in order to be more individualistic. The futility of hipsters' desperate hanging on to their sense of individuality is further highlighted by what Allan and Turner deem the "decentered subject."[19] Since everyone in this postmodern scenario is focusing so furiously on his or her individuality, the point becomes, essentially, moot. Furthermore, the hipster need to be different and desire not to be labeled (such as being called a "hipster") is actually unifying—it is precisely hipsters' radical individuality that breeds their collectivity. It is, in a way, a homogeneity of heterogeneity. On the dance floor, this translates into a visual unity as discrete elements blur together: because everyone dances uniquely, no one is out of place. Furthermore, the hipster's aforementioned apart dancing with a deemphasis on virtuosity combines with the intense focus on individuality to create an environment in which each individual is concentrated more on his or her own movement than that of any other dancer. Consequently, hipster dancers are completely permissive, if only out of indifference.

All the contradictions that riddle the genre also grant it a special license. Hipster dance is defined by being everything and nothing all at the same time—pulsing like a quasar on the brink between nonexistence and tangibility. In this fertile place of flux, hipster dance has almost unlimited potential. If a movement form denies that it exists, how do you ban it or suppress it? It simply cannot be done. If a dance is indefinable and ineffable, that also means it is impossible to do incorrectly. In a hipster club, dancers can do literally anything they could imagine because there are no defined boundaries to the medium. In this fertile liminal space, performers are granted, because of the elastic nature of the form, a unique type of social transcendence; hipster dancers, essentially, have access to a world of truly limitless movement possibilities. Thus, I believe that hipster dance is not only the most tolerant vernacular genre but also the most freeing since, at its oxymoronic core, it is defined by a lack of definition.

Notes

1. Anonymous Hipster #1, interview with the author, September 2012. All interviews were conducted in confidentiality, and the names of the interviewees are withheld by mutual agreement.

2. Based on the author's personal observations in Williamsburg, Brooklyn, September 2012.

3. Jace Clayton, "Vampires of Lima," in *What Was the Hipster? A Sociological Investigation* (Brooklyn: n+1 Foundation, 2010), 27.

4. Fredrick Jameson, *Postmodernism, or, The Cultural Logic of Late Capitalism* (Durham, NC: Duke University Press, 1991), 16.

5. Zev Borow, "Will The Last Hipster Please Turn Out The Lights? New York Cool Dies Its Thousandth Death. A Satire," *New York Magazine*, May 21, 2005, http://nymag.com/nymetro/urban/features/10488/.

6. Based on the author's personal observations in Williamsburg, Brooklyn, September 2012.

7. Audie Cornish, interview with Greg Gillis, "Girl Talk: Cataloging Samples 'All Day,'" *NPR*, last modified December 4, 2010, http://www.npr.org/2010/12/04/131791011/girl-talk-cataloging-samples-all-day.

8. "GIRL TALK—ALL DAY SAMPLES LIST," Illegal Arts, accessed September 2, 2014, http://illegal-art.net/allday/samples.html.

9. Based on the author's personal observations in Williamsburg, Brooklyn, September 2012.

10. Latika Young, "Dorky Dance, YouTube, and the New Vaudeville," *Dance on Camera Journal* (2008): 19.

11. Lola Wakefield, "#14, "Dancing," *Stuff Hipsters Don't Like* (blog), August 27, 2008, http://stuffhipstersdontlike.wordpress.com/2008/08/27/1-dancing/.

12. Yvonne Rainer, *Feelings are Facts* (Cambridge, MA: MIT Press, 2006), 263–64.

13. Leland, John. *Hip: The History* (New York: HarperCollins, 2004), 353.

14. Douglas Haddow, "Hipster: The Dead End of Western Civilization," *Adbusters*, July 29, 2008, http://www.adbusters.org/article/hipster-the-dead-end-of-western-civilization/.

15. Anonymous Hipster #2, interview with the author, December 2010.

16. Morwenna Ferrier, "The end of the hipster: How flat caps and beards stopped being so cool," *Observer*, June 21, 2014, http://www.theguardian.com/fashion/2014/jun/22/end-of-the-hipster-flat-caps-and-beards.

17. Kenneth Allan and Jonathan H. Turner, "A Formalization of Postmodern Theory," *Sociological Perspectives*, 43:3 (2000): 374.

18. Kevin Lewis, Mario Gonzalez, and Jason Kaufman, "Social Selection and Peer Influence in an Online Social Network," *Proceedings of the National Academy of Sciences of the United States of America* 109:1 (January 3, 2012): 70, doi: 10.1073/pnas.1109739109.

19. Lewis, Gonzalez, and Kaufman, "Social Selection and Peer Influence in an Online Social Network," 377.

Contributors

Jennifer Atkins is associate professor in the School of Dance at Florida State University where she teaches courses in dance history, theory, and research. Her research focuses on American social dance, gender, and popular culture. Her work on New Orleans social dance in particular appears as part of the anthology *Contemporary Scholars and Artists Respond to the Baby Dolls of New Orleans*, edited by Kim Vaz-Deville and in her own book, *New Orleans Carnival Balls: The Secret Side of Mardi Gras, 1870–1920*, which is the 2017 winner of the Jules and Frances Landry Award.

Jessica Berson is lecturer in Dance Studies at Yale University, and has previously served on dance and drama faculties at Harvard University, Wesleyan University, and University of Exeter (UK). She is the author of *The Naked Result: How Exotic Dance Became Big Business*, which focuses on the corporate takeover of the exotic dance industry. Performance artist Annie Sprinkle gave *The Naked Result* her "highest rating—two tassels way up!" Jessica regularly presents her research at national and international conferences. She holds a PhD in Theatre/Dance Studies from University of Wisconsin-Madison and is a Certified Movement Analyst. You can find out more about Jessica's work at www.jessicaberson.com.

J. Ellen Gainor is professor of Performing and Media Arts at Cornell University. She has published essays on same-sex ballroom for the *Gay and Lesbian Review*, and on ballroom dance in Athol Fugard's *MASTER HAROLD . . . and the boys*. A specialist in modern British and American theatre, she is also an editor of the *Norton Anthology of Drama*.

Patsy Gay is currently associate archivist at Jacob's Pillow Dance Festival. Previously she was archivist and associate producer for Ain Gordon and David Gordon's Pick Up Performance Co(s). Through Dance Heritage Coalition she also did archival work with Dance Theatre of Harlem, Eiko & Koma, and Lar Lubovitch Dance Company. She formerly served as an adjunct instructor for Florida State University's FSU in NYC program run by Dr. Sally Sommer. Patsy received her MA in American Dance Studies at Florida State University and is currently pursuing an MS in Library and Information

Science at Pratt Institute. A resident of Becket, MA, and Brooklyn, NY, Patsy loves vintage fashions, obsolete audio/visual formats, and rowdy dance parties.

Ansley Joye Jones is a full-time multidisciplinary artist, Official U.S. Cultural Ambassador, Hip Hop feminist, and women's rights activist. She holds a BFA in Visual and Performing Arts from Savannah State University and an MA in American Dance Studies from Florida State University. In 2014 Jones traveled to India as a cultural ambassador with the "Next Level Program," then returned in 2016 with "Cultural Vistas," a U.S. State Department urban arts program "Celebrate the Connections." In 2015 Jones received a creative performing arts fellowship from The American Institute of Indian Studies (AIIS) for her 2017 project, "The Jukeboxx Movement—From Surviving to Thriving." This program is geared toward creating safe spaces for survivors of gender-based violence through hip hop culture and cultural artistic expression. The three-month program will be based in Kolkata, with a five-city Indian tour promoting "From Surviving to Thriving," culminating in a subsequent five-city teaching performing tour in the United States.

Kate Mattingly received her PhD in Performance Studies with a Designated Emphasis in New Media from UC Berkeley. Her dissertation, "Set in Motion: Dance Criticism and the Choreographic Apparatus" examines the multiple functions of dance criticism in the twentieth and twenty-first centuries in the United States. Her undergraduate degree is from Princeton University and her MFA degree from New York University's Tisch School of the Arts. Her writing about dance has been published in the *New York Times*, the *Village Voice*, *Dance Research Journal*, *Dance Magazine*, *Pointe Magazine*, and many other journals and publications. She has served on nominating committees such as the New York Dance and Performance "Bessie" Awards and in 2005 was invited by the National Endowment for the Arts to serve on the panel determining funding for U.S. dance companies, choreographers, and schools.

Hannah Schwadron is assistant professor of dance at Florida State University, where she teaches courses in dance history, critical theory, and choreography. Many of the questions raised in Schwadron's essay for this volume are discussed in more depth in her forthcoming book, *The Case of the Sexy Jewess: Dance, Gender and Jewish Joke-work in US Pop Culture*. Schwadron received a PhD in Critical Dance Studies and an MFA in Experimental Choreography at the University of California, Riverside.

Sally R. Sommer is a writer, historian, and filmmaker. She has published hundreds of reviews and articles on dance and popular culture in numerous journals, newspapers, and magazine publications. She has articles in five encyclopedias and four anthologies, and is the author of two books, *Feet Talk to Me* and *Ballroom*. She worked on three PBS documentaries, *Watch Me Move*, *Tap: Dance America*, and the Peabody Award–winning *Everybody Dance Now!* She has taught at New York University and

Duke University and currently is a professor in the School of Dance at Florida State University. She produced and directed *Check Your Body at the Door*, a documentary about extraordinary dances and dancers of the 1990s underground club scene in New York City.

Ina Sotirova is an award-winning documentary filmmaker and internationally published multimedia journalist who specialized in documentaries at Columbia University's Graduate School of Journalism. She is the recipient of the 2012 duPont/Judy F. Crichton Award for visual storytelling. Her documentary debut, *freedom2dance*, combines her sensibility for social justice with her love of dance in a twenty-minute film about illegal dancing in New York City, which became the basis of her contribution to this book. In 2012, she presented a TEDx talk about the power of dance for personal and social transformation. Ina currently lives in Kingston, Jamaica, where she teaches at the University of the West Indies's Community Film Project, mentoring inner city youth in film and video production. She is also producing and directing a documentary TV series that explores Caribbean nature, culture, and innovation.

Dawn Springer is a dance artist and writer. Her choreography has been performed throughout the United States and she has been an invited guest artist and speaker at colleges across the country. She has an MFA from Hollins University and lives in Milwaukee, Wisconsin. You can learn more about her work at www.dawnspringer.com.

Michelle T. Summers is an active dance scholar, educator, and choreographer in the San Francisco Bay Area. Summers is currently a lecturer in the Department of Theater, Dance, and Performance Studies at the University of California at Berkeley and adjunct faculty at the Graduate Theological Union. She holds a PhD in Critical Dance Studies from the University of California at Riverside and an MA in Performance Studies from New York University. Her research interests include American religious performance and dance, the interplay between Christianity and secularism, and the politics of embodiment. For further information on her research and teaching, please see www.michelletsummers.com.

Latika L. Young, dorky dance scholar *and* practitioner, received a BA in Dance and Environmental Studies from Swarthmore College, an MA in American Dance Studies from Florida State University, and an EdM in International Educational Development with a concentration in Peace and Post-Conflict Education from Columbia University's Teachers College. Straddling the dance and international development worlds, she completed a Fulbright Fellowship in Bosnia and Herzegovina (2008–2009) as well as a Critical Language Scholarship in Bursa, Turkey, in 2011, and has long been interested in arts as social change and as a tool for reconciliation and peace-building. Latika is director of the Center for Undergraduate Research and Academic Engagement at Florida State University where she is also completing her PhD in Educational Policy and Evaluation. Although she has not yet produced any dorky dance videos for the web, you can find her busting out her best dorky dance moves in her kitchen and at her local dancehall.

Tricia Henry Young is professor emerita at Florida State University, where she founded and directed the graduate program in American Dance Studies. She has published numerous articles in academic journals, and her book *Break All Rules: Punk Rock and the Making of a Style* was nominated for the Ralph J. Gleason Music Book Award. Dr. Young is a former member of the Board of Directors and the Editorial Board of the Congress on Research in Dance (CORD), and the Board of Directors of the Society of Dance History Scholars (SDHS).

Index

Page numbers in *italics* refer to illustrations.

ABC News, 151
Abel, Marco, 219–20, 223, 224–25
Activism: dance as, 6; through dance communities, 3–4; *Descent* and, 223; Jewish, 116, 133n18. *See also* Cabaret Law
Addams, Jane, 139
Adorno, Theodor, 187n29
Aerobics, 142–43
African Americans, 193; aesthetic in dance, 62, 75; athletes, 73; black "play" and, 75; Cabaret Law and, 230–31; dances, 230; exotic dancers, 171; gestures, 195; hipster rejection of dance forms of, 257–58; identities, 66, 72, 76, 78n13; NFL percentage of, 78n13; quarterbacks, 72; racial politics in NFL, 72–73, 75–76; stereotypes, 63–64; women pole dance students, 153–54. *See also* Bgirls; Blacks
Agency and Embodiment (Noland), 83
Agora, 4, 10, 212, *213*; afterlife of *Descent* and, 223–24; dance and activity, 222–23; ending of, 224; McCarren Park pool site of, 221–23, *223*; opening, 222; publicity for, 221; scenarios and, 223–24; word meaning, 224
Ahlstrom, Sydney, 141
Air Force Band, U.S., 102
Akeela and the Bee, 188n47
Alexander, Keith, 194
Allan, Kenneth, 259, 260
Aloff, Mindy, 214, 217–18
Altporn, 112, 132n6
Alvin Ailey dance company, 166

American ballroom dance, 35; American Rhythm, 55n5; American Smooth, 55n5
American culture: fitness in, 141–42; hip hop and, 190, 203–4; Protestantism backdrop of, 155–58; underground dance and, 234–36. *See also* Breaking
Americanness: breaking and, 9; fitness culture and, 141–42; identity and, 2, 11
Anderson, Jamal, 74
Angel, Joanna ("punk princess"), 8; awards and reputation of, 11–12, 132n3; blow-up doll of, 126–27; Brous and, 112–15, 129–32; Burning Angel Studios website of, 121–24; contribution of hard-core, 128; dance studies perspective on Brous and, 112–13, 130; egalitarianism claim of, 122; interview with mother of, 127; Jewishness of, 123–27, 128; patriarchy and, 131–32; as porn celebrity icon, 123; porn star body and, 125; punk princesses and, 121; spoof Hanukkah video of, 123–24, 125, 129
Animation, dorky dance, 24–25, 29
Antwerp, "Do Re Mi" flash mob in, 101
Arzut metzach (stealing with pride), 127
Asherie, Ephrat ("Bounce"), 191
Athleticism, ballroom dance controversy over, 38, 55n13
AT&T, 95
Audience: critical stance of virtual, 20, 31n5; *Descent*, 9/11 inclusion of, 215–16, 218, 219; dorky dancing role of, 19–20; inclusion of, 219; interpretations by, 212; ownership, 219; reception theories, 212, 225n2; spectatorship theory and, 212; virtual dance community participation of, 20, 26

Auditions, *So You Think You Can Dance*, 57n36; Belfer and Kibel, 46–49, 57n31; de Vries and Jason, 50–53, 57nn37–38
Awkward dancing, 16–19, 24; hipsters and, 257

Baauer, 120, 135n27
Baby Love, 207n47
Backstage Bill's, 163, 164, 170–72, 174
Ballet Hispanico, 66
Ballroom dance: American style, 35, 55n5; athleticism controversy, 38, 55n13; competitive form of, 35, 36; cultural positioning of, 35; heteronormativity and, 34–35, 41, 43; lead switching in, 40, 42, 52; manuals and codification of, 36, 36–37; reality television and, 34–35, 41, 55n2; representations, 34. *See also* Same-sex ballroom dancing
The Ballroom Technique, 36
Barry, Dan, 70
Barton, Bernadette, 164–65
Battling. *See* Breaking
Bboys, liminality of, 200, 207n49. *See also* Breaking
Beit Shemesh Women's flash mob, 98–99, 99, 102
Belfer, Misha, 44, 46–49, 53, 57n31
Bell, David, 5
Berkeley, Busby, 90
Berlin, flash mob in, 88
The Bernie Lean touchdown dance, 74–75
Best Shape of Your Life pole studio, 137, 144–45, 160n29
Bgirl Emiko, 204n2
Bgirls: baggy clothes and, 194, 205n19, 206n21; bboy and bgirl events compared, 204n2; bboying and, 190–91; costuming and style, 195; as drag kings, 197, 202; empowerment of, 196–97; female anatomy disguised by, 196–97, 206n30; feminine qualities acceptance by current, 201–2, 207n47; hip hop culture and, 190; idealization and naming option, 191, 205n6; liminal androgyny of, 192, 197–201; mimetic category of, 191–96; 1970s and 1980s, 203; 1990s to 2005, 203; paradoxical position of, 191; personal experience, 191; phallic gestures and, 195–96, 198; race and, 192–93; rape mimed by, 191, 195; reproductive power gestures of, 201, 207n46; shift away from mimetic elements, 203; suppression performed by, 194; training of (foundation), 190–91, 204n3
Björk, 253–54
Blacks: athletic aesthetic, 73; black-owned venues, 232; black "play," 75–76; identities, 67–68; quarterbacks, 72, 80n51; stereotypes, 63–65, 192, 194–95, 205n16; touchdown dances, 73. *See also* Bgirls
Bloomberg, Michael, 241
Booth, Tiffany, 147
Borelli, Melissa Blanco, 5
Borow, Zev, 253–54
Bott, Esther, 156
BPC. *See* Brooklyn Parks Commissioner
Branding, corporate: brand as defined by Klein, 176, 187n24; brandscapes, 177, 185, 187n32; commodities distinguished from, 176–77; Disneyization concept of, 179–80; in exotic dancing, 165–66, 176–81; fantasy and play elements in, 181–83; liminality notion, 188n49; McDonaldization theory, 178, 179; vulnerability to, 183
Breaking: African American identity, masculinity and, 9; basic training in, 190–91; battling in, 192, 196–200, 203, 204n3; Foundation, 200, 204n3; hypermasculinity of, 190, 191, 192, 197, 204; liminal androgyny and, 198–200; misogyny in, 190, 200, 201, 204n3; power privileges in, 193–94; reproductive power gestures in, 201, 207n46; sexism and, 190–92, 193, 201, 204n3, 205n4, 205n18, 206n42, 206n45; womb power in, 194, 196
Brent, Barbara, 178
Brides of Christ, 153
Bridges, Chris ("Ludacris"), 194
Briginshaw, Valerie, 5
British lap dancers, 156
Brokaw, Tom, 241
Brolsma, Gary, 4, 6, 17; "New Numa" created by, 27–30; as Numa Numa kid, 16;

revolutionary legacy of, 16–17; unexpected popularity of, 20. *See also* Dorky dancing
Brooklyn, Crown Heights in: 1970s racism in, 234–35
Brooklyn Parks Commissioner (BPC), 222
Brous, Sharon (rabbi), 8; Angel and, 112–15, 129–32; awards and popularity of, 11–12, 118–19, 132n2, 134n24; best of business status of, 111; dance studies perspective on Angel and, 112–13, 130; embodied prayer and, 117; Israel/Palestine stance of, 116, 117–18, 119; Not Your Bubbe's Synagogue, 116–21; Purim Party and, 119–21, 134n26; yoga and, 117, 133n20
Bryman, Alan, 179–80
Bubbe, 112, 113, 132n4; Brous's Not Your Bubbe's Synagogue, 116–21
Building Code, 242
Burgundy Café, 232–33
Burman, J.T., 32n21
Burnett, Archie, 233, 234, 235, 237
Burning Angel Studios: female empowerment in, 122; Hanukkah spoof, 123–24; website and video content, 121–24
Burns, liminal bgirls and, 198, 200
Butler, Leroy, 61, 62

Cabaret Law, 61–62; activism against, 244; bars and, 239–41, 240; cost of cabaret license, 230; date of original, 229; enforcement, 232, 236, 238, 239, 241–42; fines, 230; First Amendment and, 244; Harlem Renaissance and, 230–31; jazz and, 231–33, 243; lawsuits, 229–30, 233, 244–45; live music clause, 232–33; MARCH enforcement of, 238, 241, 242; 1980s jazz and, 232–33; 1989 ruling, 244; noise issue, 243; NYC nightlife and, 245, 249n100; Prohibition and, 229, 232; racial relations and, 230–32; revival of, 233–34; safety justification for, 242–43; social dance in New York City and, 233–38, 235; violations, 245; zoning regulations and, 238–39
Cash Mob, 100, 102
Cat's Corner, 257

Caucasian kitsch, 258
Cavallo, Dominick, 139
Censorship, 61–62; of African American slave dance, 72. *See also* Cabaret Law
The Chad Rules, 71
Chandler, Rick, 137
Chaplin, Charlie, 18
Chevigny, Paul, 229, 232–33; in case against Cabaret Law, 244; on Giuliani, 238
Chicago Bears, 62–63, 77n8
Chicago Gay Games, 38
Christian dance fitness: aerobics and improvisation example of, 142–43; historical background, 138–41; perfectible body framing in pole dancing and, 145–50; secular fitness and, 137
Christianity: commodification of, 141; embodied, 146; exotic dance and, 9; feminism and, 161n63; fitness and, 141, 142–43; masculinity and, 140–41; Muscular, 140; pole dancing and, 8–9; sexuality and, 150–52, 153, 158; touchdown dances and, 69–70, 79n37; white God in, 162n68. *See also* Pole Dancing for Jesus classes
Cindy Davis Show, 144, 147
City of Dallas v. Stanglin, 244
City spaces, 5. *See also Agora*; *Descent*
Claire's Accessories, 85–86
Clayton, Jace, 252
Clear Channel Entertainment, 221
Clock Tower, 213–14, 214, 219, 220
Collective identity, 3, 83, 94; Generation Y individualism and, 4; of hipsters, 259; Jewish, 113
Competitions, ballroom dance, 37–41, 56n18, 56n19, 56n22, 56n25; costuming, 57n31; exotic dance atmosphere of, 174; new trends in, 54, 57n39. *See also So You Think You Can Dance*
Corporate branding. *See* Branding, corporate
Cox, Byron, 233–34, 236, 244
Crotch-grab, 191, 205n9
Cruz, Victor, 65–66, 70, 71
Culture. *See* American culture
Cyrus, Miley, 31n5

Daddy Daughter Iggy Azalea dance off, 75
Dance: activism through, 3–4, 6; communities, 3–4; competitions, 3, 7; diverse formats and spaces for, 6; Equality, 40, 50, 57n31; hipster, 255–58, 256; history of fitness and, 138–41; Internet influence on gatherings of, 2–3; policing of, 61–62; politicizing of, 9–10, 75–76; race, jazz and, 231–32; slavery and, 72; social trends and, 11; striptease as, 164–65, 186n4; virtual, 20, 26; world, 49. *See also* Christian dance fitness; Competitions, ballroom dance; *specific styles*
Dance Liberation Front (DLF), 229, 230, 231, 245
DanceSport, 37–38
DanceSport, international, 35
Dancing with the Stars, 7, 41–44, 45, 56n26; NFL players on, 62
Davis, Cindy, 144, 147
Dawkins, Richard, 23
Day of Atonement, 117
Deans, Crystal, 8–9; classes described by, 146; conversion experience of, 144; as embracing what feels right, 155; exotic dance past of, 137, 157, 183–84; interviews, 143, 144, 147, 150, 159n25; personal life of, 137, 145; Protestantism of, 157; public retreat of, 143–44, 145; stripper career of, 144; students of, 147–48; studio of, 144–45. *See also* Pole Dancing for Jesus classes
Debord, Guy, 212, 215, 226n12
Deeley, Cat, 46, 51
DeLillo, Don, 219–20
Demographics, 8; strip club, 169; touchdown dance, 65
Dérive, 212, 213–14, 224
Descent: 9/11 and, 4, 10; activism and, 224; afterlife of *Agora* and, 223–24; cast and duration of piece, 213; choreography and spectators, 213; Clock Tower location of, 213–14, 214, 219, 220; commemorative nature of, 218; first showing of, 211; official opening and transmutation of, 211–12, 213; periodicity of, 213; post-9/11 context of, 220; processions in, 215; psychogeography and, 212, 215, 221, 224, 225n4, 226n12; reception theory and, 212, 225n2; as ritualized commemoration, 217–18; scenarios and, 218–19, 223–24; staircases and, 211, 213, 214, 215, 216, 219, 220; white-powdered dancer in, 213, 220
Desperate Housewives, 66
Details, 125
Devious Maids, 66
De Vries, Willem, 44, 50–53, 57nn37–38
Diamonds strip club, 173–77, 183, 187n23
Diaspora Jews, 128
Digital communities, 2–4
Digital technology, Generation Y and, 1
Discotheque, 235, 238
DLF. *See* Dance Liberation Front
Dolores Park, cross-whirl event in, 88–89
Dorky dancing, 6, 25; audience role in, 19–20; awkward dancing and, 16–17, 24; characteristics, 16–18; commercialization and, 29–30; gender role in, 18; of hipsters, 257; marketability, 33n41; original video upload of, 16; popularity of, 17–18, 24, 30; purpose of, 19, 26; YouTube launch of, 16–17
Drag kings. *See under* Bgirls
"Dragostea Din Tei," 21, 28
"Dr. Suzy's Porn and Purim DVD Bacchanal," 125
Duck Dynasty, 158
Duncan, Isadora, 161n52
Dworken, Arye, 127

Eagleton, Terry, 183
Efforts Space, 173–74
Effort State, 174
Ehrenreich, Barbara, 243–44
Ellen show, 25
Ellz, bgirl, 195
Empowerment. *See* Female empowerment
End zone celebrations. *See* Touchdown dances
Equality Dance, 40, 50, 57n31
Essay themes, 6–10
Ethnicity, Cruz touchdown dance and, 67
Exodus International, 151

Exotic dancing, 137, 144, 175; African American, 171; age of dancers, 171, 173, 186n18; audition, 173; at Backstage Bill's, 163, 164, 170–72; basic moves and directives for strip club, 169–70; body types, 173, 184; branding of, 165–66, 176–81; brandscapes, 177, 185, 187n32; British lap dancers and, 156; choreography and, 16, 72; Christianity and, 9; class distinctions and, 168, 175, 181, 183; competitive atmosphere among dancers, 174; contracts, 170–71, 177–78; corporate branding and, 165–66, 176–81; cultural conflicts reflected in, 165; culturally-constructed sexuality and, 167; dancing sexy in, 163, 165, 166, 172, 185; decision to stop, 183–84; at Diamonds, 173–76, 187n23; Hanna's categorized moves in, 167; lessons in, 163–64, 166–67; "low class" moves in, 168; Olympics and, 167; pole dance and, 168–69, 169, 180; scholarship on, 164, 185n1; sexual intercourse references and, 172, 174; striptease as dance perspective, 164–65, 186n4; subjective experience of, 172; transgressive potential of, 185; working class and, 156–57. See also Pole Dancing for Jesus classes

Fat Boy Slim, 31n13
FDNY. See Fire Department of New York
Female body: bgirls as disguising, 196–97, 206n30; imagery of fecund, 200; Jewish Frontier and, 115, 133n17
Female empowerment, 122, 192–93, 196–97; pole dancing and, 152–53, 155–58
Female rabbis, 118–19, 134nn22–23. See also Brous, Sharon
Femininity: Bgirls acceptance of, 201–2, 207n47; Jewishness and, 114
Feminism: anti-sex industry, 184; first-wave, 152; fitness and health advocacy of early, 139–40; Griffith on Christianity and, 161n63; Jewish, 118; second-wave, 152
Fessenden, Tracy, 155–56
Fikentscher, Kai, 244–45
Fire Code, 242

Fire Department of New York (FDNY), 213, 220; Memorial Climb in honor of, 218; song composed for, 216–17, 226n21
First Amendment, live music and, 233
Fitness: American culture of, 141–42; early feminists and, 139–40; rise of Christian, 141, 142–43; twentieth-century dance and, 138–41. See also Christian dance fitness; Pole dance fitness
Flash mobs, 2–3; advertising through, 90–91, 105n34; Beit Shemesh Women's, 98–99, 99, 102; collectivity afforded by, 83, 94, 103; commercialization of, 87–103; cross-whirl event, 88–89; definitions, 87–88; distinguishing elements of, 85; early years of, 84, 85–87, 93; flash casts and, 98; Internet creating possibility for, 7–8; as kinesthetic experiences, 83–85, 87, 89, 95, 97, 99, 192–93; love rug, 86; malleability of, 100, 103; media coverage, 91–92; micropolitics of, 84; movement choirs compared with, 100; in movies, 92, 93–98, 97, 100; multifaceted roles of, 83; participation experience in, 100–101; police and, 104n24; political potential of, 89, 92, 101; September 11 and, 88; simulation and immersion theory applied to, 106n43; social change impact of, 100; spontaneity and, 88, 89; subcultural capital and, 91–92; tactical media theory of, 83–84, 86–87, 89, 95, 98, 99; temporal dimension, 104n15; Toys "R" Us, 82–83, 84, 96–97, 103n5; transformation of, 89–91; virtuosity and, 84
Football. See Touchdown dances
Foster, Susan, 139
Foucault, Michel, 157, 196
Foundation. See Breaking
Fox News, Deans interviewed by, 143, 159n25
Francus, Marilyn, 200
Frasier, Jim, 39, 41, 56n18
Freud, Sigmund, 201
Friends with Benefits, 93–96, 97, 100
Frontier phenomenon, 113. See also Jewish frontier

Frozen Grand Central, 88
Fuller, Steve, 63

Gangnam Style, 25
Ganot, Brenda, 98–99
Gault, Will ("Speedy"), 63
Gay and Lesbian Alliance against Defamation, 49
Gay Games, 37–38, 47, 50
Gay liberation movement, 236
Gay men, arrests for social dancing, 235–36
Genderfuck, 192, 197
Generation Y, 1–4
Gentlemen's clubs, 166, 177
Gerber, Lynne, 151, 155–56
Gigs: Jazz and the Cabaret Laws in NYC (Chevigny), 229, 233
Gilman, Sander, 112–15, 128–29, 133n14
Giuliani, Rudolph, 238
Goebel, Bryan, 101
Going pink, 168
Goths for Jesus, 141
Gottschild, Brenda Dixon, 63–64
Gracey, Michael, 93
Grand Hyatt Hotel, 86
Great White, 241
Green Bay Packers, 61, 77n8
Griffith, R. Marie, 146, 151, 153, 161n63
Guevara, Nancy, 207n47
Guilty nap of whiteness, 133n19
Guttenberg, Steve, 42–43

Haddour, Azzedine, 5
Haddow, Douglas, 258
Hall, Francis, 230, 231, 245
Hall, Stuart, 225n5
Hallensleben, Markus, 5
Hamantaschen (triangular cookies), 125
Hancock, Herbie, 188n48
Hanna, Judith Lynn, 165, 167
Hanukkah, spoof video of, 123–24, 125, 129
Harlem: Harlem Renaissance, 230–31; nightlife, 233
Harlem Shake, 120, 135nn27–28
Hausbeck, Katherine, 178

Heeb, 127, 129
Henderson, Katie, 32n31
Hepcats, 252
Heteronormativity: ballroom dance and, 34–35, 41, 43; reality television and, 50; *So You Think You Can Dance*, 48–49, 53
Heyden, Tom, 135n27
Hip hop: in American culture, 190, 194, 201, 203–4; patriarchy and, 196, 205n8; rape lyrics in, 191, 195, 205n10. *See also* African Americans; Bgirls; Breaking
Hipsters: age range of, 252; apart dancing of, 260; clothing and fashion of, 253–54; core dance move, 255; dance parties of, 251, 253; dancing, 255–58, 256; denial of hipsterness by, 258–59; first wave of, 251–52; identity of, 258–59; as individualistic, 259–60; mashup genre, 254; mashup style of, 255; music of, 254; name of, 252; studies on, 252, 260; virtuosity devalued by, 257, 260; whiteness fetishized by, 258
Homophobia, 38
Homosexuality, 151
Horizons of expectations, 225n2
House Dance Project, 234

Ickey Shuffle, 65, 70, 71, 79n40; Africanist aesthetic of, 74; in *Jerry Maguire*, 74
Identity: Americanness and, 2, 11; breaking and, 9; Chinese, 5; collective, 3, 4, 83, 94; dance space and, 6; hipster, 258–59; LGBTQ, 236; music and, 216–17. *See also* Jewish frontier; Jewish identity; Jewishness
IDSF. *See* International DanceSport Federation
Ikar, 111, 130; High Holiday services, 116–21; leftist perspectives in, 118; Purim Party, 119–21, 134n26
Imperial Society of Teachers of Dancing, 36
Improv Everywhere, 87, 88, 93, 95–96, 104n15
Inaugural Prayer Service, 118, 119
Inner Remote, 174
International DanceSport Federation (IDSF), 35, 39, 56n18

International Federation of Gay Games, 37–38
International Olympic Committee, 35
International Pole Dance Fitness Association (IPDFA), 149, 167
Internet, 4, 11; dance gatherings influenced by, 2–3; flash mobs and, 7–8; hipsters and, 252; memes, 23, 24
IPDFA. *See* International Pole Dance Fitness Association
Israel-Palestine conflict, 116, 117–18, 119

Jackson, Janet, 101
Jameson, Fredrick, 252–53
Jarnow, Jesse, 241
Jason, Jacob, 44, 50–53, 57nn37–38
Jazz and jazz dancing, 231–33, 243, 251–52
Jefferson Memorial, 62
Jenkins, Henry, 46, 48
Jerry Maguire, 74
Jewish Daily Forward, 119
Jewish frontier: Brous and Angel as choreographers of, 129–31; criticism of activism within, 116, 133n18; definition of, 113; female body and, 115, 133n17; feminist approach to, 114–16; Gilman model of, 112–15, 133n14; male examples of, 114; New Jews and, 127–28; revised, 114–16; self-definition struggle of Jews, 128–29; virtual, 115
Jewish identity, 8, 113; Angel and, 123–27, 128; collective, 113; Diaspora Jews and, 128; generation gap and, 127; Jewish American Princess jokes, 136n34; nonaffiliation and, 127, 128; progressivism and, 112; whiteness and, 116, 133n19
Jewishness: femininity and, 114; nose and, 124; sex and, 126, 136n34; sexy, 130
Johnson, Chad ("Ochocinco"), 71, 73
Jones, Bgirl Ansley, *197*, 202
Jonze, Spike, 31n13
Judson Dance Theater, 257

Kavka, Misha, 53
Keaton, Buster, 18
Keegan, Dominique, 239–41

Kelly, Monica ("TahXic"), 198–99
Kennedy, John F., 140
Kibel, Mitchel, 44, 46–49, 53, 57n31
KinkyJews.com, 115
Kipnis, Laura, 125
Kirshenblatt-Gimblett, Barbara, 127–28
Klein, Naomi, 176, 178, 187n24; on Starbucks, 180
Kloetzel, Melanie, 5
Koch, Ed, 232, 237
Kracauer, Siegfried, 90
Krieger, Hilary, 134n23
Kurz, Tim, 146–47, 152

Laban, Rudolf, 100
Laban Movement Analysis, 166, 173–74
Lafrance, Noémie, 4, 10, 211; as artist-citizen, 221; ideals of, 219; McCarren Pool discovery and vision, 221–22; mission statement of, 214; site-specific nature of works by, 212, 214, 224. *See also Agora; Descent*
Lambeau Leap, 61, 62, 71
Langston, Timothy ("K.T.") (Killer Tim), 199
Lash, Scott, 176–77, 187n29
Latin American Dance Technique, 57–60
Latin dances, ballroom, 36, 39, 45
Latinos, NFL athletes, 65–66
Lawrence, Tim, 234–37
Lawsuits, Cabaret Law, 229–30, 233, 244–45
Lee, Andrew, 28
Leonard, David J., 66
Let's Move initiative, 142
Levy, Joe, 22
LGBTQ identity, social dance and, 236
Liepe-Levinson, 161n53, 167, 168
Liminal androgyny, of bgirls, 192; in battling, 198–200; burns and, 200; comic element in, 199; genderfuck in, 197; masculine elements in, 197–98; mother imagery and power of, 200–201
Liminality: of bboys, 200, 207n49; corporate branding and, 188n49; hipster, 260; strip clubs and, 182, 188n49
Live Nation, 228n44
Liverpool train station, 90

The Loft, 236
London Olympics, 167
Longoria, Eva, 66, 67
Lorde, Audre, 155
Lury, Celia, 176–77, 187n29
Lythgoe, Nigel, 47–48, 49, 51

Mandela, Nelson, 102
"The Mango," 43, 44
Manhattan: ballroom competition in, 57n39; zoned venues for social dance in, 239
Manning, Susan, 100
MARCH. *See* Multi-Agency Response to Community Hotspots
Marx, Eric, 39
Masculinity: black, 190, 191, 192, 197, 204; Christian, 140–41; liminal androgyny and, 197–98
Massachusetts Institute of Technology, 39
Massey, Doreen, 222
Mass ornament theory, 90
McCarren Park pool, 227n37; closing of, 221; Lafrance vision for, 221–22; reopening of, 223; request and support for using, 228n44; as site for *Agora*, 221–23, 223
McCarthy era, 141
McDonaldization, of sex industry, 178, 179
McGonigal, Jane, 88–89, 94, 95, 103
McMahon, Jim, 63
McMains, Juliet, 48
Meatpacking District, 239
Memes, 23, 24, 32n21
Memorial Climb, 9/11, 218, 227n26
Messick, Vanicia Flores, 203
Michaels, Mia, 52
Millennials. *See* Generation Y
Million Mambo March, 229, 230
Milovanovic, Dara, 197–98
Mimetic bgirls: attire of, 194; empowerment perspective of, 192–93; era of, 203; phallic gestures and, 195–96; rape mime, 191, 195
Misogyny, in breaking culture, 190, 200, 201, 204n3

Moanne81, 198
Modern dance, 161n52
Modern Family, 92
Moon, Warren, 72–73
Moore, R. Laurence, 141
Mötley Crüe, 175
Movement choirs, 100
Mr. Safety, 29–30
Muchmore, Andrew, 230
Multi-Agency Response to Community Hotspots (MARCH), 238, 241, 242
Munson-Weinberg, Lisa, 205n8
Murphy, Mary, 47, 48, 49, 50
Muscular Christianity, 140
Muse, John, 88
Music: Cabaret Law clause against live, 232–33; of hipsters, 254; identity and, 216–17; social dance and, 244–45

Napoleon Dynamite (fictional character), 18, 24, 32n26
National Fallen Firefighters Foundation, 227n26
National Post of Canada, 237
NBC Nightly News, 241, 242
NBC Sports, on Pole Dancing for Jesus, 137
Newgrounds, 16, 17, 22
New Jews, 127–28
"New Numa," 27–30
"New Numa: The Animation," 29
Newsweek, 111
New York City: licensed social dance venues in, 237, 247n46; revenue generated from nightlife in, 245, 249n100; social dancing in, 233–38, 235; SoHo neighborhood, 237; Von Bar No Dancing sign, 240. *See also* Cabaret Law
New York Giants, 65, 68
New York Magazine, 253, 259
New York Nightlife Association, 245
New York Police Department (NYPD), 236, 238
New York Post, 239
New York Review of Books, 86

New York Times, 22, 39, 243; Deans interviews with, 144, 150; on flash mobs, 87; Tebowing article in, 70

NFL: African American percentage in, 64, 78n13; ethnic percentages in, 72; excessive celebration penalties of, 71; football culture and, 64–65; Latino and Puerto Rican players in, 65–66; revenue, 76; touchdown dance regulated by, 71, 76; white leadership of, 72; wide receivers in, 73. *See also* Touchdown dances

Nigga Twins, 200

Nike, 98, 179

9/11, 9–10; FDNY and, 213, 216; healing through social dancing after, 234, 236; Memorial Climb, 218, 227n26; time and, 216; underground dance parties in wake of, 234. See also under *Descent*

No Dancing sign, in Von Bar, 240

Noland, Carrie, 83, 89, 102–3

"No Manifesto," 257

No Pants Subway Ride, 87, 88, 96

"Not Your Bubbe's Synagogue," 116–21

"Not Your Daddy's Porn," 121–28

Noxon, Christopher, 125

"Numa Coop," 24–25, 32n31

"Numa Numa Dance," 4, 6–7, 19; animation version of, 24–25; as archetypal viral video, 21; audience likes and dislikes reaction to, 22; Brolsma's first version of, 21–22; commercialization of, 29–30; copycat videos, 23–24, 32n33; first parody of, 24; innocent posting of, 27; as Internet meme, 23; Newgrounds video upload, 16, 17; popularity of, 23; song used in, 21, 28; viral version of, 22; virtual audience role as critic spawned by, 20, 31n5

N(um)apolean, 24

NYPD. *See* New York Police Department

Oakland A's, 75

Obama, Barack, 118

Obama, Michelle, 142

Olympics, London, 167

O'Rourke, Karen, 225n4

Outgames, 38, 47, 50

Owens, Terrell ("T.O."), 71, 73

The Oxford Handbook of Screendance Studies, 5

O-Zone, 21

Pabon, Julio, 67–68

Palestine, 116, 117–18, 119

Passing, Bgirls and, 194

Patriarchy: Angel and, 131–32; in hip hop, 196, 205n8; in social dance regulations, 235

Pavlik, Carolyn, 5

Payton, Walter, 63

Pee-wee Herman (Reubens, Paul), 18

Pew Research Center, smart phone study by, 19

Phantasmagoria, 215

Physical education, dance, fitness and, 139

Picart, Caroline, 35

Pile, Steve, 215

Pinder, David, 225n4

Plant Bar, 239–43

Pole dance fitness: African-American women and, 153–54, 162n66; attire, 148; codification, 148; healthy sexuality view of, 150–55, 157–58; historical accounts, 148–49; homosocial bonding in, 149–50, 161n53; male gaze and, 154–55, 162n68; reframing strategies, 146–50, 161n52; social class demarcations in, 156–57

Pole dancing, 168–69, 169, 180; stigma of, 147

Pole Dancing for Jesus classes: actual class name, 143; Christianity and, 8–9, 137–38; contradictions in, 153–54; health and sex framing of, 157–58; media attention on, 137, 143, 144, 151–52; perfectible body rhetoric surrounding, 145–50; Spinarella studio class contrasted with, 153–54, 162n66; studio and first classes, 144, 160n29

Politics: dance, 9–10, 75–76; of empowerment, 155–58; flash mobs and, 84, 89, 92, 101; NFL racial, 72–73, 75–76

Polonetsky, Jules, 242
Pornography: alternative, 112, 124, 132n6; mainstream compared with Angel's punk, 121–22; "Not Your Daddy's Porn," 121–28. *See also* Burning Angel Studios
Porn star. *See* Angel, Joanna
"Praise You," 31n13
Prayer, embodied, 117
President's Council on Youth Fitness, 140
Prichard, Robert, 229
Processions, 215. See also *Dérive*
Progressive Era, fitness and, 138–41
Prohibition, 229, 232
Protestantism: as hidden force in American culture, 155–58; perfectible body and, 146–50; whiteness and, 156
Psychogeography, *Descent* and, 212, 224, 225n4; Situationists and, 215, 221, 226n12
Puar, Jasbir, 157
Puerto Ricans, in NFL, 65–66
Punk princesses, 121
Purim, 119–21, 125, 134n26

Rabbis: female, 118–19, 134nn22–23; jokes about, 111, 132n1
Race and racism: Brooklyn 1970s, 234–35; Cabaret Law dynamics of, 230–32; NFL politics of, 72–73, 75–76; touchdown dances and, 63–64, 66, 72–73
Rainer, Yvonne, 257
Raley, Rita, 83–84, 89, 98
Rape, 191, 195, 205n10
Rateau, Nicole ("Severe"), 195, 198, 199
Raymond, Usher, 195
Reality television: ballroom dance and, 34–35, 41, 55n2; *Dancing with the Stars*, 7, 41–44, 45, 56n26; heteronormativity and, 50; mores and tension in, 53; *So You Think You Can Dance*, 44–53, 57n31, 57nn36–38
Reception theories, 212, 225n2
Red Triangle, YMCA, 140
Regulations: dance censorship and, 61–62; NYC zoning, 238–39; social dance, 235–36; strip club, 186n16; touchdown dance, 71, 76
Reiwoldt, Otto, 187n32
Remote State, 173–74
Reubens, Paul. *See* Pee-wee Herman
The Revised Technique of Latin American Dancing, 36
Rhythm Nation, 101
Rhythm stereotype, 64
Rice, Ray, 75
Richardson, Mike ("LA Mike"), 63
Rick's Cabaret, 169, 177
"The Rising," 216–17, 219, 226n21
Ritual, 217–18, 227n26
Ritzer, George, 178
Roach, Catherine, 164
Roberts, Jonathan, 42–43, 45
Rogers, Dexter, 73
Rokafella, bgirl, 199
Rolling Stone, 22
Rosenau, Douglas, 152
Rosenberg, Douglas, 5
Rosenfeld, Kathryn, 192–93, 194, 195, 196

Sacramento DanceSport Project, 38
Salsa, Cruz's touchdown dance as, 65, 66, 67, 68
Salzer-Moring, Miriam, 176
Same-sex ballroom dancing, 7; Belfer and Kibel audition, 46–49, 57n31; de Vries and Jason, 50–53, 57nn37–38; homophobia and, 38; new trends in, 54, 57n39; normative masculinity and, 43; Tango analysis, 42–44; threat represented by, 40–41, 50. *See also* Competitions, ballroom dance
San Francisco Chronicle, 89
San San Kwan, 5
Saturday Night Fever, 172
Savage, Sean, 86
Scenario theories, 218–19, 223–24
Schlemiel, 114, 132–33n13
Schloss, Joseph, 204n1, 190–91, 203–4; on bboying, 190; on Bgirl Emiko, 204n2; on Foundation and misogyny, 204n3

Schroeder, Jonathan, 176
Scores, 177, 187n30
Scott, Christopher, 96
Screendance, 5
Screen formats, 6
Severe. *See* Rateau, Nicole ("Severe")
Sex industry, 184; McDonaldization of, 178, 179; pole dancing and, 150–51
Sexism, in breaking. *See* Breaking
Sexuality: Christianity and, 150–52, 153, 158; culturally-constructed, 167; movement-oriented approach to, 166–67; pole dance fitness as healthy, 150–55; Taylorization of, 178
Sexy dancing, 163, 165, 166, 172
Shultz, Howard, 180
Siegel, Norman, 241–42
Simulation and Its Discontents (Turkle), 106n43
Situationists, 212, 215, 221, 226n12
Skeggs, Beverly, 156
Slavery, dance censorship and, 72
Smart phones, 19
Smith, Anna Deveare, 75
Social Club Task Force, 242
Social dancing: bars in NYC and, 239–41, 240; collective experience and benefits of, 233–34; colonizers suppression of indigenous, 243; Cox on 9/11 and underground, 234; Ehrenreich on emotional need for, 243–44; ethnomusicologist testimony on, 244–45; fear of, 243; growing focus on, 1, 5; Manhattan zoned venues for, 239; in New York City, 233–38, 235; in 1970s and 1980s, 236; number of NYC venues licensed for, 237, 248n46; NYC venues 1960s compared to 2002, 237, 248n46; regulations on, 235–36; shut down of venues for, 237; Supreme Court ruling on, 62; TV and, 3; underground dance clubs, 234–36; zoning regulations and, 238–39. *See also* Cabaret Law
So You Think You Can Dance, 41, 54, 57n36; Belfer and Kibel audition, 46–49,
57n31; de Vries and Jason audition, 50–53, 57nn37–38; flash mob choreography and, 96; format, 44, 46; heteronormativity, 48–49, 53; recognition of gay dancers, 57n34; world dance on, 49
Space, 70; city, 5; diversity of dance, 6; liminal, 182, 188n49
Space Effort, 173–74
Spearmint Rhino, 166, 177–78
Spectatorship theory, 212
Spiegel, Julius, 222
Spinarella studio, 153–54, 162n66
Sports Illustrated, 140
Springsteen, Bruce, 216–17, 219, 226n22
Standard dances, 36, 39, 45
Starbucksization, 180–81, 188nn47–48
Star Wars Kid, 33n51
St. Denis, Ruth, 161n52
Stealing with pride (*arzut metzach*), 127
Step Up Revolution, 92, 96–98, 97, 100
Stern, Howard, 187n30
Stevens, Sufjan, 259
Stonewall Inn, 236
Streb, Elizabeth, 222
Strip clubs: Backstage Bill's, 163, 164, 170–72; commodities, 184–85; corporate branding and, 180, 181; demographics, 169; Diamonds, 173–76; fantasy and play elements in branding of, 181–83; independently-owned, 166, 185; laws regulating, 186n16; liminal spaces in, 182, 188n49; white heterosexual, 168
Striptease: as dance, 164–65, 186n4; early, 167–68; Liepe-Levinson on choreography and, 167–68; scholarship on 1990s, 167, 186n7. *See also* Exotic dancing
"Super Bowl Shuffle," 62–63, 64, 77n8
Supreme Court, 62, 233

Tactical media theory. *See* Flash mobs
Tango, same-sex, 42–44
Tayeh, Sonya, 47, 48, 50, 59
Taylor, Diane, 218–19, 227n26
Tebow, Timothy Richard, 68–69, 70, 79n36

Tebowing, 65, 69–70, 79n36
TEDTalk, 101–2
Tenerife, British lap dancers in, 156
Third Reich, 100
Thornton, Sarah, 91–92, 98
Throwing the cock, 191, 194, 205n18, 205n9
Tiller Girls, 90
Timberlake, Justin, 93
Times Square, Twistathon in, 230
T-Mobile, 87, 90, 91, *91*, 93, 94; viewer comments, 101
Todd, Charlie, 87, 101–2
Touchdown dances, 7; Africanist aesthetics in, 74; the Bernie Lean, 74–75; call-and-response, 73; Christianity and, 69–70, 79n37; cultural meanings in, 75–76; demographics and, 65; end zone as public space for, 70; ethnicity issues and, 67; excessive dances issue, 71; fans proximity in, 70; High-Affect Juxtaposition in, 73–74; humor in, 73–74; Ickey Shuffle, 65, 70, 71, 74, *74*, 79n40; Lambeau Leap, 61, 62, 71; local sports incident and conflict, 75, 81n65; race and, 63–64, 66, 72–73; regulation of, 71, 76; religion and, 69–70, 79n37; salsa, 65, 66, 67, 68; "Super Bowl Shuffle," 62–63, 77n8; Tebowing and, 65, 69–70, 79n36
Toys "R" Us, 82–83, 84, 103n5; unison quality of flash mobs like, 96–97
Trac 2, 204
Travolta, John, 172
Trebunskaya, Anna, 42, *43*, *45* Triangular cookies (*hamantaschen*), 125
Tso, Tammy ("Kadence"), 195
Turkel, Avram, 231–32, 238–39, 242
Turkle, Sherry, 106n43
Turner, Frederick Jackson, 133n14
Turner, Jonathan H., 259, 260
Turner, Victor, 188n49
TV: dance competitions on, 7; social dancing on, 3. *See also* Reality television
Tweed, Thomas, 151–52
Twerking, 31n5
Twistathon, Times Square, 230

Underground dance: clubs, 234–36
Use group, legal term, 12, 239
"Uses of the Erotic: The Erotic as Power" (Lorde), 155

Vagina dentata, 201
Van Doorn, Niels, 123
Variety Beats, 28
Videos: Burning Angel Studios porn, 121–24; original dorky dancing, 16; spoof Hanukkah, 123–24, 125, 129; viral, 31n6; YouTube most watched, 25. *See also* "Numa Numa Dance"
Vilaro, Eduardo, 66–67
Viral videos, 31n6; Numa Numa as archetypal, 21
Virno, Paolo, 84
Virtual audience, as critics, 20, 31n5
Virtual communities, Jewish, 115
Virtual dance communities, 20, 26
Voelker, Gary, 28
Von Bar, 240

Waddell, Tom, 37
Wakefield, Lola, 257
Walker, Jimmy, 230
Walker, Mike, 65
Wall, Travis, 96
Wall Street Journal, 230
Waltz Natural Turn, 37
Warren Chiasson et al. v. New York City Department of Consumer Affairs, 233, 247n22
Washington Post, 242
Wasik, Bill, 2–3, 82–83, 88, 89; behavior disruption and, 97; as flash mob inventor, 103; hidden identity of, 86; improvisation use by, 94; tactical media in flash mobs of, 84
WDSF. *See* World DanceSport Federation
Weight Effort, 174, 184
Weiner, Rex, 119
Wesch, Michael, 20, 25
Whitehead, Kally, 146–47, 152
Whiteness: hipster fetishizing of, 258; Jewish identity and, 116, 133n19; Protestantism and, 156; strip clubs and, 168

Wickstrom, Maurya, 182, 187n32
Wilson, Otis ("Mama's Boy"), 63
Woods, Elbert L. ("Ickey"), 65, 70, 71, 79n40
Woods, Tiger, 71
Works Progress Administration (WPA), 221
World dance, 49
World DanceSport Federation (WDSF), 35, 39–40, 44
WPA. *See* Works Progress Administration

"Y" freeze, 202
YMCA. *See* Young Men's Christian Association
Yoga, 117, 133n20
Yom Kippur, Brous and, 116–21

Young, Latika, 257
Young Men's Christian Association (YMCA), 140, 141
YouTube, 7, 20; collaboration on, 25–26; dorky dancing launched on, 16–17; dorky dancing promoted by, 17; flash mobs on, 86, 91, *91*; impact of, 16; launching of, 19; most-viewed flash mobs on, 91; most watched video on, 25; "New Numa" on, 27–30; number of daily uploads on, 19; T-Mobile flash mob on, 91, *91*, 93, 94, 101; touchdown dances on, 71; viral videos and, 31n6

Zumba, 141–42, 154

www.ingramcontent.com/pod-product-compliance
Lightning Source LLC
Chambersburg PA
CBHW022001220426
43663CB00007B/907